THE CENTENNIAL HISTORY
OF THE
AMERICAN BIBLE SOCIETY

•The M Co•

THE MACMILLAN COMPANY
NEW YORK • BOSTON • CHICAGO • DALLAS
ATLANTA • SAN FRANCISCO

MACMILLAN & CO., LIMITED
LONDON • BOMBAY • CALCUTTA
MELBOURNE

THE MACMILLAN CO. OF CANADA, LTD.
TORONTO

JAMES WOOD
President of the American Bible Society, 1916

The Centennial History of the American Bible Society

BY
HENRY OTIS DWIGHT

VOLUME II

New York
THE MACMILLAN COMPANY
1916

Set up and electrotyped. Published, April, 1916

PREFACE

In dealing with so serious and significant a subject as the effort of a Society to increase the circulation of the Holy Scriptures in the world the point of view has been that of an humble servant acknowledging that success in the effort can proceed only from the guidance and help of Him to whom these ancient writings belong.

The plan of this book has excluded many things which may have been expected to appear in a review of labours covering a whole century of the world's progress. Its aim was to make a book to be read by the people rather than a manual of reference for the student.

It is natural, then, for this Centennial History to seek in every chapter the glory of God. The pervasive, living power of the word of God is emphasised by the facts of distribution in many lands, and these facts suggest praise and thanksgiving on the part of all who have shared in the development and progress of the Bible cause.

The author would frankly confess his obligation to the Rev. Dr. William I. Haven and the Rev. Dr. John Fox, his colleagues as Secretaries of the Society, for kindly criticism of the manuscript, much to its advantage.

In publishing this record of the first hundred years of the labours of the American Bible Society we would suggest that it is only the beginning of a story which, please God, will continue until the knowledge of the Lord shall cover the earth as the waters cover the sea. The future is impenetrable to the vision of the present writer as it was to the men who founded the Society a hundred years ago and bravely set forth on unknown paths. Many things clearly ought to be done in the years immediately before us. In the meantime all may look forward with yearning and pray with the beloved disciple, that the Lord Jesus Christ may hasten His coming.

CONTENTS

FIFTH PERIOD 1861–1871 (*Continued*)

CHAPTER		PAGE
XXXV.	The One Talent Hid	297
XXXVI.	Peoples Who Know Not God's Law	308
XXXVII.	The Jubilee Celebration of 1866	318
XXXVIII.	Forget Not All His Benefits	326

SIXTH PERIOD 1871–1891

XXXIX.	Paying the Cost of War	337
XL.	Events and Emergencies in the Bible House	347
XLI.	Making the Bible Speak with Tongues	357
XLII.	Distribution in the Home Land	368
XLIII.	The Bible Sent as a Foreign Missionary	379
XLIV.	Systematizing the Distribution Abroad	390
XLV.	The Call of the Far East	401
XLVI.	Japan and Korea	411
XLVII.	Mediating between Europe and Asia	420
XLVIII.	Seventy-five Years of Service	431

SEVENTH PERIOD 1891–1916

XLIX.	At the Bible House	440
L.	Changes in the Auxiliary System	451
LI.	New Methods at Home	460
LII.	Latin America	470
LIII.	Opening Doors of the Far East	482
LIV.	The White Elephant and the Dragon	490
LV.	America in the Orient	503

CONTENTS

CHAPTER PAGE

LVI. The Bible in Apostolic Fields 512

LVII. The Problem of Means 521

LVIII. Thy Ordinances are My Delight 530

Appendices 538

Index 579

LIST OF ILLUSTRATIONS

VOLUME II

James Wood . . . . *Frontispiece*

FACING PAGE

Travellers in Brazil 304

100,000 Gospels leaving the Bible House in Yokohama . . 314

The Philippines — A catastrophe in Bible transportation . . 380

A daughter of Modern Mexico 394

The Union Mandarin Revision Committee 406

Selling Bibles in Korea 418

The Constantinople Bible House 422

Dr. Bowen and the colporteurs in Egypt 426

A great work well done 448

Carrying Bibles to an isolated South Dakota farm . . . 460

Quechua Indians of Bolivia 476

Binding Scriptures for the American Bible Society in Yokohama 490

Bishop Schereschewski 498

A Fisher of Men 522

CHAPTER XXXV

THE ONE TALENT HID

THE tendency of Bible ideas, words and phrases to take a permanent place in the language is of exceeding interest. Because of this tendency all is an understatement that can be said of the Bible as a mine of wisdom. The Book unobtrusively moulds thought and surrounds the reader with a pure atmosphere which nourishes spiritual growth. It is a precious treasure which the humblest may use, like the talent in the parable, for the increase of his intellectual and spiritual capital. Merely as a civilising agency Bible distribution, for this reason, should commend itself to the support of all.

For various reasons a good many people in their treatment of the Bible follow the notorious example of the man who buried his talent in a napkin. Some make the reading of the Bible impracticable by giving it ponderous weight and massive binding; some make the reading by common people a crime which merits anathema; some, without going so far as to punish readers, see to it that the book can only be found wrapped in gorgeously embroidered cloths on the altar of a church, and some, though free from such restrictions, cordially neglect reading the book that lies open in their hands. The one possession which might make all rich is buried out of reach.

What the Society has done in some of the countries where the Bible is neglected or hidden is an essential part of this story. The undertaking has been simple conformity to the purpose of the Master, in the same way that the builder of a palace tries exactly to embody in stone the thought and plan of the architect. American Baptist Missionaries in Sweden, and Methodist Episcopal missions in Norway and in Denmark asked and received during this period $5,150 for Bible distribution. In Denmark the use of a grant of $650 illustrates how widely even a small sum may serve the destitute. Scriptures bought with the grant were sold at cost or less whenever possible. With the proceeds of sales more books were bought and sent on "missionary excursions." After five years the missionaries through this grant had circulated 8,686 volumes, and their expectation of typical fruits from the sowing was as well grounded as that of the farmer who expects to reap wheat when he has sown wheat.

During the period of the Civil War (1861–1871), the Methodist Episcopal Mission at Bremen, Germany, received grants amounting to $52,947, applied to making three sets of plates of the German Bible and two of the New Testament, and printing and distributing the books among the people. The scarcity of Scriptures among the common people, and the advantage of supplying the Book to emigrants to the United States at the port of embarcation, made this work like the despatch of shiploads of provisions for famishing families in Ireland and Russia. Bible distribution was opposed by Roman Catholic priests just as people in India oppose the health officers who try to save them from the plague. But Dr. Jacobi, the missionary, remarked with satisfaction, "The old man (the Pope) will surely be convinced that Protestantism has a much greater force than he imagines."

In 1864–65 Prussia made war on Denmark over Schleswig-Holstein; in 1866 on Austria, and in 1870 on France. In all these wars our little Testaments went to barrack and hospital. One wounded man said to the colporteur who gave him a Testament: "What on earth shall I do with it?" But a few weeks later, when he was leaving to rejoin his regiment, he said to the colporteur, "I am studying the little book in earnest, and thank you for it." In the war with France a German lady had to give up her only son for service in the Army. Six weeks later, the battle at Sedan which overthrew the Emperor Napoleon bereaved this lady. Comfort came to her like a voice from the spirit world, however, when in her dead boy's effects she found a little Testament given by the "American Bible Society" on which were marks of use such as showed that her son had lived in harmony of purpose with her and with her God.

In Russia during this period 20,000 Testaments were printed at the expense of the Society by the Committee which supplied the destitute Esthonians of the district of Reval. Later on money was sent to the Committee at St. Petersburg to buy from the depot of the Holy Synod Russian New Testaments for exiles in Siberia. When the books arrived at Nikolaievsk (about 4,000 miles from St. Petersburg), they were sent up the Amur River 500 miles, and rejoiced the hearts of the poor exiles. Grants for the Russian work during these nine years amounted to $17,497. Good will in the name of the Lord knows no limitations.

In France at that time any failure to use the Bible was due, perhaps, less to government restrictions than to fear of the Church hierarchy. Here is a reason, if one must needs be given, for the Society's labours in such lands. Old friendship for France, too, was a special reason for aid rendered to the French Bible Societies. The French Protestant Bible Society, organised in 1818, in 1863 changed its constitution and began to publish an imperfect version of the Bible. Upon this a minority of its managers resigned and in 1864 united with the French and Foreign Bible Society forming a new body called the Bible Society of France. To this new organisation the American Bible Society gave some $13,000 in this period. The money was used in printing and distributing Scriptures in France. In 1870 the French Society reported that in the six years since its organisation it had put in circulation 60,000 volumes.

The Board of Managers in 1863 made a re-statement of its policy toward the nations more or less destitute of the Bible. It declared that while the Society is under obligation to enter every open field where American missionaries ask its aid, America, excepting Canada, is its special field. Latin America, including Mexico, Central America and South America with their island dependencies, should be supplied with all diligence in addition to the vast home field. From 1861 to 1871 the expenditures in Latin America amounted to $10,486, besides grants of books.

Mexico both attracted and repelled efforts to supply its people with Scriptures. Until 1861 the Rev. James Hickey, a Baptist minister in Texas, had been actively distributing

Scriptures and tracts among Mexicans near the Rio Grande. When the Civil War blazed up, hoping to continue his work unhampered by the crisis in the United States, he removed from Texas to Monterey in Mexico. There he received occasional grants of Scriptures from the Society and put some nine hundred volumes into circulation chiefly by sale.

The earnestness and devotion of Mr. Hickey led the Board in the latter part of 1862 to appoint him Agent of the Society for Mexico, expecting him to live in Mexico City. Meanwhile, England, France, and Spain had intervened to regulate the chaos in Mexico, and had disagreed as to the measures to be adopted. France was left to act alone. In June, 1863, French troops captured Mexico City, to the great joy of the clerical party, which opposed Juarez. The country was full of fighting men — partisans of the French, partisans of Juarez, and plain, unblushing bandits; but Mr. Hickey was not afraid to travel. His adventurous excursions took him into the states of Tamaulipas, Zacatecas and San Luis Potosi. The marvel of his ventures was that everywhere he aroused interest in the Bible which he carried. But the roads, he said, were "such as to smash any wagon not made of spring steel."

The fame of the Bible spread through the country. Mr. Hickey wrote in 1865: "So soon as the Heavenly Father sends peace I propose to send four colporteurs into Tamaulipas to distribute Scriptures in every town and ranch in the state." But this was not to be. Again and again Mr. Hickey had to make the difficult journey of some two hundred miles from Monterey to Brownsville because there was no other way of securing the books sent from New York. Early in 1866 he suffered from exposure on a journey for books, and was laid up with pneumonia at Brownsville for nearly two weeks. He went to work again while still far from well, and toward the close of the year he took the same hard journey again to replenish his stock. Illness followed his arrival at Brownsville, and on the 10th of December, 1866, this brave servant of Christ rested from his arduous labours.

The impression of such a life on the country was lasting. General Lew Wallace later passed through the region where Mr. Hickey had laboured and was surprised at the profound respect in which the people held his memory. The reason of this respect was partly the high character of the man, but chiefly the quality of the Book. It quickly won the love of the soul-hungry people. One Mexican on hearing some verses read, instantly said to his wife, "That is a book to open a man's eyes; buy it!" And she did. "Is not my word like as a fire, saith the Lord, and like a hammer that breaketh the rock in pieces?"

Upon the death of Mr. Hickey, Mr. Thomas Westrup was appointed agent of the Society. He was prepared for the work by missionary labour on the border and well-seasoned for its extraordinary demands. The obstructiveness of the priests whose cause seemed to be looking up since the advent of the Emperor Maximilian, was less of a hindrance to Bible work than the outlawry which flourished under cover of resistance to the French invasion.

Maximilian's exotic Empire was doomed, however, as soon as the end of civil war in the United States permitted Mr. Seward, with some hundreds of thousands of seasoned soldiers at hand, to speak seriously to Napoleon III concerning French armies in Mexico. Early in 1867 Bazaine and his troops embarked for France. The tragedy of Queretaro, June 19th, 1867, was the natural consequence — a shock to the whole civilised world, a cup of gall to Napoleon III, and an ominous beginning for the new freedom of Mexico.

The clerical party was much enfeebled by this catastrophe. Local officials, Mr. Westrup wrote, declared that the new constitution made Bible burning illegal. In the three years of his agency he put in circulation about 8,000 volumes of Scripture in Tamaulipas, Nueva Leon, Chihuahua, Durango, San Luis Potosi, and Zacatecas. The proceeds of sales in 1869 were $1,100 — good evidence that the book was wanted by the people. There were little groups of Bible readers in many places, and the Bible could be seen to be changing brutes into men. Colonel Rodriguez in Tamaulipas described the revolution wrought in his own life by saying, "I have not changed my profession. I have only changed my commanding Officer!" Miss Melinda Rankin, always vigorously at work, reported converts to New Testament Christianity of all ages — an old woman of sixty-nine and a boy of thirteen — in the place in Nueva Leon where she now laboured. Two men who had threatened to shoot any one who should bring Bibles to their village were found among the humble students of the words of Jesus Christ.

By the beginning of 1870 the new order of things in Mexico led to the opening of missions by different denominations. The Society made grants of books and money, 500 Bibles to the Protestant Episcopal Mission, $2,750 to the American and Foreign Christian Union for Rev. H. C. Riley, its missionary in Mexico City. The missions found instant response among Bible readers, particularly in the six states named above, where to this day are found a large proportion of the adherents of Protestant missions. Mr. Westrup had taken part in laying foundations, he now yearned for a share in the building. In 1870 he resigned in order to enter the service of the American Baptist Home Mission Society, in Northern Mexico.

Entreaties of the American Missionaries in Buenos Aires decided the Board in 1864 to appoint an Agent for that part of South America. Mr. Andrew Milne, a young Scot living in Buenos Aires, was selected for the post. With a delicate sensitiveness to comity, the Board instructed him to establish the Agency in Montevideo because the British and Foreign Bible Society had labourers in Buenos Aires.

Mr. Milne was connected with a mercantile house, but hours that were his own he had long devoted to missionary effort among the people of the city. He gladly began service of the Society in June, 1864. From his appointment dates the opening of serious work of the Society in behalf of the Spanish speaking parts of the southern continent. The vision of a Christian worker always outruns his immediate surroundings. While Mr. Milne in 1864 was advised to begin his efforts in Entre Rios, one of the fourteen provinces of Argentina, he foresaw that one day the Bible would nourish the lives of divers tribes and nations, from the Atlantic to the Pacific and from the equator to Cape Horn.

Since by this time the British and Foreign Bible Society had opened a depository in Montevideo, Mr. Milne, to avoid appearance of rivalry, established his agency at Rosario, on the Parana River. From Rosario Mr. George Schmidt, an energetic colporteur, was sent to explore the northern country. He visited many of the chief cities, besides the villages and ranches as far west as Jujuy in the skirts of the Andes, some seven hundred miles from Rosario.

When the work of the Agency began in 1864 the Bible was the rarest of books in that region. By slow and patient methods Mr. Milne and one or two colporteurs in the first six years of his agency had placed in the hands of the people of many towns and villages as far as to the borders of Brazil and of Peru a total of about 25,000 copies of Scripture. The wide dispersion of these books prepared the way somewhat for missions of many denominations. A salient feature of this work was the ceaseless and even virulent opposition of leading men of the church which for three centuries had dealt with the nation as though its existence depended upon keeping the book inactive. This opposition in turn brought to light evidences that the Bible frees men's minds from arbitrary control. At a little mud ranch in the country which seemed hardly worth a visit, Mr. Milne in 1870 discovered a refined lady who said, "I have a Bible already; it is worth more to me than an ounce of pure gold! The priest ordered me to give it up to be burned but I told him I would as soon think of burning my clothes!"

To Peru the Society sent Scriptures through Rev. Mr. McKim, missionary of the American and Foreign Christian Union at Lima. Chile, settled by the Spanish in 1541, lies between the crest of the Andes and the Pacific Ocean, and the Society treated its needs as a problem separate from those of Mr. Milne's Agency. Rev. Dr. Trumbull at Valparaiso completed in 1871 his twenty-fifth year of hearty co-operation with the Society. During this period the Valparaiso Bible Society, organised in 1862, with Dr. Trumbull as president, pressed Bible distribution among English, Germans, and Americans in the city and reached out among Chilians in adjoining districts. During seven years the Valparaiso Bible Society in 1870 had put in circulation 7,000 copies of the Scriptures.

In regard to Central America, and Colombia then known as New Granada, little can be said except that the Board intently watched for opportunities of Bible distribution while the unrest of revolution bubbled and boiled like a witch's mixture in a cauldron. In 1863 the Rev. W. H. Norris was appointed Agent of the Society for Central America and New Granada. But early in 1864 Mr. Norris' health gave way, and he was obliged to resign. The Rev. W. H. Gulick of Caraccas, Venezuela, and Mr. F. Hicks of Panama, independent and self-supporting missionaries, were now furnished Scriptures for distribution. In 1866 the agency of the British Society was withdrawn from Bogota and the American Society took steps to aid American missionaries in Colombia as it had always done. In the West Indies the work of the Society, during this period, was still rather desultory in character, books being sent in small parcels to missionaries or other Christian workers in Cuba, Hayti, and Porto Rico; but nothing being attempted in the way of a permanent Agency for the islands.

When American missionaries began to establish themselves, far south of the eastward straggling islands, in Brazil, they were glad to handle Scriptures for the Society. Rev. Mr. Simonton and Rev. Mr. Blackford of the Presbyterian Mission in Rio Janeiro, during this period employed colporteurs at the expense of the Society. Farther north the Rev. R. Holden of the American Protestant Episcopal Mission at Para, each year after his arrival received grants from the Society, employed colporteurs and himself travelled widely to distribute Scriptures until 1864. Then he was formally appointed Agent of the Society. The Board was rather surprised, however, to learn that before the notice of this appointment had reached Mr. Holden he had been engaged as Agent of the British and Foreign Bible Society.

In all such distributions the Bible permanently wins the hearts of some. Here and there people were reading the Bibles bought from Mr. Fletcher, the former Agent of the Society. Mr. Blackford wrote joyfully of results of the sower's work that came under his own eyes. The story of a convert at São Paulo suggests that in many places the Bible even now may be working silently and imperceptibly. A very old woman rebuked this man when a boy for noisy play on

TRAVELLERS IN BRAZIL

Sunday, and read to him out of a book the command to keep the Sabbath holy. She also let him read in the book, which was the Bible. When he grew up he sent to Rio Janeiro to get a Bible; but could not, for the price was twenty-five dollars. Some time afterward the teacher of the public school gave him a Spanish Bible, printed by the American Bible Society in 1824. The man learned Spanish solely for the purpose of reading the Bible. For twenty years that man had privately studied the Bible, and when the missionaries arrived in São Paulo he was entirely ready to make public profession of his faith in Jesus Christ. Mr. Blackford wrote in this connection: "Results may seem small as compared with the outlay, but such facts as this prove the work to be worth while!" The sincerity of the Brazilian lovers of the Bible received further testimony when the little church at Rio Janeiro out of its poverty sent a donation of twenty-five dollars to the Society as a token of the gratitude of its members.

At the beginning of this period a few governments of Europe served the clergy, guarding the Bible with the sword. In the Papal states as well as the small countries in central and Southern Italy, the police constantly watched against the admission of Bibles. Even an American who went to Rome would have his Bible taken from him as soon as he crossed the line. A species of madness seemed to possess the authorities. After Italy became one united kingdom the police restrictions were removed excepting in the Papal states and the Society speedily took advantage of this situation. The Rev. William Clark, formerly a missionary in Turkey, was sent by the American and Foreign Christian Union to Milan and the Society furnished him with money to circulate Scriptures. It also made grants to the Geneva Italian Committee whose work in the north of Italy it had long aided, and to a Waldensian Committee in Florence, first to print Scriptures, and finally for making a complete set of plates of the Bible in Italian to be used at Florence. The grants of the Society for printing and distributing Scriptures in Italy through these channels amounted during the nine years to $24,240. During this period the British and Foreign Bible Society and the Scottish National Bible

Society were working with great vigour in all parts of Italy and the American Society refrained from placing colporteurs in the field.

Toward the close of this period the great Vatican Council assembled in order to declare as a dogma of the church the infallibility of the Pope in matters of spiritual guidance. On the 18th of July, 1870, this dogma of infallibility was proclaimed with all the pomp and ceremony of which the ancient church of Rome is capable. On the same day France, whose troops were protecting Rome against liberty, declared war against Germany. Within two months the French Empire had been overthrown; her troops were recalled from Rome, and Italians occupied the city, and temporal sovereignty was wrenched from the paralysing grip of the church!

In Spain almost more than in Italy arbitrary power forbade the people's access to the book that gives men understanding. Worthy men were imprisoned for reading it. After the revolution of September, 1868, when Queen Isabella fled the country and Marshal Serrano was installed at Madrid as Regent, freedom seemed to have displaced tyranny even in the domain of religion. The American and Foreign Christian Union established a mission at Seville and the Board granted it 5,000 copies of Scripture. But the Spanish Custom House stopped the books. By the intervention of General Daniel E. Sickles, the American Minister, the Custom House released the books one full year after their seizure. The boxes of Bibles were viewed by every official "with deepest malignity," wrote Rev. H. C. Hall at Seville, for they contained the first Bibles, perhaps, ever regularly passed by that Custom House. As we shall later see, they were not the last.

Thus the treasure long hidden has been gradually put into use among multitudes. The word "talent" used to be a Greek word of money value. Its adoption into many languages with a nobler meaning reveals the wide dissemination of the Bible, where our Saviour's parable attached to the old Greek word the sense of an endowment or gift available for success in life. The Bible itself is such an endowment, for neglect of which none can escape accountability. Hence the effort to give the book free course in lands where men have concealed or neglected it appeals to the sympathy and support of every true Christian.

CHAPTER XXXVI

PEOPLES WHO KNOW NOT GOD'S LAW

WARM as was interest in the nations among whom the Bible was hid from the common people, sympathy and yearning to help could not but go out toward the millions of pagans and Mohammedans whose lands seemed to form a sort of anarchistic reservation on the earth, where the law of God was not known.

India, one of the countries of this class, had held for many years a place in the hearts of the members of the Society. The aid of the Society was given to American Missionaries in Ceylon, at Madura, and in the Arcot region of South India, in Lucknow and the Lodiana district in North India. The languages of India in which Scriptures were published or circulated during this period at the expense of the Society were Tamil, Telugu, Marathi, Uriye, Urdu, Hindi and Panjabi. The cost to the Society of printing and distribution from 1861 to 1871 in different parts of the country amounted to $57,859.

In 1866 the Rev. Dr. Jacob Chamberlain of the Reformed Church Arcot Mission, made a tour for the Society in the territories of the Nizam of Hyderabad, little known because of the surly fanaticism of the population outside of the great cities. The tour was an exploration, an opportunity for distribution of Scriptures among all classes, and an undertaking adventurous and even dangerous to the devoted missionary. Many of the people in their ignorance could not make out the sense of a Gospel unless some one expounded it. One man in South India, after buying a portion brought it back because he said "it had offended his household god." Another one liked the little book so much that he came to ask the missionaries if he ought not to offer it worship. On the other hand there was some intelligent use of the books. An inspector of police, a Brahmin, said to a missionary: "There never was a being like Jesus Christ, and never a book like the Bible. Though I have eaten a meal, if I have not read my Bible I am hungry still."

In Siam with money furnished by the Society, the Presbyterian Mission Press at Bangkok printed during this period 29,000 copies of Scripture, including the four Gospels, St. Paul's Epistles to the Romans and to the Corinthians, Genesis, Exodus, and Leviticus, all in separate portions generously distributed.

An atmosphere of romance hangs about the palm-clad atolls of Micronesia. But the missionaries of the American Board found little of romance when they visited one island after another where the unclothed people were sunk in ignorance, without an idea of reading or writing, or of an alphabet. During this period, however, the Society printed Scriptures pretty continuously at the Bible House and at Honolulu for use in these little islands; schools having prepared the natives to read. The English alphabet was used, as in the Hawaiian Islands, for writing the different languages. Portions of Scripture for the Marshall Islands, for the Gilbert Islands, and for Kusaie (Strong's Island) were printed at Honolulu at the expense of the Society, and a large family Bible in Hawaiian as well as a New Testament in Hawaiian and English in parallel columns were printed at the Bible House in New York. There was large demand for both of these last named books, although it was the opinion of the missionaries that the natives of the Hawaiian Islands, at least, would gradually lose their identity by mingling with foreigners who were taking up their abode in those charming surroundings.

The acceptance of the Scriptures in Micronesia is shown in a letter of Rev. Mr. Snow of the American Board's Mission in Kusaie, who had been absent from the island for many months, leaving the people the Gospel of St. John for their instruction. On his return in 1864, he found that some forty persons had made up their minds during his absence to surrender to Jesus Christ. In a Sunday School were 118 pupils of all ages in twelve classes studying the Gospels. Many had committed the Gospel of St. John to memory. Mr. Snow brought them the Gospel of St. Matthew, just printed. The people were over joyed. In groups of three or four that evening they were lying around their little lamps reading the new book. The Society could not but hasten the printing of the Bible for people giving it such a welcome.

In China, as a thorn in the flesh of translators, the "term question"[1] persisted because missionaries were unable to unite upon a Chinese term for "God." A compromise usually permitted the printing of either *Shangti* or *Shen* in editions of the Bible for the missions which respectively required either term. By Dr. Schereschewski a curious experiment was made in his Mandarin Old Testament. He introduced the term *Tienchu,* supported by the fact that it had been used by Roman Catholic missionaries for two hundred years. It never came into use, however, in Protestant missions, and it did not appear in the Mandarin Old Testament after 1899.

Bible translation at the expense of the Society steadily went on, driven by the needs of China's vast multitudes. The Board had recognised in 1852 a committee composed of Bishop Boone and Rev. Dr. E. C. Bridgman, once members of the "Delegates'" Committee, Rev. Dr. Culbertson, Rev. Dr. Jenkins, of Shanghai, and Rev. Dr. McClay of Fuchow, as a Committee of translation with power to publish the Bible when completed. The version of the New Testament prepared by this American Committee was published in 1854 and that of the whole Bible in 1862. Dr. Bridgman did not live to complete the work, passing from this life in 1861. Dr. Culbertson had the privilege of seeing the work finished before he died in 1862. This version was more faithful in rendering the original, but less elegant in Chinese style than the Delegates' version. It had a very large circulation during forty years, being the first complete Bible in Chinese published by the Society. Even now the demand for it requires it to be kept in stock at the depository at Shanghai.

During this period the printing of the Fuchow colloquial

[1] See Chapter XXIX.

version of the Bible and tentative portions of a Mandarin version called for grants. The Society in May, 1869, requested the Board of Managers to hasten the publication of a Mandarin version since it is generally understood throughout China. A committee at Peking, of which Bishop Schereschewski was a member, took up the work and in 1872 the New Testament in Mandarin was published at the joint expense of the American and British Bible Societies. This was a new practical illustration of federation, cautiously tested in the field by missionaries, its timid inventors, and thus commended to the Boards at home.

Up to the year 1866, grants of the Society to missions in China had been designated for the expense of translation and printing; the missionaries distributing the books commonly without asking payment from the people. As early as 1866 the Presbyterian Mission in Shanghai experimented with sales. Five colporteurs were sent out who left some part of the Bible, generally by sale, in 30,000 Chinese families; and when a proposal was made by this and other missions that a part of the money granted by the Society should be used to support colporteurs, the Board could not very well refuse. A good colporteur in a pagan land is the face of a personified, smiling, well-wishing Christianity. Accordingly, the missionaries were authorised to use some part of the Society's grants for maintaining colporteurs.

Such a development of the activities of the Society might be suspected by some to be partly owing to the weakness of a people unable to resist energetic foreigners. It was, however, encouraged by the reception given to the Bible by the Chinese. A missionary cautioned some country people to whom he was giving Bible portions to take care of the books. One of the peasants said to him: "Do you mean that you think we would destroy printed books? Never!" A certain amount of discrimination and intelligence was always shown by the people after the practice of selling Scriptures drew more thoughtful attention to the books. Rev. Mr. Mills, a Presbyterian Missionary of Tungchow, travelled far afield and sold a considerable number of Scriptures in the very birthplace of Confucius. Rev. Dr. Blodgett of the American Board's North China Mission, happened upon a little company of Chinese studying the Bible by night. They were weavers who had to work late in finishing some special order, and one of their number would be asked to read the Bible to them while they worked. In one of these serious groups of weavers the reader was a woman. As among all other races, some among the Chinese, too, learned faith in Jesus Christ through the unaided reading of the Scriptures. Rev. Dr. Martin, of the Presbyterian Mission, wrote of a Chinaman who had never seen a missionary, but had become convinced of the truth by poring over a Bible which years ago had somehow fallen into his hands. Such incidents thrillingly show the fitness of the blessed book for inner needs of every race of men.

Several times the question of appointing an Agent for China was raised in the Board of Managers. Both the British and Foreign Bible Society and the National Society of Scotland were represented in China by Agents, and many of the American missionaries thought that Bible distribution could be more effective under supervision of an Agent of the Society. The Board, however, did not wish to incur the expense. As late as 1868 it decided again that so long as missionaries were willing to superintend distribution, the money might well be committed to them for that purpose. Five years later, however, Bible distribution absorbed so much time that the Board appointed the Rev. L. H. Gulick, M.D., a missionary who had served long in Micronesia, to be Agent of the Society for China and Japan. The books in Mandarin, in Classical and in local colloquials printed at the expense of the Society in Shanghai and Fuchow, were being sent to Nanking, Hankow, Peking, Tientsin, and far up the Yangtse River as well as among the coast provinces. Grants were being made to the American Board, to the Methodist Episcopal, the Protestant Episcopal, the Presbyterian, and the Reformed Church (Dutch) missions. From the beginning (in 1833) of the Society's serious work in China until the appointment of Dr. Gulick as Agent in 1874, 1,594,818 volumes of Scripture had been printed in Chinese, and 1,300,000 of them had been put into circulation. The cost to the Society of this great work was $215,280.93.

In 1837 the Board made a grant to Rev. Dr. Gutzlaff in the hope that Gospels translated into Japanese by him might carry an appeal to the unknown empire of Japan. But the first words from America heard by the Japanese were the English words of the hymn, "Before Jehovah's awful throne ye nations bow with holy joy." The Japanese could not understand these words, but they were mightily astonished at the music of the band upon the deck of Commodore Perry's flagship as it led with the tune of "Old Hundred" the singing of a thousand manly voices engaged in divine worship on a Sunday morning in July, 1853.

Fully six years passed after Perry's first visit to Japan before the treaty with the United States was ratified. Then only could foreigners venture to live in Japan. The objection of the old feudal system to any breaking down of the wall of exclusiveness was like the objection of a bat to the rays of the sun. Happily some Japanese preferred the sun. In 1859 the first American Missionaries went to Japan; Rev. Mr. Liggins and Rev. Mr. Williams of the Protestant Episcopal Church, Rev. Mr. Verbeck of the Reformed (Dutch) Church and Dr. Hepburn of the Presbyterian Church. These men were instantly confronted with the need of Bibles for the missions. There was no Bible in Japanese. Dr. S. Wells Williams, the Chinese scholar, and Dr. Gutzlaff, the learned free lance of China missions, had long ago attempted something in the way of translations into Japanese; and later Rev. Dr. Bettelheim, a converted Hebrew from Hungary, who had been sent by British naval officers as missionary to the Lu Chu Islands, had translated portions of Scripture which had been printed by the Society for the Promotion of Christian Knowledge. Otherwise no word of Scripture existed in Japanese. Application was made at once to the Society for aid.

So far as the Board was concerned, this newly opened empire was little more than a name in the year 1860. In June of that year the Board invited the Japanese ambassadors making a tour of the Western nations to visit the Bible House. The ambassadors came; went over the whole building; minutely inspected the machinery for printing and binding; were especially amazed by the hydraulic presses used to smooth the printed sheets, and went away delighted with the Society and its wonderful works. The visit of the Japanese Embassy put Japan on the map of the Society, although the name was still followed by a question mark.

In the same year Rev. Dr. B. J. Bettelheim, who had returned from the Lu Chu Islands and established himself in the state of Illinois, offered to give the Society his translation of parts of the Bible, assuring the Board that all Japanese scholars would testify to the high quality of the language used. The Dutch interpreter of the Japanese Embassy, said that the ambassadors thought educated people in Japan might discover the meaning of Dr. Bettelheim's translation, but that the masses could not understand it at all. Meanwhile Dr. Hepburn at Yokohama advised on general principles that if Dr. Bettelheim's manuscript could be had for any reasonable sum, it might help other Bible translators. After consideration, however, the Board decided not to accept Dr. Bettelheim's offer.

In view of the phenomenon of a knowledge of the Dutch language by many Japanese, the Board in 1861 sent a supply of Holland Bibles to be distributed among those Japanese who had been in trade with the Hollanders living on the little island in front of Nagasaki which had been a trade mart of the Dutch during some two hundred years. Taking these Scriptures to the Japanese was at best a forlorn hope, since the strictly commercial vocabulary of Dutch which was used at Nagasaki could hardly throw light on theological terms. But in this urgent case more than one order for these Scriptures came from the missions in Japan. Since all educated Japanese could read Chinese, the missionaries also ordered Scriptures in that language. In their hope that the Bible might speak to the Japanese before they themselves could, like the ancient alchemists, they cast various materials into the crucible and watched to see if base metal was transmuted into gold.

The Society placed in the hands of missionaries of different denominations in Japan during the period from 1861 to 1871, $4,800 for use in translation of the Bible, and for purchase of Chinese Scriptures. It also sent out 1200 volumes of Dutch and of English Scriptures for direct

AMERICAN BIBLE SOCIETY
BIBLE SOCIETY
One Hundred Thousand Gospels,
Shipped Feb. 3rd 1914, from the Bible House, Yokohama
三台の馬車に満載せる四福書拾万部
大正三年二月三日.横濱米国聖書會社より発送.

100,000 GOSPELS LEAVING THE BIBLE HOUSE IN YOKOHAMA

distribution. The money granted for translation was used for supporting the Japanese assistants. The formal beginning of Bible translation in Japanese was about 1865, and by the year 1866 the missions had agreed to organise for Bible translation a select committee so that there might be for all but one Japanese version.

During this preliminary work the people showed interest in the Bibles offered by the Americans. The nation had been awakened by cannon. A considerable number of the people were eagerly asking how they, too, could get such cannon. But some of them actually found food for hungry souls in the American book. People who read the Bible for the first time enjoy the vividness of a first impression; the new thought remains a topic of meditation. We to whom the ideas in general are old, often fail in meditation because we think we know the truths taught by the Bible. The importance of the fresh first impression had not occurred to Abbé Huè when he sneeringly inquired if Protestant missionaries thought they would convert China by placing a few Bibles on its shores. At all events it does not seem to have occurred to him that the spirit of God is able to use His own word. By the time, in 1868, that the Gospel of Matthew was ready for the press, the missionaries had already been rejoiced by learning that a young man in prison had been converted through Bible study recommended by a Chinese teacher. In that same year two Japanese of education and rank were baptised, having found faith in Jesus Christ through copies of the Bible in Chinese sent out at a venture from mission stations. The faith of the missionaries was justified. The rock had in it a soft spot that having once been reached by the elements, all external things began to work together to reduce the granite to powder.

For Africa the first serious work taken up by the Society was aid to the Gaboon Mission of the American Board, and to the Cape Palmas Mission of the Protestant Episcopal Church. African tribes had neither writing nor alphabet. Hence distribution of Scriptures must wait upon mission schools. In 1870 the entire New Testament in Mpongwe was printed at the mission press on the Gaboon at the expense of the Society. Grants of Scripture portions were made from the stock in New York, and curiously enough some copies in Arabic were called for to be read by the Mohammedan negroes engaged in trade in all that region. On the eastern side of the African continent the American Board's Missionaries in Natal were translating the Bible. The book of Genesis in Zulu was printed in Natal at the expense of the Society, together with several additional portions of the Old Testament. By such slow stages the Society pursued its path of help to American missions in what was then almost literally the unknown continent.

Beyond the confines of Christendom the only lands in which the Society at this time had an agency were in the region at the eastern end of the Mediterranean known as the Levant. Rev. Dr. I. G. Bliss, the Agent, wrote with fluent optimism of successes in Bible distribution. There was opposition from some of the Greek and Armenian clergy, and many ingenious devices of obstruction were used by the Turkish authorities, but the Bible made its way among the people so rapidly that in 1870 the Society had no more promising field abroad. In that region, where no inherited conviction of Christian truth gives support to Bible work, there were fifty principal Bible depositories of the Society with 175 branch depots. These depositories were found in European Turkey, in Greece, in the storied islands of the Ægean Sea, on the shores of the Dardanelles, in the old Roman provinces of Asia, in Syria and Mesopotamia, on the banks of the Nile and in the Empire of Persia — wherever there were American missionaries. Forty colporteurs and six Bible women were engaged in distributing Scriptures.

In Persia a colporteur exploring the country went through Hamadan, the city of Esther and Haman, as far as Ispahan, and came back delighted with the reception given to him and his books. In Egypt, Rev. Dr. Lansing took a colporteur to a great fair at Mansoura. The Patriarch of the Coptic Church was at the fair and his presence was dreaded by the men of the Book. The tactful colporteur, however, went straight to the Patriarch asking if he had forbidden the people to buy Bibles. "Oh, no," said the Patriarch, "God forbid that I should do such a thing!" The colporteur then suggested that he might buy one himself. The great prelate bought, and the whole stock of Bibles was quickly taken up. Mohammedans in different parts of Turkey bought Bibles or Testaments and one expressed the feeling of many when he said: "This is the best and the holiest book I ever saw; it cannot do me harm." It must not be supposed from these incidents that the work of the colporteur comports with ease. Such labour requires too great self-denial for any but the most devoted Christians. The incidents of this period, however, justified belief that every Bible or Testament sold kindles a light which cannot be extinguished.

Rev. Dr. Bliss returned to the United States on furlough in 1865, with a plan, elaborated lovingly in detail, for a Bible House in the heart of Constantinople. As a centre of all forms of evangelism such a building would send out light to every part of the Levant. The Board could not consent to use funds of the Society for the purpose; but it authorised Dr. Bliss to raise money by special subscription, letting it be understood that the Society took no responsibility in the matter. Dr. Bliss presented his case with such contagious zeal in different parts of the United States that he succeeded in raising about $60,000 for the construction of the Bible House and returned to Constantinople with a glad heart.

During the period from 1861 to 1871 the cost to the Society of supplying Scriptures in the languages of this great Agency amounted to $230,951. Including this amount the expenditure during this period in non-Christian lands whose people had erected their various civilisations in ignorance of the Bible and of its existence was $411,385. This great sum represented a part of the cost to American Christians of their obedience to their Lord, of their compassion for men who grope in spiritual and ethical uncertainties, and of their conviction that the Bible makes men and makes nations. It represented the worship by free-will offerings of many thousands of our people; and by every token the gift had found favour with God.

CHAPTER XXXVII

THE JUBILEE CELEBRATION OF 1866

In May, 1865, the Society entered its fiftieth year of service. At the same time a new era dawned in the United States with the end of civil war. The rattle of small arms and thunder of cannon were stilled. The passions of those who fought passed away like bad dreams. The great armies dispersed. Long separated families were reunited. Officers and soldiers packed up their regimental trappings and returned to their ordinary occupations. Throughout the land useful production gradually displaced waste and destruction. There was a general revulsion of feeling from distress and anxiety to thanksgiving and joy. The Bible Society, also, had special occasion for joy as it entered its fiftieth year. It could look back upon a half century of struggle and often of anxiety, cheered, however, by constant gains of strength through the support and leadership of its Master. To the Board it seemed a happy and providential coincidence that the beginning of so notable a year of its history should be associated with the beginning of a new order of things in the history of the republic. For this the Managers offered humble and hearty thanksgiving to God.

At its regular meeting, May 4, 1865, the Board appointed the current year to be observed as a Jubilee, delegating to the Anniversaries Committee all necessary arrangements. The Committee appealed to all the churches in the country, to observe the Jubilee year by special services, and invited the Auxiliaries to change each regular annual meeting into a little Jubilee meeting that would commemorate the increased circulation of the Bible as well as the multiplied evidences of its power. The Committee also suggested four particular objects which might be undertaken by the Society as appropriate to a year of praise and thanksgiving: First, the supply of destitution in the South; second, a general supply of the needy throughout the home land; third, the electrotyping of the Arabic Bible, and fourth, the issue of the revised Spanish Bible. There would be no general call for special contributions, but Auxiliary Societies might well take up one or more of these objects and do what they found possible to make it a success.

The appeal sent out by the Committee was written by the Rev. William Adams, D.D., and rang out clear and penetrating like the old Hebrew trumpet call at the beginning of each Jubilee year. Dr. Adams pointed out how the Society had surpassed the most sanguine expectations of its founders, receiving the cordial confidence and support of the entire country; multiplying its Auxiliaries in all parts of the land; sending out millions of copies of Scriptures in all directions which, like those placed in the army during the war, could be reckoned as seed cast on a subsiding flood, and destined to reappear with blessed results in future growth. He noted the changes since the organisation of the Society throughout the world, in sentiment, in forms of government, and in religious devotion to God with a new regard for the Bible; and he called upon all the people to expect quick progress of the Kingdom, like a tree long in growth, which after maturity, in one season blossoms out and bears abundant fruit.

Responses to these appeals came from all parts of the land, Auxiliaries and ecclesiastical bodies heartily pledging action in the line proposed. Congratulations were received from the British and Foreign Bible Society, the Bible Society of France, and other Societies in Europe.

The Board arranged as a part of the exercises of the fiftieth year a series of sermons by eminent clergymen to be delivered in the first instance in New York City. The first Jubilee sermon, on the "Advantages of a Written Revelation," by Rev. William Adams, D.D., was preached October 15, 1865; the second by Rev. Dr. Vermilye, November 19, on the "Purity of the Bible"; the third by Rev. Dr. Charles Hodge of Princeton Theological Seminary, January 21, 1866, on the "Inspiration of the Bible"; the fourth, February 18, 1866, by President J. W. Cummings of Wesleyan

University on "The Bible and Civil Government"; the fifth by Rev. R. S. Storrs, D.D., Jr., March 18th, on "The Bible the Book of Mankind"; the sixth by Rev. Dr. W. R. Williams of the Baptist Church, April 15, on "What the Bible has done for the World during the Last Century"; the seventh by Rev. Dr. Alexander Vinton, April 22, on "The Humane in the Bible"; and the eighth by the Rev. Isaac Ferris, D.D., LL.D., Chancellor of the University of the State of New York, May 6th, on the "History of the American Bible Society."

These sermons were listened to by large and interested audiences; several of them being repeated in the House of Representatives at Washington, and the most of them in Philadelphia, Boston, Cincinnati, and other cities. Taken together they constituted a powerful agency to turn the thoughts of the people to the Bible and the memorial celebration which would reach its climax on the fiftieth Anniversary of the day on which the Society was organised.

That anniversary day was Thursday, the 10th of May, 1866. The Board of Managers met as usual at the Bible House, where they welcomed as representatives of the British and Foreign Bible Society the Rev. Thomas Phillips, senior District Secretary, and the Rev. Thomas Nolan of St. Peter's Church, Regent Square, London; of the Bible Society of France the Rev. Cæsar Pascal; of the Bible Society of Upper Canada, the Rev. Lachlin Taylor, D.D., and Rev. William Ormiston, D.D. Besides these men from other Bible Societies, representatives were present of twenty-nine Auxiliary Societies from Massachusetts to California. After transaction of the formal business of an Annual Meeting, the Society with its guests adjourned to the Academy of Music where the celebration of the fiftieth Anniversary took place, President Lenox taking the Chair at ten o'clock.

The platform was filled with an assemblage of eminent and venerable men such as are not often brought together. The Bible Society Record in describing the meeting, said: "Rarely have we seen so large an audience equally interested, patient, and deeply affected with the spirit of the occasion."

A very interesting feature of the Jubilee Anniversary

was the presence on the platform of the Rev. Dr. Gardiner Spring, who briefly addressed the meeting. As the youngest of the founders of the Society in 1816 and one of the three surviving members of the Convention, he presented to the meeting, after giving thanks to God for the experiences of his own life, the single thought, "It is my earnest desire that the God of the Bible shall be honoured in your future career as He has been in some measure in the past."

Immediately following the words of Dr. Spring, Bishop C. P. M'Ilvaine of Ohio arose, giving as an excuse for his doing so that, while he was too young in 1816 to be present at the organisation of the Society, he remembered his impressions as a boy on seeing Dr. Boudinot and some of the delegates; and how later, in college, he was moved by an address by Dr. Spring. He added that he felt unable passively to hear the words, perhaps the farewell words, addressed to the Society by this venerable father, and therefore he requested that the audience rise in testimony of respect to Dr. Spring. Immediately the vast audience rose and remained standing for some time in silence and in tears.

Among the addresses at the Jubilee Anniversary we can only mention a few. Rev. Thomas Phillips, of the British and Foreign Bible Society, pointed out that a Jubilee is an opportunity which may occur only once in a lifetime to review the past and stimulate new zeal for the future. He rapidly described the Jubilee of the British and Foreign Society in 1854 as a time for thanksgiving, a time for reasserting the nature and source of the Bible, and a time for urging Bible lovers to become Bible givers. He brought to the American Bible Society the salutations of the older Society, gracefully suggesting that she had been in the habit of considering herself a parent to the American Society, but now that the younger Society had attained to the respectable age of fifty, he would salute her as a sister and heartily thank God for her work in the world. The Rev. Thomas Nolan emphasised the fostering care of God shown in the history of the Bible Societies. The stereotype process was invented just a short time before the British and Foreign Bible Society was organised and required a method of quick multiplication of Bibles. Again the Society with the appliances for printing available at the mission presses in Beirut and Smyrna working full speed, would have required 6,000 years to print a supply of Arabic Bibles for the 120,000,000 who ought to have them. But shortly before the need arose the invention of electrotyping solved the difficulty. Mr. Nolan thanked the Society for the gift to the British Society of a set of Arabic plates of the Bible, and rejoiced that both Societies had fostered the Christian feeling expressed by Lord Bexley: "If we cannot reconcile all opinions, let us try to unite all hearts."

The Rev. Cæsar Pascal, representative of the French Bible Society, followed up this topic of the favour of God shown to the Bible Society by remarking what an amazing thing it seemed to friends in Paris that the American Society in the midst of the war, with a financial crisis pressing and a national debt computed by the thousand millions, could still increase its operations and enlarge by many thousands its circulation of Scriptures. In expressing the warm regard of the French Society he added that it is the Bible which gives the United States its prominent place in the world, and makes the destiny of the United States rest under God to a great extent with Societies like this.

Major-General O. O. Howard of the United States Army, who one year before on that day was still commanding the right wing of General Sherman's army in North Carolina, made a warm appeal for attention to the needs of the South, and especially of the poor whites and the freed slaves.

There were also strong addresses on the Bible in action. Rev. Dr. Rufus Anderson, Secretary of the American Board, pointed out that the American Bible Society in fifty years had spent about $800,000 for printing and distributing Bibles in foreign lands and chiefly in pagan countries. He said that more Bibles had thus been distributed outside of Christendom since the Bible Society era than were in all the world from Moses to the Reformation. By trying to form some impression of the vastness of the influence of this distribution, it is possible to see how essential the Bible is to the missionary.

Rev. I. G. Bliss, Agent of the Society in the Levant, having to watch over an area of 1,200,000 square miles, made a strong appeal for adequate support. In the eight years of his service the proceeds of books sold in his Agency amounted to $22,000. This sum had been paid by the poor; the books for the most part being sold for only one-third of their cost.

Rev. Dr. Jonas King of the American Board's Mission in Athens, Greece, who had received during forty years grants for Greek Scriptures, emphasised the truth that missionary work shows the Bible to be the centre of the moral world as the sun is the centre of the physical world.

The Hon. Robert C. Winthrop of Massachusetts, the statesman and orator who followed Daniel Webster in the United States Senate, invited his hearers to think of the influence of the 21,000,000 volumes of Scripture sent out by the Society during these fifty years. They have gone to people who were without them, and it were better to endure war or pestilence or any other variety of famine than a famine of the word of God. "The influence of these Bibles," he said, "has nothing to approach it in importance in all the boasted achievements of mankind." And then he appealed to the people to reflect that "if the Bible stands alone, in measureless superiority, in peerless pre-eminence, so have Societies devoted to its publication a paramount claim upon the support, the sympathy and the co-operation of all Christians."

The addresses were eloquent and in some passages very impressive. For full five hours the large audience kept up its interest. Then President Mark Hopkins of Williams College, pronounced the benediction, and the assembly dissolved, with hearty good wishes for the future of the American Bible Society.

That passage of Mr. Winthrop's appeal was needed which reminded his audience that Societies devoted to Bible circulation have a paramount claim upon the support of all Christians. A great number of new schemes of benevolence had sprung up during the war period. The Agents of the Society and its Auxiliaries reported strenuous efforts being made throughout the country to raise money for colleges, theological seminaries, denominational extension schemes, endowment of hospitals, homes for disabled soldiers and sailors, and similar institutions throughout the South as well as schemes for the education and uplift of freedmen. The difficulty of maintaining interest in the Bible Society work was felt very strongly in cities. Churches absorbed in purely denominational work were very glad to have supplies of Scriptures from the Bible Society, but did not feel under special obligations toward it since it was an undenominational institution. In the cities there was more and more difficulty in finding churches willing to put the pulpit, even for a single Sunday in the year, at the disposal of the Society.

In this careless attitude toward the support of the Society people forgot that their missions, both at home and abroad, were receiving large sums in aid of their work from the Society; that the churches in the days when missions were young had urged the Society to take up work in Turkey, China, Japan, and other countries. The Society had become involved in and attached to this work; the churches should not lose their interest, lest they be classed with certain unthrifty farmers who will set out acres of choice peach trees and then leave them to the borers and the weeds. The people forgot, too, that if the Bible Society were left to go to pieces for want of support, they themselves would be the first to suffer from such a catastrophe.

It was with pleasure, therefore, that the Board learned that many stimulating sermons on the Bible and the claims of support for its circulation had been delivered at this time in different parts of the country. Here we can give space to a brief mention only of the charge of Bishop Eastburn of Massachusetts to the clergy of the diocese. The subject of this document, issued May 2, 1866, was "The Bible Society's Jubilee Year." The paper reviewed the history of the formation of the Society which was within his own memory. It then, in eloquent terms, pointed out "what a distinct assertion this great institution is every day making in the face of the whole country of the inspiration and divine authority of the Holy Scriptures." On this account prayer and labour is due, he said, for the continued prosperity of the work of the Society.

A time of transition is always one which sifts aims and motives. The period of the Civil War was to the Bible Society such a period of sifting. Such experiences as have been noted during the period of the war developed in the Society inspiration to undertake and vigour to execute. From these experiences, hard and wearing as they were, the Bible Society had occasion to rejoice with thanksgiving as it came forth, entering upon its second half century as a new, well-equipped body assured of success, through divine guidance, in all the undertakings of its destiny.

CHAPTER XXXVIII

FORGET NOT ALL HIS BENEFITS

A PROVERB of the Zulus in South Africa says, "You can count the apples on one tree, but you cannot count the trees in one apple." It is a breezy thrust at him who knows too much, and a quiet hint that attention may yield profit as well as interest.

In the fifty years whose close was celebrated with thanksgiving in May, 1866, the Society received $10,434,953.74. Aside from the proceeds of sales of books at or below cost, important sources of the receipts were:

Donations from Churches, Societies and Individuals, ...	$1,500,470
Donations from Auxiliaries	1,386,146
Donations from Legacies	1,145,149

These large sums, like the apples on the Zulus' tree, are obvious and important facts of the Society's arduous labours during half a century. But many important details of the present, the future, and the permanent usefulness of the Society can only be observed by a closer examination of the relations of past events.

In such a retrospect one is particularly struck with the enormous additions to the home field of the Society since the close of the first quarter century of its history. Texas was then a foreign country; California, which included a vast expanse of territory to the eastward of the present limits of the state, then belonged to Mexico; and in the northwest the great undefined region known as "Oregon" was of uncertain ownership, being occupied by British as well as American hunters and explorers. All of these vast regions at the end of another twenty-five years were included in the United States. Hundreds of thousands of immigrants had come into the country and were fast settling the lands west of the Mississippi. Willing or not willing, the Society had been irresistibly driven to attempt the supply of the great, needy populations thus placed within its reach.

The temporary rending of the Union by the Civil War with the severing of relations with the Southern Auxiliary Societies, and with the immense demand upon the Society for the supply of the army and the destitute South seemed to have nothing but strain and pain for the Board of Managers and the Executive officers. In after-thought, however, none could but see a providence in the building of the Bible House at Astor Place, without which the Board would have been helpless in this emergency. All saw, too, that through this terrible stress of supply, the ties uniting associates in the Bible House, the bonds holding together the Auxiliaries all over the country, yes — and those linking the Society with brethren of the Southern States, were more firmly knit; very much as the fellowship of a fierce campaign binds members of the same regiment to one another almost as members of one family.

Engrossing anxieties in the home field had not hindered the expansion of the Society's fields abroad. Those fields had increased to a degree never imagined, in most sanguine moments, by the executive officers of the first twenty-five years. Europe, France, Germany, Russia and even Italy, had received thousands of volumes of Scriptures through the solicitude of the men who looked upon the world from the windows of the Bible House. Bible Society colporteurs were ranging over the Turkish Empire from the Danube to the Persian Gulf, distributing Scriptures in languages which, like Bulgarian for instance, had not been heard of in New York during the first quarter century of the Society's existence. In China the Bible was being printed for the Society in at least six different dialects and American funds were joined with those of the two British Bible Societies to secure the preparation of a truly union version of the classical Chinese. Japan had come to light. Japanese Ambassadors had inspected and praised the Bible House in New York. Copies of the Scriptures in Dutch and in Chinese had been disseminated for the Society in Japan, turning a chosen few men to Christianity; and a Committee of scholarly missionaries were preparing for a Japanese version of the New Testament.

American Missionaries in Mexico, Central America, in both Spanish and Portuguese South America were dispensing to eager inquirers Scriptures provided by the Society. From India and even from Africa missionaries were calling for additional grants to reach multitudes that might now be won to the knowledge of Jesus Christ. Missionary ships in the Pacific Ocean were carrying Bibles printed by the Society to numbers of the little Micronesian Islands and bringing back word of the wonderful influence of the word of God upon the people. This was not the fruit of well-planned enterprise on the part of the Board. All that its members could say on seeing the great fields inviting them to foreign lands was, " What hath God wrought! "

Expansion in the foreign field cheered the members of the Board by bringing them into touch with men converted abroad, and helping the Bible distribution of the Society. Dr. Bliss of the Levant Agency described in 1866 some of his colporteurs working in the city of Constantinople. One was a Greek — tall, sallow, sorrowful, and taciturn, who had been working twelve years as a colporteur, dealing largely with his own people, the Greeks; selling many books also to Mohammedans until the government interfered, and selling some too, to Jews. He had succeeded in inducing people to buy about 8,000 volumes of Scripture. Another was a thin, nervous Armenian named Avedis who went about burdened like a pack-horse, with a basket of books hanging from his shoulder and a carpet-bag full of books to balance it in front, another carpet-bag, also full of books, in his left hand, and two or three sample New Testaments in his right hand. When any one raised objections to buying the Scriptures, Avedis would talk the caviller into buying if it took an hour. This colporteur had a mind of his own. He objected strongly to selling the Ancient Armenian Bible because in his view that unintelligible language has been used by Satan to ruin the souls of multitudes of his fellow countrymen. Another successful colporteur was a blind theological student. After his study hours he would feel his way carefully along the street, offering Scriptures to any whose attention he could gain. Taking a portion of Bible in raised letters in his hand and reading with his fingers passages to the people helped him to dispose of his books when a man had been induced to open a Testament and find in it the verses which the blind man was reading. Simple minded followers of Jesus Christ like these, in South America, in the United States, in Europe and in Asia had been doing an important service as pioneers who open the way for the missionary.

Of the manner in which missionaries opened a way for the Bible Society much could be seen in the important languages in which Scriptures were printed during this period at the Bible House. Of German and French Scriptures large editions had been printed almost every year from 1817 onward. For the Jews the Old Testament in English was printed without chapter headings, running title, or other accessories. Among the Asiatic languages, besides the Arabic of which detailed mention is given below, the Modern Armenian Bible and the New Testament, and a pocket Testament in Modern Syriac (the colloquial language used by the Nestorians of Persia), were electrotyped and printed during the second quarter century.

Among the languages of the American Indians the New Testament in Dakota, translated by Riggs and Williamson, missionaries of the American Board, had been electrotyped and printed, along with parts of the Old Testament in the same language, and the New Testament in Cherokee. From the West Indies the Society had received a curious manuscript of the Gospel of St. Mark in Creolese, the dialect of the mixed coloured population of the Islands of Curacao. The translation had been made by the Rev. S. Van Diessel, a missionary labouring in that island, and the Board was glad, on being assured of the faithfulness of the version, to add it to the list for which the Society is responsible.

For the Islands of the Pacific the Hawaiian family Bible had been electrotyped and printed, together with portions for several of the Islands of Micronesia, and the latest work for the healing of the nations undertaken at the Bible House during this period was the electrotyping of the Bulgarian New Testament with the old Slavic in parallel columns.

Among these numerous versions of the Bible, the Arabic

version deserves more than a casual glance which it has had. The Arabic version used for forty years or more by the British and Foreign Bible Society was the work of Sarkis, a Maronite Bishop of the Seventeenth Century. He translated the whole Bible from the Vulgate for the use of the Roman Catholic Church in Syria and the work was published at Rome in 1671. In the form there printed the Latin original accompanied the Arabic in parallel columns. This version being the best available was adopted by the British Society in 1818, the Apocrypha and the Latin of the diglot being of course discarded. Scriptures of this version were the ones first purchased by the American Bible Society to supply American missionaries in Syria, and were generally used in that region until about 1864.

A new Arabic translation free from the inaccuracies of the Vulgate seemed absolutely essential. "The Arabic translator" wrote the missionaries in urging their plea, "is interpreting the lively oracles for forty millions of an undying race whose successive and ever augmenting generations shall fail only with the final termination of all things. . . . To give to them a Christian literature, or that germinating commencement of one which can perpetuate its life and expand it into full grown maturity is to put in their hands gigantic verities taking fast hold on the salvation of myriads whom no man can number in the present and all future generations!"

Books in Arabic printed from type made in Europe are intolerable to Oriental readers, because the curves and slopes of the letters are not artistically proportioned. Rev. Dr. Eli Smith, who commenced the great work of translation, first took the finest available specimens of Arabic caligraphy, and by long, patient labour reproduced perfectly all the graceful forms for which Arabic manuscripts are remarkable. The pattern letters which he drew averaged about three inches in height. Mr. Hallock, the printer, with a pantograph then traced the letters, reduced to the required diamensions, upon polished steel from which he finally cut the punches with which matrices were formed. So perfect were Dr. Smith's models that the form of the letters has never been modified in the least. They satisfy the reader most finical, and by triumphantly outdoing efforts of past type-founders they disarm the Mohammedan hatred of everything Christian. The form of type having been fixed, the work of translation could go on with high hopes.

This translation of the Scriptures begun by Dr. Eli Smith, revised and completed by Dr. C. V. A. Van Dyck, was brought to a conclusion in sixteen years. The laborious solicitude with which accuracy was sought should be noted. Of every form thirty proofs were taken and sent to as many scholars of all nations, their suggestions and criticisms being carefully considered before the form was released for printing. After several editions had been printed from type at Beirut, the mission unanimously requested the Society to electrotype the book in ten different sizes and the request was warmly urged by the American Board; with the result that one of the great works signalising the Jubilee year was the making of electrotype plates for the Arabic Bible, Rev. Dr. Van Dyck, the translator, supervising the work in New York. The first plate was electrotyped March 15th, 1866.

After completing three sets of plates, of which one set was sent to the British and Foreign Bible Society and one retained in New York for safety, the work of electrotyping was transferred to Beirut, the Society furnishing a complete equipment and a skilled electrotyper to instruct the Syrian workmen in the process. Since that time this Bible has been electrotyped and printed at the Presbyterian Mission Press in Beirut, the American Bible Society paying all expenses of publication year by year.

It was pleasant to render the kindly service to the British and Foreign Bible Society as to plates of the new version. That Society wished to buy a duplicate set of the Arabic plates and the Committee to which the matter was referred brought in a report of which the noble principle was expressed as follows: "No particular part of this broad work belongs of right to either Society exclusively, except so far as God in His Providence may afford to one a more ready access and greater facilities than to the other. In this great work of evangelising the world we should press forward side by side, with one heart and one purpose.

Neither should 'they call aught of the things they possess their own,' but all things should be 'in common' for the Master's sake. Translations should be used interchangeably, and any advantage or facility secured by one Society should be a gain to the cause and to all who love it."

The Board of Managers approved the recommendation of the Committee and voted to furnish the duplicate electrotype plates without charge. It accompanied this decision with the largest liberty for the free and unrestricted use of these plates by the British Society with its own imprint, conditioned only by the provision that no alteration be made in the plates without the consent of the American Society. Rev. Dr. Bergne in communicating a graceful resolution of thanks from the Committee of the British and Foreign Bible Society wrote to Dr. Holdich: "You resolve that the word of God shall not be bound, and give us unrestricted liberty to the use of a translation which owes its existence to the able scholarship, laborious toil, and indomitable perseverance of one of the best missionaries America has sent forth, and whose name will be held in loving veneration not only in the land where he has personally been known but wherever the Arabic tongue is spoken and the Arabic Bible is circulated. For this we heartily thank your Board and shall long cherish the pleasant remembrance of a transaction upon which we believe the blessing of God will abundantly rest."

Besides this progress with new versions many events during this period favoured the task of the Society. But some hindered it; like the burning of Bibles by a priest in Massachusetts and like the suspicion of some good people in Connecticut that the Society was mismanaging its affairs. This history cannot give space to details of trials which in the retrospect seem trivial. The Roman Catholic priest who burned Bibles in 1869, probably really thought that he was doing God service for he said, like one who boasts a good deed, that he had gathered Bibles from the parish enough to last him "all winter for kindling." Connecticut is near enough to New York for its people to learn for themselves exactly what the Society is doing at any moment, but in 1864, some of the good people of that state made known to the Congregational General Association distrust of the wisdom and practical management of the American Bible Society. The Association appointed a Committee to investigate the management in detail. Two years later, in June, 1866, the Committee reported through its chairman, Rev. M. N. Morris, that it had made a full and careful investigation by repeated visits to the Bible House. Upon the recommendation of the Committee, the Association adopted resolutions entirely clearing the Bible Society of any mismanagement or carelessness, and giving thanks to God for the ability and fidelity with which its affairs were conducted. To these resolutions the Association added another asking the Society to study the question whether a way could not be devised, without detriment of the missionary work of the Society, for supplying its Bibles everywhere through the ordinary trade, instead of limiting their sale to a few only of the more important centres of business. By such kindly action what seemed like a needless burden cast upon the Board became a favouring word.

Three of the events which favoured the task of the Society during the war period are worthy of emphasis. One of these was the sequel to the daring scheme of building the new Bible House on a great scale. This scheme was entirely foreign to the purpose of the Board until disappointment had forced the giving up of the smaller plans which the members of the Board had formed at the beginning. In the sequel it was clearly seen that without that great Bible House the comprehensive service of the Society for the army a decade later could not possibly have been rendered. Then as a secondary consequence of the building of the Bible House, the Young Men's Christian Association was established under that roof. From that association sprang the Christian Commission which co-operated in the work of Bible distribution in the army in a most efficient way, using its hundreds of agents for the purpose, while the Society had comparatively few agencies available for work among the vastly increased masses of soldiers.

Another of these notable events was the sudden disappearance of an insurmountable obstacle like a failure of income at a time when general distress made larger contributions improbable. The story of the change in the financial condition of the Society at the height of the war reads like a fairy tale of a good child liberally cared for, by a mighty helper, for his good will and diligence. "The Treasure House of the Lord is the hearts of His people." During the five years after the Southern States seceded until the armies were disbanded donations from churches and individuals amounted to $263,681, an amount considerably larger than donations of the same class in five years before the secession. During the five years of the war period, donations from Auxiliaries amounted to $375,754. This amount was contributed to the Society after more than six hundred Auxiliaries in the South had withdrawn, and it exceeded the gifts of all the Auxiliaries in any previous period of five years. Again during this same five years of dire need on the part of the Society, receipts from legacies amounted to $475,733. This was a larger sum than had been received from legacies in any other period of five years since the Society was founded, and it was $200,000 more than the total of legacies in the next largest and next previous five-year period. If the Society had possessed a wishing cap which would enable it to procure gold at a moment's notice, the effect could not have been more startling.

One more notable event of this period was the astonishing agreement of the governments and generals of the two conflicting armies to allow hundreds of thousands of Bibles and Testaments to pass through their lines under a sort of special truce almost inconceivable in war time. Great as was the benefit of this episode to the soldiers of the South while the war was waging, the kindly spirit which moved the Society was thus made known to the Southern States and prepared the Southern people to welcome the Society after the war as if war had not been. The Society had not been brought into collision with the strong sentiment against union of the States which existed before the war because its very object held it aloof from purely civil questions. Therefore, it gladly undertook to act when it could, as an Agent of the Lord to aid and renew the religious activities of the South. It was the more ready to pour the living waters into the Southern States through every channel since there can be no real or enduring pacification without the Bible at the foundation of government and civilisation.

These and many similar occurrences in Bible Society history incline men to say, "Events have favoured the enterprise!" Events have neither eyes, brains, nor hands that they should favour or oppose. A truly intent mind will ask Who caused those favouring events? A similar question often arises in the ordinary life of the community. One man goes out to do what his hand finds to do. His task is perfectly done. Another man fails in all that he tries to do; when he looks at the first he will only say, "Lucky dog!" But when the successful one has controlled all his powers in the name of his Master, it comes to light that he has a secret which makes him stronger. The secret is that he is controlled by the thought, "My God helping me, I can and will succeed in this thing!" Like the Hebrews in their long and checkered history, the members of the Society were taught during this time that when they were weak God was still Almighty; when their plans seemed about to fail, God's plans for them were most firmly founded.

The men in the Managers' Room did their best. Workmen in any great factory finish perfectly the single piece of wood or of metal assigned to them, knowing that from these detached pieces the general management will cause to be built up and sent forth beautiful machines perfectly adapted to work. What these men did in the Managers' Room in the Bible House was of the same class; they did the duty next at hand, believing God would use their service for His great ends. It is in the periods which come afterwards that the proofs of the Bible appear; and one great thing evident to the later reader of this history is that this was a reason to expect the interposition of the Most High at this time, not in behalf of the Society, nor in behalf of the men representing it and sorely tried by their burdens, but in behalf of the task laid upon them and the Book which they had to send out. The cause at stake was a great one. A failure at New York would be felt throughout the home land, with its growing population, and abroad among the inarticulate masses of India, in China, in Japan, in Africa, and in Siberia. The benefit of the events which favoured the task of the Society was no personal gain. The gain was to the people who needed and received the Bible and gave glory to God Himself.

SIXTH PERIOD 1871–1891

CHAPTER XXXIX

PAYING THE COST OF WAR

GREAT and heroic deeds of the soldiers fill the thoughts of the common folk at the end of a successful war. Painful surprises await the people, however, when the dolorous task begins of adjusting the war's cost. After the civil war, when business depression befogged the whole country, the people at large were taken aback. Anxiety prevailed in the land; in some places money almost disappeared from the markets; suffering fell upon many a family; even a church, here and there, found it impossible to pay the salary of the pastor, and until after the return of the United States Treasury to specie payments in 1879, uncertainty hampered all plans for business or benevolence.

As the nation tried to struggle up from the enfeebling wastes of the war, local catastrophes added to the general uneasiness. In October, 1871, the great fire in Chicago destroyed 18,000 buildings with money losses estimated at two hundred millions of dollars. The population of a wide region was thus bereft — the Christians, of a noble rallying point, and the pleasure-seekers, of the kind of values which the Revelation describes as lost in the fall of Babylon. This fire, by the way, occasioned a grant by the Board of $5,000 worth of Scriptures to the Chicago Bible Society which had 7,000 Bibles in stock, paid for, as one might say, by sweat of the brow, and entirely destroyed in one day. A year later, in November, 1872, was the great fire in Boston, where granite buildings supposed to be absolutely fireproof melted in the fervent heat, and where the cost of the catastrophe to the city was at least eight millions of dollars. It was in Boston at this time that love for the Bible had noble fruit in the circumstance that three of the larger Episcopal churches of the city gave the Society $2,500 for its work — an amount considerably more than their gifts the year before.

The relation of these painful experiences to the story of the Bible Society is that in several states financial stringency and local anxieties made men quite willing to shut their eyes to the needs of the Bible cause. A little later people would become accustomed to smaller incomes and then they might perhaps begin to afford something toward forwarding the interests of their great Master.

The Bible Society in 1867 reported its total receipts as $734,089.14. Twelve years later, in 1878, its report of receipts was $446,954.04. This gives some impression of the financial stress which the period of recovery from the effects of war brought to the Society. A comparison of the receipts during each period of five years for twenty-five years after the Jubilee Anniversary will give a clearer idea, perhaps, of the anxieties of the Board of Managers.

Receipts for the five years ending March 31, 1871	$3,565,453.94
Receipts for the five years ending March 31, 1876	3,128,734.66
Receipts for the five years ending March 31, 1881	2,667,534.89
Receipts for the five years ending March 31, 1886	2,853,409.22
Receipts for the five years ending March 31, 1891	2,660,603.32

The situation during this period verged on the desperate in several years when the receipts of the Society were over $100,000 less than the expenditures.

Receipts from sales of books offered no relief to the Treasury, although they amounted to $7,785,459; for the larger part of the Society's issues do not return their cost to the Treasury. A great part of the books sold to the poor, particularly in backward foreign lands, bring no adequate price. The ten per cent. discount allowed to Auxiliaries and to the book trade, taking from the receipts the element calculated to cover cost of rent, supervision, wear and tear of plates, etc., like whole or partial grants of books is entirely a charge upon the Society's general resources. Books given in a single year to worthy denominational evangelistic enterprises with which the Society co-operates, frequently exceed in value the whole sum contributed by the denomination toward the support of the Society. Taking at random the year ending March 31, 1884, grants of books amounted in value to $195,041. The same year the donations received from church collections and from individuals amounted to $31,363.92, a sum less than one-sixth of the value of the grants, and the donors probably hoped that they had paid for numbers of Bibles besides those furnished for the uses of their own denomination.

During the same five yearly periods from March 31, 1866 to March 31, 1891, donations from churches and individuals were, respectively, $300,623, $176,907, $159,072, $154,310, and $149,029. Since these figures show that contributions from churches and individuals in the last five years (of the period ending in 1891) were one half less than they were twenty years before the question may arise how the great development of the Society's work at home and abroad was possible; for, as was stated by President Allen early in this period, in fifty-six years the income of the Bible Society had increased twenty fold, but the volumes issued had increased two hundred fold! A verse in Revelation pronounces a benediction upon the dead who die in the Lord and rest from their labours, adding, "And their works do follow them." This verse might find interpretation and exemplification in this epitome of financial troubles. Legacies of saints who had passed away during this period formed the largest single source of income for the Society. The aggregate of legacies received during the twenty-five years was $3,350,460, while the total of donations of churches and individuals was $939,941; or, adding the total of Auxiliary donations which amounted to $1,378,529, as belonging to the same category of church collections, an aggregate is reached of $2,318,470. That is to say, the donations of twenty-five years were over $1,000,000 less than the legacies of the same period.

Difficulties which obstructed the collection of money for the Bible cause naturally tended to weaken Auxiliary Bible Societies, for they, too, looked to the churches for their support. Many of those which had shared the lights and shadows, and borne the burdens of Bible Society progress since 1816 were still strong and active. Of such were the old state Societies in Massachusetts, in Virginia, and in New Hampshire, the latter so influential as to send in seventy-five years to the national Society $116,371 in donations. Among these earlier Auxiliaries, too, were county Societies, like that of Westchester County which has furnished presidents and vice-presidents to the national Society; or like Orange County, Albany County, Saratoga County, Washington County, Rockland County, and the Long Island Bible Society, in New York, the Cumberland County Society in New Jersey, and the Charleston, South Carolina, Bible Society, all of which appear as Auxiliaries in the very first report of the American Bible Society.

Other state societies, like those of Maryland and California, and hundreds of county Societies of later origin in almost every state from Maine to California, were sturdily pressing forward in Bible work like young athletes in a Marathon race. The good women of Auxiliaries in Ohio, Delaware and New York were still relied upon with confidence. In Texas the Bible Societies at Galveston and Houston, which were organised before Texas was fully disengaged from Mexico, and at Austin, formed as soon as the Mexican War came to an end, were trusty helpers of the national Society. Two score or more of Welsh Auxiliaries, one of them being in New York City and quite a number in Wisconsin, maintained a noble reputation for self-denial for the sake of sending to the Bible House, money which would carry Bible light into dark places.

These few out of the long list of active, self-sustaining Societies, are names used merely as illustrations of the working of the original plan by which the national Society would combine and harmonise the efforts of local Societies willing to help as Auxiliaries. In this list, as labouring against peculiar encumbrances, the New York Auxiliary may be mentioned. It always felt handicapped by the fact that the city was the head-quarters of the national Society. While its work of distribution was marked with vigour, the collection of money for the support of the work was not easy. Churches and many individuals in the city often preferred to give for the world-wide enterprise of the national Society rather than for merely local undertakings. The situation was like that of a son keeping a haberdashery shop in the city where his father has a department store, and the business depression which came to a crisis in 1873 seriously affected the New York Auxiliary. During the Civil War the parent Society had aided it to supply troops and sailors by granting to it about $35,000 in books or in money. In 1873 this Auxiliary's indebtedness for Scriptures, used in the main for immigrants and sailors, was cancelled to the amount of $35,485. Two years later a new indebtedness of $20,500 for books had accrued, which was also cancelled. At the same time the Board decided to aid its struggling helper by regular monthly grants on applications submitted to the Distribution Committee. During the next sixteen years, from the 1st of April, 1874, to the 31st of March, 1891, the New York Auxiliary drew from the depository under this arrangement books valued at $187,609, toward the cost of which it had paid $8,669. In its 66th annual report (1890) the New York Auxiliary mentions the fact that it had received in that year from the American Bible Society books valued at $9,148, and adds: "Thus that Society saved us from a serious deficit, if not from a cessation of our work, instead of receiving financial benefit from us." These circumstances naturally added to the burdens of the Managers. But the Board was full of sympathy for the Auxiliary because ever since 1829, when as the New York Young Men's Bible Society it asked recognition by the national Society, it had spent much money upon the expensive task of seeking and supplying the destitute in this great city.

During the financial stringency which followed the war, a considerable number of Auxiliaries seemed to be overcome by an epidemic paralysis which carried alarm into the Bible House in New York.[1] The Auxiliaries which slowly dried up like herbage on the edge of a desert were chiefly in the newer and more sparsely settled territories, but some of them were found also in the most favoured states. Numbers were found to be irresponsible as well as inefficient and were kept alive by the costly system of agencies. In 1891, out of 2,100 Auxiliaries only about 1,200 had enough physical force to order books from New York. Many of these did nothing more than to keep books for sale in depositories. Out of this number 364 had collected money for Bible distribution, sending the surplus to the national Society. Only 990 of the whole number of Auxiliaries sent in reports, and out of these only 110 reported that they had been engaged in general operations in their respective fields.

The original plan for an Auxiliary system laid a heavy burden upon local Bible Societies in expecting of them both labour in distribution of Scriptures, and activity in collecting the money to cover expenses of the distribution. It is impossible to review the history of those Societies without a suspicion of a parallel with men expected to "make bricks without straw." The assumption of the founders of the national Society was that Auxiliaries would always be stable in purpose, one in mind with the national Society which had just been organised. Robert Louis Stevenson defines what such unity of mind is. "To be of the same mind with

[1] Numbers of Auxiliaries expected the Society to send Agents to relieve them of the labour of book-keeping, of stock-taking and even of making out orders for books. In 1877, out of 1968 Auxiliaries 267 remitted to the Treasury money for books and as donations, 1117, for books only, and 57, as donations only. Five hundred and twenty-seven Societies sent nothing for either books or donations. The indebtedness of these Societies for books ordered but not paid for was $169,000. Of the Auxiliaries 919 reported $166,624 as cash received by their Treasurers. Of this sum they reported $38,277 as expended on their own fields; for books and donations they had sent to New York $114,213. This left $14,134 unaccounted for. At the same time, taking reports from 919 Auxiliaries as a basis, it was estimated that the 1968 local Societies had in their hands and entirely under their control, books valued at $427,465. The situation pictured by these figures made the Auxiliaries Committee at the Bible House reluctant to withdraw the Agents upon whose advice and assistance growth in efficiency seemed to depend.

another," says he, "is to see all things in the same perspective. It is not to agree with him in a few things near at hand and not much debated. It is to stand so exactly in the centre of his vision that whatever he may express, your eyes will light at once on the original; that whatever he may see to declare, your mind will at once accept." Now such a oneness of mind among Bible Societies implies not only stability in purpose, but the existence of a permanently helpful constituency and environment.

Besides the influences already suggested as combining to hamper the support of Bible work, one cause should be borne in mind as constantly affecting the Society as well as its auxiliaries. A generation which has studied and appreciates the necessity of Bible work is always passing away. A new generation "which knows not Joseph" is always receiving its heritage of control and direction in secular and religious affairs. Yet the new generation may lack knowledge of the relation of the Bible to national welfare. That the need of the Bible is as absolute in any nation as the need of scientific education, has to be taught again and again. The rising generation has to learn that the supply of every family in the nation with God's word is as much a public utility as the introduction of electric light into the streets. To many the idea will be entirely new that the circulation of the Bible has the power of God behind it, as certainly as has the flow of sap in an apparently dry tree when the spring sun stirs it to life. Again and again the new generation has to be taught that for their own welfare the Bible Society should be enrolled on the schedule of every church for an annual and adequate contribution. Upon this sort of educational work depends the adequate support of interdenominational enterprises like the Bible Society and its Auxiliaries, even when their activities are most clearly needed by the churches.

To all who love the Lord Jesus Christ the time here described offered wonderful opportunities for fruitful effort. The stimulus which emerged from the complex of influences left by the Civil War was felt in all the churches as it was in the Society. It was a glorious era of expansion of missions, of establishing schools, colleges, institutions for freedmen, homes for the aged, hospitals, and every other concrete expression of Christian desire to benefit mankind. The churches were electrical with longing to serve and honour the Lord. In these various enterprises the Society heartily rejoiced. Perhaps the Bibles distributed broadcast in the land during and since the war had prepared the way for these various undertakings of the different denominations. The Bible was often a pioneer in home evangelistic activities; while home missions, on the other hand, fostered need of the Bible. Thus all worked together to advance the kingdom of Christ. These splendid and most timely undertakings of the denominations could not succeed without money. Insensibly, this need of money displaced in some churches the annual collection for the Bible Society, although the Bible is so essential an element in home evangelisation.

Men of business principles like the laymen who conduct the affairs of the Bible Society again and again must have felt it their duty to reduce the large expenditures abroad and at home in view of the steady falling off in the contributions of the churches to the support of the Society. But a permanent failure of support for Bible work was almost unthinkable. The labours of the Society at home and abroad, like other missionary operations, continually called for larger ventures, as will be seen in later chapters. The task of Bible Societies cannot be ended until every family on the face of the earth has received, or at least has been offered a copy of the Bible. Many attempts were therefore made to increase contributions to the Bible cause.

An attempt was made with some success in some parts of the country to enlist Sunday School children for the support of the Bible cause. Another measure in the same direction was a decision that in districts where Auxiliaries were inert or careless the Agents should go directly to the churches proposing to them to make their contributions to the Treasury in New York without reference to the moribund local Auxiliaries. This rather drastic action was approved by many ecclesiastical bodies in different parts of the United States and of different denominations, since this arrangement would bring the churches into direct relations with the Society. When the fourth General Supply of the destitute in the United States was decided upon in 1882, a general appeal was sent out for special contributions, since the Society would have to spend considerable sums for distribution by means of colporteurs. The Board also sent a strong appeal to lovers of humanity everywhere to become Life Members of the Society in order to aid in its support.

Several times an urgent proposal was made to change the price of books so as to make it possible to offer the book trade attractive discounts and thus secure aid in Bible distribution; this, however, after long study by experts was steadily refused by the Board. As the Connecticut Congregational Association pointed out in 1866: "The laws of trade or the principle of profit will never carry the gospel to heathen lands nor distribute the Bible to the poor at home or to those who need its influence but do not realise its worth. If these are to be supplied it must be by other means."[1]

These various measures availed little. Then the number of colporteurs employed in the United States in connection with the fourth General Supply was reduced, and reduction of aid to missions abroad seemed imminent. The Society had already withdrawn from Greece, where it had been working for more than fifty years. The withdrawal was due partly to the closing of American missions in that country, but chiefly to the lack of money in the Treasury. And now, in 1891, for the first time in its history, inadequacy of receipts compelled the Board to defer making important appropriations for its foreign work. In 1880 the Board decided upon the absolute necessity of establishing a reserve fund which should protect the work of the Society in times of financial stress and emergency, but the provision of such a fund now seemed impossible. The administration of the Society seemed to be, like Othello, "steeped in poverty to the very lips."

At each of the most difficult moments of this period legacies brought a respite. Several large bequests were received, of which $10,000 from the late W. B. Astor was a type, and many small ones charged with love, like a legacy of about $900 from an aged coloured woman who had been a slave

[1] *Bible Society Record*, July, 1881, p. 98.

in Georgia. Nevertheless, the continual threats of the financial situation called to mind St. Paul's allusion to the "thorn in the flesh" which he found disagreeable enough to justify prayer for its removal. His allusion does not describe, it merely suggests; moreover, it does not give a hint as to the sequel. It merely says that the Lord rated His grace as sufficient for the sufferer. Doubtless, the members of the Board and the Secretaries, if they could speak to us to-day, would tell us that the grace of the Lord *is* sufficient for any man, for it permanently turns the mind from pain.

From the point of view of the Board and the Executive Officers, financial weakness did not prove an unmitigated evil. It insured discovery that money is an incident and not the soul of success in missionary work, it kept them from thinking that their own wits accomplished results, kept them near to their Master, and it forced upon these servants of God alertness and concentration of mind in the prosecution of the work committed to their care. In the strength thus cultivated they performed their tasks, trying meanwhile to suggest to the minds of the people the idea found in the old rule of the Talmud for work which is incumbent upon all: "If some complete the work effectively, the duty performed is credited to the whole body; but if through failure of some the cause suffers, the sin of it lies upon the whole body!"

CHAPTER XL

EVENTS AND EMERGENCIES IN THE BIBLE HOUSE

In times of stress such as the last chapter introduced, able, broad-minded, and consecrated leaders became known to every active Christian. That men of weight are numerous, even exceedingly numerous, in every denomination is one of the surprises encountered whenever several denominations work together. In the rapid procession of choice and earnest men who pass through the pages of this history, each successive group owed its dependence for strength and ability upon God alone. The Society is inclusive. It brings together in practical and effective co-operation men of different theological views in order that their very differences may brighten labour for God's Kingdom; the word of God being an inviolable bond of unity. The changes which occurred in the Society from year to year emphasised the religious basis of many a noble life. The end of such a life on earth to the labourers who remain is a painful emergency, but its revelation that the departed one was led of the spirit of God is a memorable event.

Of the sixty men of 1816 who met in the Garden Street Church to lay foundations for the institution whose development has been followed during nearly three score years, the Rev. Gardiner Spring, D.D., LL.D., died in 1873. He had been identified during fifty-seven years with the history and progress of the Society. During eighteen years he was Chairman of the Committee on Versions, retiring in 1864 by reason of the infirmities of age. As pastor he was always active in forwarding the interests of the Society, and the Board gave thanks to God for the long and valuable services of this eminent man. One man only of that distinguished body remained until 1875. Mr. Henry W. Warner was one of the representatives of the Auxiliary New York Bible Society in the Convention of 1816. He served for a time as President of that Society. In his own time he had been well-known as a cultured writer and lawyer in New York, but in 1875, when he passed away, Mr. Warner was remembered by younger men as the father of Susan Warner, author of the "Wide, Wide World," "Queechy," and other books, and of Anna B. Warner, who wrote under the pen name of Amy Lothrop.[1]

The changes in the presidential chair during this period were unusually many. President James Lenox became a Manager of the Society in 1838. In 1854 he was chosen Vice-President, and in 1864 President of the Society; performing the duties of his high office with grace and dignity. In 1871, cherished schemes of Christian benevolence demanding his constant attention, he urged that it was impossible with justice to himself to give attention longer to the duties of his position, and he resigned, to the great regret of the Board. On the 17th of February, 1880, Mr. Lenox passed away.

Dr. William H. Allen of Philadelphia, President of Girard College, was elected President of the Society in 1872. His character displayed a rare blending of simplicity and dignity, of firmness and gentleness, and he was held in the highest esteem by all who knew him. After eight years of service of the Bible cause he felt obliged to resign his office. Once before he had signified his intention to retire, but his associates in the management of the Society persuaded him to continue. After his resignation the Board elected him Vice-President, so that his counsel and influence might still be enjoyed. In August, 1882, he finished his work on earth. His funeral was held in the Arch Street Methodist Episcopal Church in Philadelphia.

Dr. Allen was succeeded as President by the Hon. S. Wells Williams, LL.D., who took up the duties of office March 31, 1881. President Williams was the son of one

[1] Who remained a warm friend of the Society until her death in 1915. The beautiful home of the family on Constitution Island opposite West Point is now the property of the United States Government, through a generous and happy thought of Mrs. Russell Sage.

of the founders of the Bible Society. In 1833 he went to China as a missionary of the American Board. After twenty-five years of enthusiastic missionary service, he entered the diplomatic service of the United States, from which he retired in 1876. He was a man of deep missionary convictions and of international reputation as a linguist, a sinologue, and a statesman. His counsels were invaluable to the Society. It was with peculiar sorrow, therefore, that the members of the Society learned of his death in February, 1884. He died as he had lived, with a simple, childlike personal trust in Christ, and a radiant assurance of the triumph of Christ's Kingdom in all pagan lands.

In November, 1884, the Hon. Frederick T. Frelinghuysen, Secretary of State, and for twenty-one years Vice-President of the Society, was elected President. He accepted the office, intending to take up its duties as soon as his term as Secretary of State was completed; but on his return from Washington to his home in Newark, New Jersey, he was ill, and on the 20th day of May, 1885, he passed away, not having entered upon the Presidential office.

Judge Enoch L. Fancher, Vice-President of the Society during eighteen years, was elected President in December, 1885. Judge Fancher had been a justice of the Supreme Court of the State of New York, and was arbitrator of the Chamber of Commerce, being a jurist of prominence and of irreproachable Christian character. For many years he had been an active member of the Missionary Society of the Methodist Episcopal Church.

The series of great men who have served the American Bible Society as Vice-Presidents illustrate the importance of the office, as well as the dignity which they have imparted to it. Many of them resided too far from New York often to meet with the Society, but the death of such was a loss to the Society as serious as though they had been in daily converse with their associates in the common work. Let this place be devoted to mention of the Vice-Presidents who died during the twenty years ending in 1891.

John Tappan, Esq., of Boston was one of the founders of the Massachusetts Bible Society, a Congregationalist of benevolent activity. It was privately recorded that he came one day to the Board with a thousand dollars in hand which he wished to give for sending a richly bound Bible to each of the rulers of the earth. The scheme was carried out; and one wonders what the rulers of the earth thought of it. But in the archives of the Society are letters from a number of Presidents, Kings, and Emperors courteously acknowledging the gift.[1] Mr. Tappan's good works on earth came to an end in 1871.

The planning of measures of supply for the United States Treasury during the Civil War fell to the lot of the Hon. Salmon P. Chase of Ohio, Secretary of the Treasury. Later he became Chief Justice of the Supreme Court of the United States. From 1843 until his death in 1873 he was actively interested in Bible work as President of the Cincinnati Young Men's Bible Society and in 1865 he became a Vice-President of the American Bible Society. To be a lawyer of eminence, a Governor of the State of New Jersey term after term, and minister of the United States to Berlin does not militate against the possessor of these distinctions being a warm-hearted, devoted member of the Reformed (Dutch) Church and during thirty-four years a Vice-President of the American Bible Society. Such was the Hon. Peter D. Vroom, who passed to the higher life in 1873.

The Hon. William A. Buckingham, as governor of Connecticut during the Civil War, was a counsellor and friend of President Lincoln, and from 1869 until his death in 1875 he was United States Senator from Connecticut. He was Moderator of the first Congregational National Council, and became Vice-President of the Society in 1865. An eminent lawyer of New Orleans, Joseph A. Maybin, Esq., Vice-President twenty-three years and President of the Southwestern Bible Society twenty-six years, entered into rest in 1876, full of honours and full of days. Hon. H. P. Haven of Connecticut, a mighty Sunday School champion, died in 1876. Myron P. Phelps, Esq., a prosperous business man of Lewiston, Illinois, during twenty-six years Vice-President of the Society, reached the term of his life on earth

[1] Volume marked Miscellaneous Correspondence 1843–1857, at the end.

in 1878. After twenty-eight years as Vice-President Hon. Abraham B. Hasbrouck of New York, finished in 1879 a life of service to the church, the state, and the school. The Chief-Justice of the territory of Utah, an officer in the Civil War, and a warm-hearted Methodist, Hon. James B. McKean, passed from this life in the same year. Two eminent Vice-Presidents who died in 1880 were the Hon. Edward McGehee of Mississippi, of the Methodist Episcopal Church South, a distinguished jurist, and the Hon. Lafayette S. Foster, a Connecticut Congregationalist, Judge of the Supreme Court of that state, United States Senator, and an intimate friend of President Lincoln. Upon Mr. Lincoln's death in 1865, Mr. Foster became Acting Vice-President of the United States. The Hon. Horace Maynard of Tennessee was an elder in the Presbyterian Church and served his country well as Senator, as Post Master General, and as Minister to Turkey. In that strange land, too, he served the Bible Society by clearing away illegal restrictions on colportage. His death was in 1882.

C. C. Trowbridge, Esq., of Detroit, long a member of the Standing Committee of the Protestant Episcopal Diocese, died in 1883. He had grown up with Michigan from the period when it was a vast and little known territory. The President of the Charleston, South Carolina, Bible Society, a financier of renown born in Germany, Secretary of the Treasury of the Confederate States, the Hon. C. C. Memminger, died in 1888 after fifteen years' service of the American Bible Society as Vice-President. It is not easy to picture in the mind Chicago as a hamlet of eight small houses. But a pioneer who built and lived in one of the eight little structures that fixed the site of the great city was Judge Grant Goodrich. During twenty-three years he was a Vice-President and in 1889 received the summons to appear on high. In 1889, too, Jacob Sleeper, Esq., a merchant of Boston, a Methodist unceasing in efforts to increase churches and schools, one of the founders of Boston University, and President of the Massachusetts Bible Society, rested from his labours. In the same year death took a distinguished Baptist, Prof. W. Gammell, LL.D., of Brown University, and that great captain of the forces of the Kingdom, George H. Stuart, Esq., of Philadelphia, merchant, banker, President of the Christian Commission during the Civil War and during twenty-five years Vice-President of the Society.

Every Vice-President of the Society, by virtue of his office, is a member of the Board of Managers. In looking over the records of the Board, one is struck with the number of Vice-Presidents living in and about New York whose names appear in every emergency. The loss of the counsel of such experienced men in the committees was deeply felt. By grouping together the names of Vice-Presidents and Managers who were members of the Finance Committee, for instance, and who passed away during this period, the seriousness of the loss appears. Vice-President F. H. Wolcott (d. 1882) was one member of this group. During thirty years he served the Society first as Manager and then as Vice-President. Besides his work on the Finance Committee, he was active in the Committee on Distribution. Vice-President Frederick S. Winston, elected member of the Board in 1839, and Vice-President in 1865, was for thirty-two years chairman of the Finance Committee. Occupied in all this time with business affairs of his own which attained success of colossal proportions, he was so identified with the Society that there was no part of its work of which he was not a part. He died in 1884. During twenty-one years a member of the Finance Committee was Vice-President Hiram M. Forrester, Esq. (d. 1888), a lawyer, and a master of wise, clear, concise statement. Vice-President James M. Brown (d. 1890), the head of the banking house of Brown Brothers and Company, and President of the New York Chamber of Commerce, served in the Finance Committee, and in the Committee of Publication. He was Senior Warden of the Episcopal Church of the Ascension.

A member of the Board who served with ardent love in the Finance Committee was A. P. Cumings, Esq., an editor and proprietor of the *New York Observer,* who died at Nice, France, in 1871, and on the day of his death spoke tenderly of the Board which would meet that day. James Donaldson, Esq. (d. 1872), who was thirty-one years a member of the Board of Managers, a leader in the Finance

Committee and in the Committee on Publication. Charles N. Talbot, Esq. (d. 1874), who had been a merchant in China for some years, was a member of the Committee on Finance and the Committee on Publication twenty-six years. Washington R. Vermilye, Esq. (d. 1876), an elder in the Presbyterian Church (who began his business life, by the way, as a clerk in the Society's house in Nassau street), well-known as President of the Greenwich Savings Bank, served in the Finance Committee twenty-three years. George W. Lane (d. 1883), a financier, was also a member of the Committee on Finance. William G. Lambert (d. 1883), another member of the Committee, was a successful business man in New York City who for nineteen years had been a member of the Board. The finances of the Society were always in efficient hands. And when vacancies occurred the Board filled them with other men of the same choice type.

Other Vice-Presidents prominent in the Board of Managers were Marshall S. Bidwell, Esq. (d. 1872), eminent at the bar, distinguished for learning, culture, and intellectual power, as well as for a spotless Christian life, who served in the Committee on Legacies and the Committee on Distribution; James Suydam, Esq. (d. 1872), of an old Holland family of New York, and a member of the Reformed (Dutch) Church, successful in business, during twenty-four years a member of the Committee on Legacies; Charles Tracy, Esq. (d. 1885), a member of the Protestant Episcopal Church, a prominent lawyer in New York City, who during a whole generation used his special knowledge of the law of wills as Chairman of the Legacies Committee; Norman White, Esq. (d. 1883), who deemed it his highest honour to share in the work of Bible distribution and was prominent during forty years in all the affairs of the Society; Richard P. Buck, Esq. (d. 1884), a true Puritan of the ancient stock in modern times, who during twenty years was rarely absent from a meeting of the Board; A. Robertson Walsh, Esq. (d. 1884), who became a Manager of the Society in 1844 and during forty years made his abilities felt especially in the Committee of Publication; Robert Carter, Esq. (d. 1889), who became a member of the Board of Managers in 1855. As he was a member of the well-known publishing house of Carter and Brothers, he naturally found his work, too, in the Committee of Publication.

Members of the Board of Managers passed away during this period who showed a variety of abilities and temperaments: George D. Phelps, Esq. (d. 1872), was a man outspoken in his strong convictions, and very efficient in work for the Board. Edward J. Woolsey, Esq. (d. 1872), a Presbyterian of an intellectual ancestry, who served well the Bible cause during twenty-eight years. Jonathan Sturges (d. 1874), a successful merchant, warm-hearted and generous, who concentrated his whole mind on the problems of the Committee on Distribution and of the Committee on Legacies. William H. Aspinwall (d. 1875), son of John A. Aspinwall, of the Society's first Board of Managers, a man of affairs, clear judgment, devotion and tact, worked with the Legacies Committee. A ruling elder in the Presbyterian church, member of the State Legislature, and for twenty-three years a member of the Board of Managers was Chandler Starr, Esq., who died in 1876. The good work of Stephen Van Rensselaer of the first Board of Managers was taken up and carried forward during forty-five years by his son, Alexander Van Rensselaer (d. 1878). The Hon. Nathan Bishop, LL.D., member of the Board of Indian Commissioners, and Trustee of Vassar College, who served in the Board of Managers as one of the representatives of the Baptist Church, finished his useful life in 1880. Dr. James L. Banks (d. 1883), a physician long a member of the Committee on Publication, spent the last day but one of his consciousness in that Committee. William E. Dodge, President of the New York Chamber of Commerce, passed away in 1883. During twenty-five years he had shown in the Board the enterprise, sagacity, and integrity which won him a commanding position in business life. John Earle (d. 1891) was connected with several important financial institutions in the city, a member of the Protestant Episcopal Church, and gave his valuable time to the Society as a true missionary institution during eighteen years in the Committee on Legacies.

Men's lives often consist of a round of simple activities important to a small circle of friends, but not notable to mankind at large. The members of the Board of Managers, although making no noise or bluster about their work, were of a quality to give it weight in the city where they were known. Belonging to different denominations whose diversities formed a considerable safe-guard against unwise or careless action, their character imparted serious importance to all decisions of the Board. Such were the men who led the policy of the Society during the larger part of this period.

The Board relies on the Secretaries of the Society for important information respecting past action of the Board or relations with Societies, churches or individuals. Hence it is a somewhat serious matter when an efficient Secretary resigns his office. In 1871 the Rev. T. Ralston Smith, after five years of service, resigned in order to return to the attractive duties of pastoral work to which he had been urgently invited. His capacity, his industry, and his affable manner, had won the regard of all. The Rev. Edward W. Gilman, D.D., pastor of the Congregational Church in Stonington, Connecticut, was then elected Secretary of the Society. It was no small privilege to Dr. Gilman to have during seven years the advantage of the counsel and experience of Secretary Holdich. It was thought at the time that two Secretaries only might watch over the correspondence, but after a fair trial the Board decided that the work of the Society was too great for this, and in 1874 the Rev. Alexander McLean, D.D., of Buffalo, was elected Secretary and given the supervision of the District Superintendents and the Auxiliary Societies.

With profound regret the Board in 1878 accepted the resignation of Rev. Joseph Holdich, D.D., for twenty-nine years Secretary of the Society. Dr. Holdich had been for some time unable to perform his duties because of partial blindness. He resigned because unwilling to be a Secretary in name only. If the Managers of the Society can rely upon receiving from a Secretary at a moment's notice a well-digested statement of policies or experiences of the Society, the Secretary must have been long in the service. In 1878 the service of three great Secretaries, Milnor, Brigham and Holdich, had covered the sixty-two years of the existence of the Society, each inheriting knowledge and experience from his predecessor almost as Elisha inherited his master's grace and power. Dr. Holdich believed that the Society must penetrate all the dark places of the home land, and to the Agencies abroad he was like a father. During seven years before his withdrawal he made known his hopes and his cherished plans to Secretary Gilman. Upon the resignation of Secretary Holdich the Board elected Rev. Albert S. Hunt, D.D., pastor of St. James' Methodist Episcopal Church in Brooklyn, Secretary of the Society. Dr. Hunt was an eloquent speaker, a warm lover of the Bible, and otherwise eminently fitted for this position.

The Society has always been happy in its Treasurers. Vice-President William Whitlock was elected to that office in 1840. He was a vestryman and warden of St. George's Episcopal Church in New York, at the time of his appointment as Treasurer being owner of a line of packets between Havre and New York. A picturesque incident of this part of his career was his providing and fitting out at his own expense the ship on which in 1824 Lafayette came from France to New York when he visited the United States as its guest. Mr. Whitlock's active service as Treasurer continued, but for two years of absence in Europe, until his death in 1875. The Society was peculiarly dear to him and in its financial arrangements he did much to promote its prosperity. The actual handling of funds and keeping of accounts was the duty of an Assistant Treasurer; Henry Fisher, Esq., having served in this capacity from 1853 until his death in 1869, and A. L. Taylor, Esq., having been appointed to the office in 1869. After Mr. Taylor had performed his duties with fidelity during seventeen years, in 1886 he resigned. At this time an amendment was made in the Constitution of the Society by which the office of Assistant Treasurer was abolished. When the Annual Meeting took this action, William Foulke, Esq., a vestryman and Treasurer of St. George's Episcopal Church, was elected Treasurer and has given his whole time to the heavy duties of the office. At the time of his election he was a merchant in the West Indies trade as his father and grandfather were before him.

CHAPTER XLI

MAKING THE BIBLE SPEAK WITH TONGUES

In the early days of the Society its greatest work was the production of Bibles. The Society's work to-day would be simple if limited to the production of books to be handed out at the door of the Bible House. The Board very shortly felt, however, responsibility for seeing that the Bibles were circulated, and after the first year or two, distribution was added to production as the Society's essential duty. By and by, when American missionaries abroad began to wrestle with the difficulties of their undertaking as in a prize ring among thousands who hoped to witness their defeat, it was found that in a large part of the earth translation must have precedence over production and distribution. This was an almost unexpected revelation.

These words therefore — production, translation and distribution — stand in the history of the Society like milestones of development. Translation, printing, distribution are all equally essential enterprises of a Bible Society, making the beneficent scheme complete. The extent of the enterprise has ever led to confidence in the triumph of the gospel through enabling its words of power to penetrate the minds of people using the different languages.

Language naturally lends itself to evil, and until it is Christianised it resists the translator like a living enemy. Translation of the Bible is the capture of a whole language by aliens who lay hands on it and force it to speak the messages of God. The fitting words have to be almost torn by force from the speech of the common folk that the sentences may find welcome in the heart of the child even though they nourish the life of the sage. In the words of the Rev. W. J. Tucker, " Christianity is thus forcing itself into languages without letters, into languages elaborated and defended by pagan or Moslem literature, and the privilege of Pentecost is ours. By the patient effort of the church, Christianity tries to do what at Pentecost the apostles did through miraculous power. Those who succeed in this effort are men the fame of whose translations will exceed that of the greatest heroic deeds of arms!"

In pagan languages the translation of the Bible meets resistance perhaps most difficult to overcome. Words and phrases long hallowed in our thoughts by devout associations, such as the names for God, grace, faith, sanctification, holiness, peace, love, joy, and the glories of the heavenly world, can be found perhaps in such a language, but have "very meagre meanings" put into them by many of the people who read them. In the Japanese there was a similar lack of words by which to express spiritual ideas. The Rev. Dr. Greene wrote, "Even the long and involved sentences of the Pauline Epistles are often easier to manage than some of the apparently simple verses of St. John's Gospel in making the translation." A further difficulty encountered by the missionaries in Japan was a perverted taste of the Japanese literary men. They revered Chinese as the only language worthy of printing. It has no affinity to Japanese, but because it was regarded with veneration by Japanese scholars, it might easily be suffered to dilute the Japanese flavour of the version, besides being unintelligible to common folk. The same difficulty was encountered in Turkish, where there was no proper literary standard, Turkish writers regarding Arabic with profound respect, although it has no affinity to the Turkish language, so that it was brought into some early versions of Scriptures to such an extent as to make them unintelligible to the common people. Obstacles of this class require patient vigilance on the part of the translator. Dr. Gundert of the Basle Missionary Society remarks: "Every language is a work of art and an inexhaustible mine. The missionary must listen with his ears pricked up. He must be swift to hear and slow to speak; and must learn to admire beauties in the language before he dares to finish any piece of translation." This implies that knowledge of the every day native idiom is most important; and only a native can handle the native idiom properly.

An illustration of the method used to overcome the illiteracy behind which a language is often fortified, is seen in the story of the Dakota Bible. Rev. Dr. T. S. Williamson went to Lacquiparle in 1835. He found himself in the midst of Indians, some of whom had a smattering of English which enabled them to transact business, and the best instrument for acquiring the language (for he had to make his own dictionary and grammar) was a half-breed fur trader named Renville. This man took an interest in Dr. Williamson's mission. The first question to be settled was how to write Dakota, which knew no alphabet. Dr. Williamson took the Roman alphabet, threw out x, v, r, g, j, f, and c, which were not required for Dakota words, giving to the discarded letters sounds of "clicks," etc., which could not be rendered by Roman letters. As a beginning of Bible translation Dr. Williamson worked day after day for two or three winters in Mr. Renville's great warehouse warmed by a fire of logs standing on end in the huge fireplace. He would read verse by verse from the French Bible. Mr. Renville would then give the verse in Dakota, Dr. Williamson writing it down from the trapper's lips. By that process translations of the Gospels of St. Mark and St. John were completed. Dr. Williamson had been joined in 1837 by Dr. S. R. Riggs, and when both had learned some Dakota, they compared this tentative translation with the original Greek. It was not until 1843 that they ventured to offer the Society a corrected gospel to be printed. The translation of the Dakota Bible from that uncertain beginning proceeded during nearly forty years. Dr. Williamson did not live to see the work finished in 1879. As it approached its end, he remarked that in forty-four years he had built four houses. Two of those houses had fallen or been destroyed; the other two would soon go. But in his labour on the Bible he had shared in building up human souls. That work would remain forever.

Another fact which resists the turning of an unwilling language to the service of the Bible is the great expense of the work. The translation of the Japanese New Testament was completed in 1879 and it was published early in 1880, when a public thanksgiving service was held by Christians in Tokio. The American Bible Society had paid about $4,000 a year for some five years, for translation and editorial work alone, upon this Testament. The printing of it was also at the expense of the Society.[1]

In 1882 the Rev. I. G. Bliss, D.D., the Society's Agent for the Levant, reported that in twenty-five years since his taking up that agency the cost to the Society of translation and editorial work in Turkey upon different versions was $64,955. The versions which entailed so great expense were Armenian, Turkish, Hebrew-Spanish, and Bulgarian. The last named Bible was translated by Rev. Dr. Elias Riggs with the assistance of two native scholars, and in the New Testament with the aid, as already mentioned, of the Rev. A. L. Long, D.D. The New Testament only was printed at the joint expense of the American and British Societies. The version as a whole was paid for by the British and Foreign Bible Society, the volumes required for the supply of American missionaries being bought from that Society as needed.

The work of promoting translations for missionaries carries the Society far afield. In 1882, when Korea was beginning to open its gates a little, so that missionaries could hope for freedom to enter, an educated Korean, of whom we shall hear more in another chapter, was found in Japan who had been converted and was eager to make translations of the Gospels into his own language. These were printed by the Society and served the earliest American missionaries in Korea. At the same time the Society was helping Presbyterian missionaries in upper Siam to issue a translation of the Gospel of Matthew in the Laos language, while nearer home steps were taken for a revision of the old Portuguese version in use in Brazil and the Rev. H. B. Pratt of Bucaramanga in Colombia was engaged in 1885 after some attempts at revision of the Valera Spanish Version, to make a new Spanish translation.

[1] Of course the work was placed at the disposal of the other Bible Societies also. The Agent, in fact, was authorised to allow any responsible party to reprint the Japanese Testament on condition of making no changes in the text.

In 1873 a great work for China was accomplished in the completion of the Old Testament in Mandarin translated by the Rev. Dr. Schereschewski at the expense of the Society, and printed for the Society on the press of the American Board's Mission in Peking. Bishop Stevens of Pennsylvania, in speaking of this achievement by Dr. Schereschewski, a minister of his own church, said: "The grandest conquests of the world's mightiest heroes sink into littleness beside the work which our faithful missionary had done when he made the Bible speak in Mandarin and herald out salvation over half a hemisphere." During this period besides some local colloquial versions, the Chinese New Testament in Easy Wenli was prepared as an experiment at the expense of the Society by Dr. Blodgett, Bishop Burdon and others. In May 1890 a general missionary conference at Shanghai decided upon a revision of the Chinese styles known as Wenli, Easy Wenli, and Mandarin in order to have a union standard version of the Bible in these forms. This noble thought was approved by the American, British and Scottish Bible Societies which agreed jointly to share the expense of this new version of the Bible for China.

One of the important translations in the promotion of which the Society has had a share is that already mentioned as proceeding in Japan during this period. After a good deal of experimental work by Dr. Verbeck, Dr. Hepburn, Bishop Williams, Mr. Goble and others, a conference of missionaries in 1872 set apart as responsible translators and revisers for the New Testament, Rev. S. R. Brown, D.D., of the Reformed (Dutch) Mission, Dr. J. C. Hepburn of the Presbyterian Mission, and Rev. D. C. Greene, of the American Board's mission. Rev. R. S. Maclay of the Methodist Episcopal Mission was added to the Committee and they finished the work in 1880, having had notable assistance from Mr. Matsuyama and other Japanese scholars. The year 1889 will always be marked in the church history of Japan as the year when, after fifteen years of patient waiting, the whole Bible was at last published in Japanese. Rev. John Piper and Rev. P. K. Fyson, both of the Church Missionary Society, were added to the Committee for this work. The great expense of translating the Old Testament was divided between the three Bible Societies; two-fifths to the American Society, two-fifths to the British and Foreign, and one-fifth to the National Bible Society of Scotland.

Another great translation aided and printed by the Society was the one made by American missionaries in South Africa for those tall black warriors known as the Zulus. The Zulu Bible grew up through many years' slow, careful work by different missionaries of the American Board. The New Testament was printed on the mission press in Natal at the expense of the Bible Society, while the covers for binding it were made at the Bible House in New York and shipped to Africa for native binders to apply. When the translation of the Old Testament was complete, the manuscript was brought to New York to be printed at the Bible House under oversight of Rev. Dr. Pixley of the Zulu mission. This version was important not only for the missions of the American Board but for its use in various adjoining regions occupied by Norwegian, German and Scottish missionaries. North of Natal during this period the American Board missionaries, B. F. Ousley and E. H. Richards, prepared a version of the New Testament in the Tonga language; and later some Gospels in the Sheetswa language translated by Rev. B. F. Ousley were accepted and published by the Society.

In those groups of islands in the Pacific Ocean called by the one convenient name, Micronesia, a considerable translation work was carried on by the missionaries of the American Board and in this period the New Testament in the language of the Mortlock Islanders, translated by the Rev. Mr. Logan, in the Ponape language translated by the Rev. Messrs. Doane and Sturges, and the New Testament in the language of the Marshall Islands translated by Rev. E. M. Pease, were made ready, and finally the translation of the whole Bible into the language of the Gilbert Islands, by Rev. Hiram Bingham, was finished in 1890. The Gilbert Islands Bible was used by the London Missionary Society stations in islands under their care besides the ones for which it was designed. Some copies were called for from Samoa.

Some experiments were made in beginning a version of the New Testament in Kurdish by Rev. Dr. Andrus, who by long residence in Mardin, Turkey, had opened relations with various tribes in that vicinity. The Gospel of Matthew in Kurdish was sent to various scholars for criticism and after passing this test, it was approved for printing. A version needed for the Society's Persian field was in the dialect called Azerbaijan Turkish. Rev. Dr. Wright undertook the work but died before much had been done. The well-known "Tennesseean in Persia," Rev. Dr. S. H. Rhea, was then assigned by the mission to the task, but he too died shortly afterward. It almost seemed as if a divine hand had laid a ban on the undertaking, but Rev. Benjamin Labaree in 1882 translated the Gospel of St. Luke into Azerbaijan Turkish which was printed at Urumia at the expense of the Society. The 2,000 copies printed were sold almost immediately. Work upon this dialect was afterwards given up when it was found that the British and Foreign Bible Society had arranged for preparing the version.

The British and American Societies were pleased as builders of some splendid palace in uniting forces and means and prayers for translations such as have already been mentioned or for a revision of a Bible long in use by missionaries from both nations, as in the case of the version which spoke the musical language of the Telugus of the eastern parts of South India. Two scholarly men, Rev. Dr. Jacob Chamberlain, the American, and Rev. Dr. Hay, the British representative, and others carried forward this revision in this period. The high purpose of bettering the expression of gospel truths unites the men and no difference of nationality or of creed can limit their free sense of doing the Master's will, or their content in doing it together in His name. If natives of the country had possibly suspected two discordant sects in the Christian teachers from England and America this joint work upon the Telugu Bible removed the suspicion.

When the Bible or any part of it is translated so as to speak in an alien tongue it has to be printed that it may give its message to the minds of thousands. The production of printed Scriptures turns one's thought toward the Bible House in New York. In common opinion the work of the Society is represented by the Bibles and Testaments in the salesroom window or continually passing out of the shipping office in boxes labelled for the ends of the earth. In the same way when a railroad is spoken of, people think only of the cars, the rails, and the signal lights at night. But in each case there is somewhere a center where may be found the mind and soul of the institution. Thence lines go out in all directions to execute plans carefully worked out at the center. The maintenance of a printing establishment is quite incidental to the work of the Society, but the maintenance of the Bible House is essential, for there all plans for work are thought out and decided.

The duty of studying and advising the Board respecting translation and printing various versions, for instance, is in the hands of a committee at the Bible House called the Committee on Versions. Of the choice men composing it during this period some were members of the American Company of revisers of the English Bible and all were Bible scholars and linguists from different religious denominations. The undertaking by the Society of enterprises in languages largely depends upon the recommendations of this important Committee.

Some plans of administration at the Bible House were changed during this period. Changes were made by the Legislature of New York in the charter of the Society giving it the right to take real-estate given it by devise. A change was made in the Constitution of the Society, also, in consequence of a new law of the state which required that no person receiving salary from a benevolent institution shall have a vote in its management. This amendment to the Constitution excluded the Secretaries and Treasurer from voting in the Board of Managers.

Another amendment to the Constitution was introduced in 1877 because of changes in the character of the population since the organisation of the Society. The seventh article originally provided that Directors could attend and vote at all meetings of the Board of Managers, while the sixth declared that any one subscribing $150 at one time should be a Director for life. A criticism of the Society, welcomed as it should be by men who are above seeking first the comfort of self-esteem, secured a change. Some one speaking disparagingly of the Society remarked that atheists or Roman Catholics by subscribing comparatively small sums could gain control of the Board and shut up the Bible House. The statement suggested the inference that mere payment of money does not qualify a man for direction of a Bible Society. So this weak spot in the Constitution was mended, the seventh article being altered with notable haste. Directors by this amendment were entitled to attend and speak, and if constituted before June 1, 1877, to vote at meetings of the Board.

During this period there was betterment, also, in the making of books at the Bible House. The Committee of Publication was composed of practical business men, some of them the heads of well known publishing houses. It aimed at efficiency as well as economy in the manufacture of books. As immigration caused increase in Scriptures in foreign languages, electro-plates of the Bible were imported from Europe; newly perfected printing presses and machines for the bindery were bought and substituted for the older styles and finally in 1889 the Bible House was fully repaired, elevators and other improvements were installed, and an entire sixth floor was added to the building, without, however, using any money contributed for Bible distribution. A mortgage for $100,000 was executed as security for a loan to be repaid by rents from rooms not required by the Society.

The printing of Scriptures in the Bible House included in the main those necessary for use in the United States. From 50,000 to 100,000 volumes, however, were annually sent abroad, chiefly to Latin America in Spanish and Portuguese. In 1876 a special reference Bible known as the Centennial Bible was issued as a souvenir of the one hundredth year of the American Republic. About the same time a beginning was made of publishing a new kind of embossed Scriptures for the blind by a system known as the New York Point Print. The presses were busy during the whole period with printing Scriptures for Africa in

Zulu, Benga and Mpongwe. In June, 1883, the first large shipment of the Zulu Bible went out of the door of the Bible House on its way to South Africa. It consisted of 12,000 volumes in all. There was also printing for the Indians, portions of the Muskokee or Creek, and Dakota Scriptures being printed as the translations of the Bible went on towards completion, and reprints of Scriptures in the Ojibwa of which the first edition was printed in 1844 and the second in 1856, and also a reprint of the Gospel of St. Matthew in the language of the Nez Perces Indians. These were the Indians who in 1832 sent a deputation from the territory of Oregon 1,500 miles to St. Louis, vainly seeking there the "book of God" which they had somehow learned that the white man has. It was a point of interest that the proofs of this new edition as they came from the press at the Bible House were corrected by the Rev. H. H. Spaulding, the translator of the original edition issued in 1845. A further illustration of the fact that Indian languages had been made to praise God appeared in 1857 at a conference at Vinita in the Indian territory. One of the ministers read from the Bible in English, another the same verses in Chickasaw, the next in Cherokee, then one read in Muskokee or Creek, and another in the Delaware language. The version of the New Testament in Muskokee or Creek was finished in 1886. It was the work of Mr. and Mrs. A. E. W. Robertson.

While the presses in the Bible House were thus kept unceasingly at work, it is worthy of note that Scriptures were being printed for the Society throughout this period at Constantinople, Beirut, Paris, Berlin, Vienna, Bremen, Stockholm, Fuchow, Shanghai, Lucknow, Lodiana, Bangkok, and Yokohama. These Scriptures were printed on local presses generally owned by missions and largely supported by the Bible Society. An exception to the rule was the press at Beirut, where the Society owned an expensive electrotyping plant and a fine printing press with its equipment which had been sent out for printing the Arabic Scriptures. In 1878 the Board transferred by gift to the Presbyterian Board of Foreign Missions this printing and electrotyping apparatus at Beirut, valued at $16,094.61.

This class of the Society's labours, little known in any detail, was continually calling for money. The problem of cost constantly hampered the Board. But the Society was called into existence in order to solve just such problems which were beyond the ability of the separate and local Bible Societies. When, therefore, the appeals of the Society are heeded, every contributor along with all workers of the Society who labour with brain or with hand is a translator or producer or distributor of books. Each one shares with the men at the Bible House or at outposts on the other side of the globe the "Well done" which rewards every sincere effort for the glory of God.

CHAPTER XLII

DISTRIBUTION IN THE HOME LAND

Bishop Janes of the Methodist Episcopal Church, formerly Secretary of the Bible Society, was the author of an address to the people which on the decision in 1866 to undertake a third General Supply of the destitute in the land, was sent out from the Board of Managers. This address set forth the belief of Christians that to make universal the knowledge of God, His will and His grace in Jesus Christ, is the first great interest of the nation; yet while the Society in fifty years had distributed, mostly in this country, over twenty-one millions of volumes of Scripture; while more than thirty commercial publishers were sending out each year some 400,000 volumes of Scripture; and while large importations of Bibles from England and Europe were constantly adding to the stock, a recent examination showed an amazing and alarming destitution of Scriptures in the United States. The case of the coloured people in the South was an instance. Many thousands of former slaves were learning to read, ought to be supplied with Scriptures lest they forget that God is their Master, but faced a famine of the Word. The white people of the South were still unsupplied with Bibles, notwithstanding all efforts to help them. In three wards of such a city as Washington, D. C., 1,400 families had been found destitute of the Book of God. Immigrants, Indians, and furthermore thousands of the old stock even in the oldest states, were living without association with the great teachers of the Bible. The rapid natural increase of population and the continuous arrival of immigrants explains in part why such destitution existed. If distribution is intermitted for one day destitution is visibly increased.

The question sometimes arises, What is the real advantage of such strenuous effort to increase the circulation of the Bible in our land? The answer of course is, Seed does not grow unless it is sown. This form of work supplies a need of the whole nation. John Bunyan used to say with what now seems prophetic insight, "Want of reverence for the word of God is the ground of all the disorders that are in the heart, life, and conversation of Christian communion." What happens when the people have not the Bible may be very properly deduced from investigations which social workers have made into the results of carelessness about moral and religious training. Dr. Harris produced a profound impression in 1875 by giving the history of a small girl many years before left homeless and without education in a country village in the state of New York. Her descendants in less than one hundred years numbered 673 persons, almost all of them criminals, paupers, or prostitutes. The neglect of that little girl cost the county and the state thousands of dollars, besides causing untold damage to the whole community in its morals as well as in its property.

Such an investigation by contrast shows the beneficent quality of Bible distribution. The nobility of this work comes from above, but responsibility for effective distribution of the Scriptures in the United States does not rest upon the Society and its Auxiliaries, but upon the Christian people of the land.

The third General Supply of the destitute in the United States was completed as fully as such an enterprise can be completed, in 1872. The work had been done mainly by the Auxiliaries, the Society employing colporteurs under the direction of its agents in parts of the country where settlers were few and the idea of an Auxiliary Bible Society had not yet taken root. In 1872, at the end of five years of effort, it was found that 2,990,119 families had been visited, 283,186 were found destitute, of which 228,807 families were willing to take up the reading of the Bible; not included in these families, 213,302 individuals more had been supplied with a Bible or Testament by sale or gift. These figures, large as they were, were admittedly incomplete. Moreover, 253,757 volumes not included in the statement above had been granted by the Society and distributed in different parts of the country by the American Sunday School Union, the American Tract Society, and the denominational book and tract societies. Five years of effort had accomplished a great work for the nation.

In any extensive national enterprise, criticism of the workers is natural and not always cautious about its ground. Swift's apothegm applies in many cases: "Censure is a tax a man pays to the public for being eminent." Although the executive officers had no vote on the Society's policy, they felt keenly certain public strictures upon its management during the first decade of this period. In 1873 one such criticism advanced by an Auxiliary Society in New Jersey and shared by some ecclesiastical bodies in Central New York, was that the Board of Managers ought to let its books be distributed by pastors and by denominational Societies already engaged in book publication, so saving the expense of Agents and colporteurs. In actual fact, the Society had learned by painful experience that while help in distribution is always rendered by pastors and denominational Book and Tract Societies, large areas would be left untouched unless the Bible Society explored and supplied them.

Nevertheless willingness to experiment with measures of economy led the Society in 1875 to diminish the number of its District Superintendents. In that year Rev. Dr. Ward and Rev. W. R. Long in New York State, Rev. Mr. Pearce in Kentucky, and Rev. S. P. Whitten in Western Tennessee and Northern Mississippi retired from the service where they had been remarkably successful. Rev. H. H. Benson of Indiana, Rev. C. A. Bolles of South Carolina, Rev. W. Herr of Ohio, Rev. J. Mosser of Illinois, Rev. W. A. Parks of Georgia, Rev. W. B. Rankin of Tennessee, and Rev. S. Reynolds of Wisconsin, retired the following year. More responsibility was thus thrown on the stronger Auxiliaries and the fields of the remaining Superintendents were enlarged.

Again the Society was assailed as wasteful of the people's money because the price at which its books were sold had never covered the cost of distributing them. The least reflection would reveal the injustice of such an attack. The very object of the Society is to supply the careless who neglect the Bible and the poor who do not patronise book stores which include in their prices profit as well as expenses. Pungent articles later attacked the Society because it would not publish "helps" desired by Sunday School teachers. The crudeness of this criticism was apparent, also, for as soon as the Society should begin to publish notes and comments on the Bible it would break the harmony between the Methodist, Presbyterian, Lutheran, Baptist, and other members of the Board.

A later series of strictures touched the character of members of the Board. The fancied grievance of a man in New England who had eaten the bread of the Society found expression in a bald charge that the reports of the Society and the financial statements of the Treasurer were untrustworthy, wilfully concealing assets. These charges which came, by the way, from parties not contributors to the support of the Society, were repeated with keen enjoyment and impromptu variations by secular newspapers in New England. This gave opportunity to some of the New England Auxiliaries for criticising the rule that limits the Society's work to "increasing the circulation of the Scriptures." In the eyes of the critics the Society's colporteurs were "mere book peddlers." One of these Auxiliaries employed men in behalf of the churches to take a religious census of country districts, and even sent missionaries on evangelistic campaigns.

A belittling of the value of Bible distribution underlay this turning of a local Bible Society to general Home mission operations. The view of the men who organised the Society, on the other hand, was that supply of Scriptures to the needy and persuasion of the careless to read the Bible would fully occupy its energies. A Bible Society, too, could not support preachers by contributions from different denominations, since it would have to defend one and another from the charge of partisanship. Here a direct issue was made between the Board and its critics. From 1878 to 1882 this campaign was pressed, now against the policy and now the personality of the Managers. As to the reports of the Treasurer, nothing in them was defective or unintelligible to men having some acquaintance with book-keeping. Yet the attacks undoubtedly had effect in diminishing current receipts. The Board could only go forward patiently following the course fixed by the Constitution, and approved by contributors. But like sincere men who put their best into all their doings, the members of the Board questioned every department of work at the Bible House from the point of view of the critics. The Publication Committee called in important publishing houses to get their opinion of the efficiency of their manufacturing department. It even induced publishers to consider on what terms they could contract to produce the Society's books. The Committees on Finance, Distribution, Publication, and Agencies jointly studied during many months the whole subject of production and distribution.

Some members of the Board felt that the more finely bound Scriptures ought to be sold at a rate which would bring a profit to the Bible Society. The expression of this idea was: "The pearl itself is above all price. We should not make merchandise of that; but only of the casket which contains it and which adds nothing to the intrinsic value of the treasure within." The calm judgment of the Managers, however, obliged them to reject this suggestion. The report of 1884 showed that the issues of the Society in the United States were 1,357,051 volumes, costing $414,000. Out of this total 17,604 volumes, costing $29,747, were bound in cheaper leather or in cloth, with gilt edges, and 1,235,460 volumes, costing $298,295, were in cloth binding with plain edges. This last named class of books represented the attainment by the Society of its main purpose. This mass of books of the cheaper class supplied the destitute. Any attempt to make profit through elegantly bound Scriptures would tend to divert attention from the great needy class to supply which the Society was called into being. In its appeal to the public for support of the fourth General Supply the Board had this helpless class in mind when it said: "We are no longer a homogeneous people, but have gathered into our midst representatives of all nations. A grave responsibility rests on the Society at this time to enter upon a distribution of the Holy Scriptures largely in excess of any former effort of this kind undertaken in the United States." The country was rapidly becoming a foreign mission field.

A great obstacle to such a distribution of the Bible is diversity in language, little appreciated by the average bystander. In St. Paul's Cathedral the Bishop of Bath and Wells once preached a sermon on the results of Bible Society labours. After speaking of the great multitude which he saw in his mind's eye, and whom he could imagine speaking discordant tongues in his very ears, he said: "As I look, there arises in the midst of them a fair figure crowned with charity, girded with knowledge, and clothed with Christian Faith. A great chest is at her feet which she unlocks, and opens, and from which she draws forth countless volumes of great price. Without distinction of race or creed, of barbarian or Scythian, bond or free, she distributes them to all nations and peoples around her, and as each opens the book he has received he finds it a copy of the word of God, uttered many hundred years ago but now written in the tongue wherein he was born. And as I watch those who receive this precious boon — whether the process takes years or centuries matters not — I see a gradual and most blessed change. The knowledge of truth takes the place of ignorance, superstition and error. Oppression and cruelty yield to justice and mercy. Christian civilisation springs up in the barren wilderness. Such an image represents I believe fairly the work of the Bible Society."

Something of what the Society was doing for foreigners in the United States was told as concretely if less beautifully to an audience at a Bible meeting in Philadelphia. It was with utter amazement that the congregation listened when different people, mostly foreigners, came to the front of the platform, read verses from the Bible in twenty-seven different languages, and thus made clear what the Bible could do for aliens both in America and in their own birthlands.

For the fourth General Supply the Society sent colporteurs of its own into sparsely settled fields. A colporteur is a Christian who is convinced that the Bible can change the bent of mankind. From experience he knows that unless the Bible is established in new settlements, the tavern, brothel, and gambling house will pre-empt the town-site. Like a homesteader in a primeval forest who has only an axe wherewith to clear his acres, he may be impeded but not discouraged by the magnitude of his task. A colporteur in Florida describes a typical day's work. He travelled twenty-five miles in woods full of undergrowth, stumps, and also snakes. In the first house he came to the family had an old Bible and did not need any of his. Five miles farther the family had no Bible and bought one for twenty-four eggs. Six miles beyond this no one in the house knew how to read and none could understand need of a Bible. At the next house the colporteur found a Testament, from which two-thirds of the pages were missing. To this family he sold a Bible for one hen. Some distance beyond was another house where the people were glad to buy a Bible, paid twenty-five cents on account and promised to pay the rest when they got some money. In the next house was a sick woman. After reading her some comforting verses, the colporteur prayed with her. A Bible was very much wanted in that house, but there was no money with which to buy. So the colporteur gave a Bible in the name of the Society and went his way. No task is so onerous as to outweigh the privileges of the colporteur's life.

Volunteer workers in this Fourth General Supply often took up Bible distribution with hesitation, but as in any form of evangelistic work, they found quick response, and wondered at the shrinking which had held them back. At Coleman, Texas, for instance, two ladies volunteered to distribute twenty-five dollars' worth of Bibles for a local committee. They placed a copy of the Scriptures in every family, store, and office where it was acceptable, and the dwellers in solitary places were made glad. Then the committee wrote joyfully to the Society in New York remitting $22.50 receipts from sales and adding $27 to pay for another shipment of Bibles.

One of the means used by the Society for reaching the careless with Scripture was the railroad companies. The Board proposed to put Scriptures in the cars on condition that the companies provide book-racks. Eighty different railroads availed themselves of this offer, and about 5,000 volumes were placed in the cars for passengers to read as they journeyed.

In 1876 President Grant wrote for a Sunday School newspaper a message to the Sunday Schools of the United States. This was the message: "Hold fast to the Bible as the sheet anchor of your liberties. Write its precepts on your hearts and practise them in your lives. To the influence of this book are we indebted for all progress made in true civilisation, and to this we must look as our guide in the future. 'Righteousness exalteth a nation, but sin is a reproach to any people.' U. S. Grant."

It was a similar earnest yearning to deal justly with children that led the Society in 1890 unanimously to approve the Board's proposal to supply with a Bible every child in the United States under fifteen years of age and able to read. The number of Bibles issued in the United States during the year by the Society was 31,000 volumes more than the issues of the previous year.

Unexpected help in the general task of making the Bible known was rendered by Roman Catholics who felt the strong impulse given to Bible reading through these efforts and could not resist or overcome the pressure. Even children sometimes thwart a parent by persistent asking. The result in this case was that for some time the Roman Catholic clergy tried to increase the use of the Douay Bible among their people. Another unexpected encouragement came to the Society during this period from Mormon congregations in Utah, which passed resolutions of thanks for Bibles sent into that territory. Colporteurs had met with opposition in Utah, and this was like the veering of the wind when a ship has been tossing on the billows of an opposing gale.

After eight years of strenuous labour the fourth General Supply was concluded. The Society had employed some two hundred colporteurs to supplement the labours of several thousand persons sent out by Auxiliary Societies. During the eight years 8,146,808 volumes of Scripture were distributed by sale or gift throughout the United States. This total included books granted during this period to the

Sunday School Unions, Tract Societies, etc., for distribution through their regular channels. It is notable just here that while the Board of Managers in its first years looked forward with hope to having the Bible in four or five languages, before the seventy-fifth year of the Society its distributions included Scriptures in twenty-seven languages spoken in the United States.

In these efforts of the General Supply it was estimated that at last 1,000,000 persons refused the Bible. Many were disbelievers in revealed religion, many were under the thrall of superstition, but a great many refused the Book because they could not read. The census of 1880 reported in the United States more than 6,000,000 children of school age who did not go to school. The number of people to whom the Bible was sealed up through inability to read was alarmingly great. Here the missionary society with its schools comes to the rescue and here the colporteur must wait on the missionary. The distribution work of the Society is a partnership work with all who accept the Bible as the word of God and the foundation of true wisdom. Sometimes this work goes in advance of other agencies, but as a rule it is closely linked with the missionary. No report of the work of the Society is complete in itself for no evangelising agency stands alone; but every year piles up records that prove the maxim that "the power of truth is like the force of gravitation," certain in its orderly, irresistible action although silent and invisible.

Sometimes it is an immigrant, sometimes a man who ought to have Bible truth by inheritance, sometimes it is an Indian, sometimes a black man who supplies proof of this inspiring fact. Mr. Lambdin in Grundy County, Illinois, in one day distributed Bibles in eight languages at Coal City. One of the men, a Bohemian, the next day brought money for the Bible and to the astonishment of Mr. Lambdin he bought several Testaments for his children. Such an appreciation gives a colporteur rest from much weariness. In Lewis County, Kentucky, a colporteur met a man who asked, "Do you remember me?" He could not remember him. "Well," said the man, "eight years ago don't you remember going toward a man who was cutting down a tree and who told you with an oath that you would be killed if you didn't look out? I was that man; you came on and gave me a Testament. I was a hard drinker, a gambler and a fighter; but that Testament held me up." For two months this "bad man" had read the Testament and judged himself by its standards. Of course, it led him into the Slough of Despond, but it led him out again, and he told the colporteur the joy which he found in trying to lead others to Jesus Christ. About 1830, during the first general supply, one of the Society's Bibles was given to a lad at work in a cotton factory. The book took hold of him, gave him aspirations. He determined to find some way to go to school and college. After completing his studies he was ordained a Baptist minister. In the Fourth General Supply he revealed himself to a Bible Agent. He had been twenty-six years a pastor and had welcomed into his church more than one thousand persons. All that he was, had done, or hoped to do he owed under God's favour to the Bible given to him in that first General Supply of the destitute.

One class of people reached in the distribution was the Indians. Often in their relations with white people they were like children who measure the love of a parent by its accord with their whimsical wishes. It was in 1876 that General Custer and his command were destroyed in Montana by the Sioux; but the Sioux were among the eight tribes of Indians for whom missionary translators prepared the Bible in the tongue wherein they were born. Of the Dakotas or Sioux in 1881 about 1,500 professing Christians were connected with the Presbyterian and the Protestant Episcopal Missions, besides some 3,000 adherents. Hundreds of Dakotas had been changed in character: the worthless made useful, and the ignorant wise, through the Bible. Buffalo Bill, on one of his tours, took his Wild West show to London. During the rest between the plays some Englishmen noticed two of the Sioux Indians sitting by themselves and reading. Curiosity led to inquiry what this book might be in which they were interested. "Why, it's the Bible," frankly answered the Indian. These two men, hired for the Wild West show, had brought their book with them, and that book had defended them from the vices of the so-called Christians who surrounded them.

The story of the home distribution in the twenty years of this period can be summed up in the statement that through the simple instructions of a Bible "a nobler few have dared to stray upward"; the interest of thousands had been aroused; violence and license had been checked among thousands who influenced succeeding generations, and something had thus been done to prepare a peaceful future for the land. In this respect Bible Distribution is entitled to unhesitating recognition in the history of the United States.

CHAPTER XLIII

THE BIBLE SENT AS A FOREIGN MISSIONARY

JEREMY TAYLOR somewhere says: "All those strange things and secret decrees and unrevealed transactions which are above the clouds and beyond the regions of the stars shall combine in ministry and advantage for the praying man." The Board of Managers and the Executive Officers while struggling to perform their daily duties made prayer for guidance their habit; when acting in a case of uncertainty their humble assurance of receiving help was as far as possible from any such "tempting" of God as marks headstrong rashness in respect to divine promises. The book which it was their duty to send abroad was God's book: it was was sent abroad for His glory. In accordance with this habit the Board granted Scriptures yearly to Mr. John S. Pierson, the enthusiastic agent of the New York Bible Society labouring among the shipping in the harbour. Mr. Pierson placed considerable numbers of books in the hands of sea-captains willing to take Bibles or Testaments to the less accessible foreign countries. Rash as such ventures might appear they had results which justified this good man's faith that they had God's approval.

Curiously enough, Mr. Pierson's daring to risk his books like a venturesome agent, carried a quantity of Spanish Scriptures in 1882 through the Roman Catholic barriers at the Philippine Islands. Three separate captains came thence rejoicing like the disciples who found that even unclean spirits were subject to them. At Iloilo, workmen, stevedores, and government officials received the books gladly. At another of the island ports the captain managed to send a package of Spanish Testaments to the soldiers of the garrison who received them with thanks. A third captain said that he had no peace after the people had received some of the Testaments. Every day they came on board begging for Testaments or Portions. The ease with which the books found readers seemed, like the thought of sending them, to come from the Lord.

The same sense of a divine hand pointing to action appeared in other foreign distributions. For years the Society had been supplying through the American congregation in St. Petersburg the Esthonians of the district of Reval and the islands of Dago and Osel with the New Testament in their own language. The Agent in this work for the Society in St. Petersburg was Mr. George H. Prince, who supervised the printing and distribution of Esthonian Testaments as money came from New York. After the completion of a revision of the Old Testament by the local clergy an edition of 20,000 copies of the Bible was printed for the Society in Berlin in a handy and cheap form which could be easily used by school children. In 1878 this school Bible was electrotyped in New York and 20,000 Esthonian Bibles were printed at the Bible House. Five years later 28,000 copies of the school Bible had already been put in circulation by colporteurs.

This to the Board was like working blindly; but it was not headstrong rashness. One thing had already been learned; there was a missionary's work which each Bible might do in the narrow circle of interests of the Esthonian peasants. A labourer testified to the colporteur concerning the grip the Testament gained upon his heart. "I did not want to buy a Testament," he said, "but now I must. Last Sunday I asked a neighbour to go with me for a walk and for a drink of vodka. He was reading the New Testament. He sat as though fixed on the spot and said to me, 'Have you no book like this?' I said, 'I have no time to read.' He said, 'If you had a book like this you would not care to go about drinking vodka!' 'I am not an old man,' said I, 'that I should sit all Sunday.' He said to me, 'Just listen to what this book says.' I sat down and he read. It was good. My wife, surprised that I was not drunk when I got home, asked me where I had been. I told her. She asked where my neighbour got his New Testament. I was

THE PHILIPPINES
A Catastrophe in Bible Transportation

ashamed to tell her, lest she would ask why I had not got one for myself. I am glad to meet you and want one for myself. Now I shall read my own New Testament on Sundays."

Rev. Mr. Bidwell of Boston had suggested to the Society work among political prisoners in Siberia and aided in 1877 in making arrangements for it. At the first there was a little difficulty on account of red tape. The books were shipped from Boston 17,000 miles to Nikolaievski at the mouth of the Amur River. After permission had been granted for the first shipment a change of military officials and ecclesiastics made it necessary to go over the whole ground again. A sample book had to be sent from Nikolaievski where the books were, 1500 miles to the archbishop at Blagovestchensk on the opposite side of the Amur River from Aigun in China. But when the books finally reached the exiles in their banishment the comfort and patience which the Master's words brought to those friendless, lonely souls repaid all the labour, anxiety and expense. The soldiers guarding the convicts were equally joyful. "We have lived here like animals," said one to the colporteur; "we have no church, and we have quite forgotten about God. Then you come with your books as if sent from heaven. We begin to read and somehow the more we read the more glad we become!"

When Secretary Gilman was in St. Petersburg in 1879 arrangements were made through Mr. George H. Prince with the Imperial Bible Society of Russia by which a new work of distribution by colporteurs was undertaken in Siberia at the expense of the American Bible Society, two of the Russian Society's colporteurs being detailed for the work of the American Society. The life of these colporteurs was strenuous, now taking a ton of Scriptures from St. Petersburg to Odessa and thence by sea through the Suez Canal to Vladivostock and the Amur River; now riding 7,000 miles on horseback across the whole continent of Asia, and back; and once returning to St. Petersburg by way of San Francisco and New York where Colporteur Golubeff was an interesting and picturesque visitor at the Bible House. About 300,000 volumes of Scripture were distributed by colporteurs in Siberia at the expense of the Society during this period. They delighted and comforted prisoners, exiles, soldiers, civilians, officers of high rank. The Society spent upon this great and beneficent work $79,563; the extent of the blessings dispensed will never be written. The glad story of the wagoner on the road from Tomsk to Irkutsk is typical. He never had seen a New Testament but the colporteurs had left Testaments in every station roadhouse. By reading what he could at each halt and finding the book again at the next station, at the end of his thousand miles' journey, out of some scores of different volumes he had read the whole New Testament. Since the book thus blessed thousands of people who were out of sight and forgotten, the cost of the distribution was not to be begrudged.

Just across the Baltic Sea west of Reval and the Esthonias, at Stockholm in Sweden the American Baptist Missionary Union had a flourishing mission in aid of which the Society made a number of grants at this time. The Rev. Per Palmquist received the grants and had Swedish Scriptures printed as required, following the version of the Bible authorised by the Lutheran state Church. Here, too, the Bible sought out hungry souls and fed them, although many felt no pressing need of it. The whole amount granted during this period to the Baptist mission in Sweden was $21,512. To Methodist Episcopal missions in Denmark, Sweden and Norway $6,150 was granted, making $27,662 for efforts to increase use of the Bible among these Scandinavian populations.

A work of the Society already alluded to was that of the Methodist Episcopal mission at Bremen. During twenty-two years from 1850 Rev. Dr. Jacobi, the superintendent, distributed at the expense of the Society 300,000 copies of Scriptures mostly printed at the Methodist Episcopal Mission Press. In 1872, full of years, he retired from active work, receiving the honorary appointment of Life Director of the American Bible Society for eminent services rendered. Rev. Dr. Doering then took charge of the mission and although the British Society was pressing its own Bible distribution with great vigour, $136,692 as help from the

American Society was granted American missionaries in Germany during this period. In addition to this money grant to the Methodist Mission, Rev. Dr. Oncken of the Baptist Mission in Hamburg in 1872 printed for Baptist missionaries at the expense of the Society 35,000 German Testaments.

Two little incidents must be mentioned lest we forget that all of these ventures abroad were merely designed to place the Bible in contact with the hearts of men. One of Dr. Doering's colporteurs encountered a Jew on a railway train. The man wanted a Bible but had not money enough to pay the full price. A German fellow-traveller sneered at him. "The Jew wants," said he, "to buy the Bible cheap so as to sell it again in half an hour." Four months later this colporteur stopped at a house in a country village and lo and behold, there was the Jew! In answer to the colporteur's question he smilingly took down the Bible from a shelf, and said: "Yes, the Bible is my Bible; it has given me light, and Jesus is my Messiah also." The Book had accomplished that whereto it was sent! The other incident shows the recognition of the missionary quality of the Bible accorded by the great as well as by the small.

Miss Heye of Bremen sometimes received small grants from the American Bible Society. The New York Female Bible Society gave her a pulpit Bible for a chapel in the Tyrol at Bad-Gastein, belonging to the German Emperor. Miss Heye ventured to ask the emperor to write in the pulpit Bible a message to the congregation. He wrote this verse: "For Thou art my hope, oh Lord God; Thou art my trust from my youth." And then he added his own word of testimony: "Hope cometh by faith. Gastein, August 21st, 1872, Wilhelm Imp. Rex." The German believer and the American believers were thus united in the expression of their common faith.

The American mission at Innsbruck in Austria was another field gladly aided by the Society. Rev. Mr. Bissell had reported the difficulties of the situation, but he undertook to support one or more colporteurs with aid from the Society. The Austrian law did not prohibit the circulation of the Bible. It did not prohibit selling the Bible. In its efforts to prevent union of aims between its diverse peoples, it forbade colporteurs to deliver the Bible when a customer was found. The purchaser must give a written order and the book must not be delivered the same day. In the meantime clerical friends of the purchaser would try to dissuade him from buying it. One of the colporteurs made the mistake of giving the Bible to a poor woman who wanted it, without first taking her "subscription." He was arrested and fined for his "crime." In his pocket the police found a tract; his license permitted him to carry the Bible but made no mention of tracts. For this aggravation of crime the colporteur's license was revoked, and word was sent to the surrounding districts that he was an unworthy man. Traps were continually set by the police in the path of the colporteurs.

But all such troubles served to reveal the desire of the people for the Scriptures. They were forgotten when the colporteur could see with his own eyes the comfort rendered by the book which he carried. One day a colporteur called upon a family living in a stable. After a few pleasant words he remarked, "Our Saviour was born in a stable, and I have brought you here His own precious words." The book for which these poor people had longed had come into their abode and they were delighted. The copy they wanted cost forty kreutzers (twenty cents); but they had only thirty kreutzers, which was their reliance for food for the next two days. But rather than fail to secure the words of Jesus, they chose to suffer hunger. They gave the colporteur ten kreutzers, keeping twenty to live on for two days. The colporteur was only too glad to let them have the book they needed. The aid rendered by the Society to the American mission in Austria during this period amounted to about $10,000.

The struggles of Protestants of France to maintain their own evangelistic institutions always called out the sympathy of the Society for they were embarrassed by poverty and opposed both by the Roman Church and by its bitterest enemies. In 1872 the Protestant Bible Society of Paris received a grant in aid of printing the Osterwald Version of the French Bible and the Bible Society of France rejoiced in a grant of $5,000 for printing New Testaments and Portions. There was in France great opportunity to circulate Scriptures notwithstanding a chorus of opposition and ridicule. When a reactionary ministry came into power colporteurs' licenses were revoked without waiting until the next day. When the reactionaries were overthrown, the granting of colporteurs' licenses was resumed but slowly. Often the vexatious conditions laid down seriously delayed the work. The steps necessary to obtain a license began with obtaining a certificate of good life and manners from well-known people. Secondly, a passport must be obtained. Thirdly, the colporteur must get a local license costing from three to eight dollars, according to the rule in vogue in the region where he was to work. In each Department (district) the colporteur had also to take out a special authorisation good only for that particular district. This was always delayed and sometimes rejected on the ground that no additional book sellers were required in the district.

Notwithstanding these restrictions, warm-hearted Christians were always eager to become Bible colporteurs. The return of Liberals to power removed the most senseless of the restrictions of colportage. This produced a curious result. The French Roman Catholic clergy obtained from the Pope permission to print a French New Testament translated from the Vulgate; avowedly in order to combat the circulation of Protestant versions. During the next ten years the Bible Society of France printed more than 300,000 volumes, chiefly Testaments and Portions, at the expense of the American Bible Society. The grants during the twenty years to French Bible Societies amounted to $53,531.

During this period the Society made grants to the Geneva Evangelical Society amounting to $27,105 for specially selected colporteurs in France. The Bible men met many difficulties, but they also probed the hearts of the common people. A colporteur was arrested because the Bibles which he carried were bound in black while the one which bore the stamp of authorisation was bound in brown. But his troubles seemed light by the side of those of a day-labourer who had been won by the savour of the verses which the colporteur read aloud. He wanted to get a copy of the Gospel of Matthew which friends might read to him. His wife objected; the priest had said that the book was bad. On his hesitating she said that he ought to obey the priest at any price because he holds the key of Heaven. The husband said: "Who gave him that key?" The poor fellow had to yield to his wife's logic although he had tasted the savour of the book. He said helplessly: "Perhaps the priest lies; but I cannot read and I have to do what the priest says for I cannot instruct myself in these matters."

A well-to-do lady told Mr. Dardier, the agent of the Geneva Society, that she did not care for the New Testament. He responded by reciting verses which breathe special comfort for the afflicted. She then admitted that her heart was sorrowful; she could not worship the God of the priests; she had not been inside of a church for eight years. But she thirsted for God; she said to Mr. Dardier: "You must have known what was in my heart when you read those verses. I would like to buy your book, and I too will believe on Jesus Christ." Time and again the colporteurs received from unexpected quarters testimony to the habit which this book has of rooting its words in the mind and heart of the serious reader. One day a clerk in a government office hailed a colporteur with some friendly salutation and said to him: "You once gave me a Testament. For a long time I carried it in my pocket and did not look at it. But now for three years it has been in my heart!"

Spain, closely linked to France in one sense, was sharply separated from it in actual fact. The quality of a government, and the character of a people may mark frontiers more sharply than mountains. Shortly after the revolution that unseated Isabella of the Golden Rose, the American Bible Society sent to the missionaries of the American and Foreign Christian Union in Spain 7,500 volumes of Scripture. It was the first large consignment of Bibles to reach the home of the Inquisition. Shortly the British and Foreign Bible Society began to print Scriptures in Madrid and issued in one year over 87,000 volumes. The National Bible Society of Scotland also arrived in Spain, not to print but to circulate Scriptures. The Trinitarian Bible Society of London also commenced an extensive work of distribution by means of a Bible coach. The eagerness of Spaniards to lay hold upon the Scriptures when some degree of liberty had been introduced was pathetic. Mr. Lawrence, the Agent of the Trinitarian Bible Society, wrote to Secretary Holdich, "No little chick just liberated from its shell more instantly seizes upon its proper food than does the heart set free to do so instantly turn to the incorruptible seed which is its own food."

Rev. William H. Gulick, missionary of the American Board at Santander, wrote to Dr. Gilman in 1878 about the method of the work. He said: "Our method is that of the disciples of old. When persecuted in one city we flee into another." The reports of the American Board's missionaries showed seven or eight colporteurs employed and five or six thousand volumes put in circulation in Spain each year after the overthrow of the reactionary ministry of Canovas del Castillo. The grants to the American missions in Spain during the twenty years amounted to $21,142.

Another country offering difficulty and opposition to Bible colporteurs was Italy, a neighbour to Spain upon the Mediterranean. In 1873 Dr. Cote of the Baptist Mission in Rome, bought at the expense of the Bible Society 300 New Testaments printed in that city by the Italian Bible Society. Dr. Cote took great pleasure in circulating them. In 1874 the Rev. H. C. Waite announced the distribution for the American Bible Society of 5,000 Portions, 500 Testaments, and 200 Bibles in Rome and vicinity. It was pleasant to know that as a result of this work of the mission, 115 Italian soldiers were converted and received into the church during the year.

The Rev. L. M. Vernon of the Methodist Episcopal Mission, writing from Rome in September, 1878, pictures graphically the method of the clergy in depriving the people of the Scriptures. A labourer returning from Bolsena met a colporteur and bought a Testament of him for half a franc. He opened the book and walked along reading here and there, saying to himself: "Half a franc; why, this is worth two worlds!" After he got home to Molise one day he met the parish priest. "Oh," he said, "I want to show you a little book I have. It is wonderful. It contains the secret for becoming good," and he handed the priest his treasure. "Miserable man," said the priest, "this book — either you burn this book or you will be excommunicated and damned forever!" "What in the world?" said the labourer. "It only speaks of God; it is not an excommunicated book; it cannot be." "Great blockhead!" cried the angry priest, "how do you know whether or not it is excommunicated? Either you burn it, or you will not receive absolution!" Upon this the labourer decided to take chances with the book rather than with the priest whose absolution was of doubtful quality.

So the gospel made its way in Italy through all of this period, often cursed and destroyed by rabid priests, but sometimes greeted with joy and often read with faith. To aid the missions to circulate the Scriptures in Italy the Society granted during this period $13,741.

As in these European lands so in the islands of Latin America in this period the Bible was sent to many places to do by itself its own work as a missionary. These islands were notable as among the nearest of the Society's foreign fields and as the most repellent. The Society for years seemed to hang upon the verge of access to them. In 1870 communications were received from J. W. Zaccheus, a teacher doing some independent missionary work in the island of Vieques, one of the dependencies of Porto Rico. When he went from this island to the town of Fajardo in Porto Rico he sent earnest requests to the Society for Scriptures to be furnished him there. The receipt of the books he acknowledged in these unstudied words December 10th, 1873: "Halleluiah! Yesterday afternoon I had the joy not only to receive but to unpack the box of books. I immediately sold three Bibles. Joy inexpressible! Only think — the first box of Bibles ever brought to Fajardo!"

Another field which was attractive and yet most difficult was the Spanish section of the island of Hayti known as Santo Domingo. Here the terrible illiteracy of the people was a main obstacle to Bible work. In 1871 when "annexation" was in the air, the Rev. W. H. Norris was sent as special Agent and commissioner to Santo Domingo. He was greatly delighted with the appearance of the island, its natural beauties and riches, and pleased with several flourishing though small missionary establishments. His report did not encourage the planting of a permanent agency in the island. Nevertheless the small groups of Evangelicals at the mission stations gave a certainty that Bible distribution would be carried on by these loving hands as the Society supplied them.

In Cuba there was a distinct relaxation of opposition to the Bible as a result of the revolution in Spain. Scriptures were sent from New York to several of the seaports and distributed thence by the good offices of parties interested in the extension of the Kingdom. It was not until 1882 that the Board decided to establish a permanent Agency in the island. After Rev. Thomas L. Gulick had made for the Society a careful examination of conditions, the Rev. A. J. McKim in 1884 was appointed Agent for the island. He found immediately a welcome for his books and at the end of the first year reported that 6,400 volumes had been put in circulation chiefly by sale. A serious difficulty, however, hampered his enterprise, in the scarcity of material to draw upon for his colporteurs. As Baptist and other missions grew congregations were formed at Havana, Matanzas, and Cienfuegos and from these came forth devoted men for colporteurs. During the five years from 1882 to 1887 about 22,000 volumes of Scripture were put in circulation in Cuba, chiefly by sale.

CHAPTER XLIV

SYSTEMATISING THE DISTRIBUTION ABROAD

MR. ANDREW MILNE was appointed Agent of the Society in 1864 for the District of Entre Rios, between the Parana and Uruguay Rivers, in South America. In Chili, on the west coast of the continent, Rev. Dr. Trumbull maintained a missionary enterprise aided by the American Bible Society[1] and to some extent by the British and Foreign Bible Society, through the Valparaiso Bible Society. This work was cosmopolitan in character, reaching not only the native Chilians as opportunity offered, but carrying books into the coast towns of Peru when it seemed safe to do so, and continually offering Scriptures to the sailors of all nations whose ships brought them to Valparaiso or to Santiago. To different parts of Chili mining and railroad construction had brought numbers of German, Swiss, Italian, and other workmen who were also reached by the colporteurs of the Valparaiso Society. At that time this enterprise of Dr. Trumbull was deemed to be a separate unit.

Mr. Milne's field, beginning at Rosario and Montevideo, was slowly extended during twenty years to include the vast expanses of Argentina, the war-devastated fields of Paraguay, the wide grassy plains of Uruguay and the little known mountain regions of Bolivia. From Montevideo on the Rio Plata to La Paz near Lake Titicaca in Bolivia is a distance of about 2,500 miles within the limits of this Agency; and difficulties of transportation at that time made the distance almost a two months' journey.

Travel and its incidents were leading characteristics of the operation of this great Agency. In its earliest days Mr.

[1] During the period 1871–1891 this aid amounted to $11,540.

George Schmidt was a devoted explorer who made long journeys with his Bibles until in April, 1872, to the great grief of his associates and friends, his life came to an end at Asuncion in Paraguay. Mr. Milne wrote of him at this time, "No one ever laboured more devotedly or with purer motives than he. If any one has deserved a monument it is Mr. Schmidt in return for his labours in behalf of the La Plata Republics."

Mr. Milne, too, made long and fatiguing journeys to learn the needs and to plan the supply of this field that extended right across the continent. It was not until 1884 that he was able to say that in one year all the different countries covered by the agency had been visited. He had a band of well-chosen and faithful colporteurs occupied continually in scattering the Scriptures despite opposition which was fierce and cruel. In the early eighties he took into his service an energetic Methodist minister from Peru, the Rev. Francisco Penzotti, who after some years of arduous journeys sometimes alone and sometimes with Mr. Milne, was appointed Assistant Agent of the La Plata Agency with a special field in Western Bolivia and Peru. All these journeys made by Mr. Milne in Argentina, Uruguay, Paraguay, Bolivia, Ecuador, Venezuela and Peru, convinced him that no part of the world can possibly have a greater claim upon the loving attention of the Society than the countries of Central and South America.

In 1888 Mr. Penzotti was arrested at Arequipa for selling Bibles, but after nineteen days he was released and continued his work in Peru and Bolivia. In July, 1890, he was arrested at Callao upon the charge of having conducted religious worship which was not that of the Roman Catholic Church. The case was tried, and Mr. Penzotti was declared not guilty, but appeal was taken to a higher court. The prosecution was so clearly malicious and unjust that secular newspapers and numbers of persons not sympathising in any way with Mr. Penzotti's Bible enterprises joined in a general clamour of protest. This agitation failing to get him freedom, men began to demand a sweeping reform in the laws and even in the constitution of the republic so as to secure religious liberty. After seven months of imprisonment, and after remonstrances from the United States and the British Ministers, Mr. Penzotti was released by decree of the Supreme Court. His sufferings in prison, like those of St. Paul, were deemed light because of the result. By the good providence of God the outrages and contumely showered upon him went far to work out full regious liberty in several Latin American countries where priests still held in their clutch many officers of the law.

In 1884 the central depository of the La Plata Agency was moved into the city of Buenos Aires and the government of Argentina recognising the purely benevolent character of the Bible enterprise granted freedom from customs duties on Bibles imported from abroad. About $400 was the saving which this franchise brought to the Society in one year.

The work of the Agency was disturbed again and again by revolution, by war, and the train of evils which such disturbances bring in their train. But during this period, in spite of all obstacles and the vehement opposition of clergy in different parts of the field, 281,199 Bibles, Testaments and Portions were distributed mainly by sale.

The growth of the field of the Agency has been suggested only. But it will be admitted that such a growth is a cogent argument for placing capable and broad-minded Agents in charge of the Society's enterprises in lands too distant for direct supervision from New York. The better knowledge of results where an Agent is on hand to report growth is another argument. Cases continually come to light which invite the Society to urge greater diligence in distribution. The results of Bible reading are uniform among all the different races with whom we have to do. In the first place the book always gains more or less of a hearing. Secondly, its influence is thus certified. Thirdly, among the people the Bible is granted a real monopoly not only of truth but of intellectual might. And in the fourth place, in all the regions to which it goes, the Bible finally becomes a leader of a more or less considerable group of people. It does its work slowly, perhaps, but when it gains a hearing the gain is permanent.

In one of his letters Dr. Trumbull describes the process

by which the Bible makes its own way among the people. The beginning of an endless chain was with an Englishwoman who advised a Chilian to read the Bible. The Chilian bought a Bible, read it, and then casually recommended a friend to read it also. This friend borrowed the book which had been commended to him. The Chilian then bought himself another book, lent it to another friend and bought a third Bible. By that time the others had read sufficiently to wish to buy the Bibles which they had borrowed. In the meantime the original mover in this matter had become thoroughly convinced of the truth. He invested the money from the sale of the two books in two more Bibles, and openly urged all his friends to read the Bible. "You will acknowledge," said he, "that this is gold. Get it, then, fresh from the mint. Do not content yourselves with coins which have become defaced from long circulation." The appreciation of the Bible shown in this Chilian's argument comes to some with surprising celerity.

Mr. Milne wrote of one of his colporteurs who gave a copy of the Gospel of St. John to a girl. A week later the colporteur was offering his books in a coffee shop when an elderly gentleman bought a Bible, saying: "You gave a Gospel to one of my girls. It was lying on the table, when a priest came in and put it in his pocket. I want this Bible to take the place of that Book. The priest will not get this!" The Bible thus produces radical changes in the thought and belief of many people. In Peru the Rev. Dr. Drees of the Methodist Episcopal Mission organised a church at Callao of thirty-one members and ninety-five adherents which had been built up entirely through Bible distribution, no missionary having ever spent any time in organising or any money in sustaining this little congregation.

Mexico afforded many instances of the same kind of a result. At Ville de Cos, in the state of Zacatecas, in a mining community fifteen people who had received the Scriptures through Mr. Hickey or Mr. Westrup agreed in 1868 to worship together and study the New Testament. Later a missionary from Monterey visited this band, administering the rites of baptism and of the Lord's Supper, and organised an evangelical church. In 1872 out of this beginning had grown a strong church of one hundred members with a meeting house which they had constructed themselves. General Casey of the United States Army, who had served in Mexico and had become interested in the beginnings of Bible work there, wrote to a friend his views as to the future. One sentence of this letter touches the root of the whole matter and applies to all the countries in Latin America. "What Mexico needs," said he, "above everything else, is that religion which is drawn solely from the word of God. Let it have that and material prosperity will come in like a flood." Systematic, continuous dissemination of the Scriptures is essential in a field which is in this condition.

Various experiences in other fields of the Society served in this period as reasons for the establishment of permanent Agencies abroad. The overthrow of the French Empire in Mexico was the beginning of American missions on a large scale in that country. As we have already mentioned, Mr. Riley of the American and Foreign Christian Union established himself in Mexico City and received liberal help from the Society in fitting out his workers with Bibles. The Society of Friends established a mission in 1871 at Matamoras, in the state of Tamaulipas, and Mr. S. A. Purdie, the leader, was very glad indeed to receive from the Society grants of books or of money. By the time that President Laredo (who succeeded to power after the death of Juarez) was ousted by General Diaz in 1877, so that quiet was established for a time in Mexico, there were American missions of seven different denominations receiving aid from the American Bible Society in that country. It was clearly impossible for any single denomination to represent the Bible Society in supplying the others. Yet it was not an efficient method to ship small grants to several missions. The time was ripe for sending out an Agent.

The Board from the beginning of its history had shrunk from supporting Agents abroad if circulation could be increased by any other means. It had not avoided the appointment of Agents to supervise the work of the Auxiliaries in the United States; but up to this time it had appointed but two permanent Agents in all the vast expanses

A DAUGHTER OF MODERN MEXICO

of its foreign field. It clung to the idea that missionaries would naturally be glad to take some trouble in distributing books freely given them by the Society.

The missionary's side of this question after a time began to assume importance. As the work of missionaries increases the difficulty increases of finding time for efficient distribution of the Scriptures which the Society has granted. A time may come when any offer to relieve him of the duty will be accepted like help from the angel of God.

Out of the seven or more denominations having missionaries in Mexico two or three denominations had their headquarters in Mexico City. It came to pass that an Agent of the British and Foreign Bible Society came up from the South and opened a depository. He thus began to make himself useful to all these denominations; they would not have to write separately for small consignments of books from New York, but could obtain books as they needed them in Mexico City.

Whether this object lesson had effect in New York is not absolutely sure. The perplexity of dealing with different denominational missions at such a distance was sufficient to account for the fact that in 1878 Dr. Arthur Gore of Boston was appointed Agent of the American Bible Society for the republic of Mexico and established himself in the City of Mexico with a depository in an eminently suitable place for representing effectively his Society.

Dr. Gore felt obliged to resign his office before a year had passed; and Rev. H. P. Hamilton, who had just graduated from Union Theological Seminary in New York, was appointed Agent in his place. In 1826 Rev. Mr. Brigham had estimated that no more than 2,000 Scriptures had ever gone into Mexico. During the twenty years before Mr. Hamilton took up the Agency the Society had sent to that country more than 250,000 volumes of Scripture. In 1883 there were connected with the American missions in Mexico 264 Evangelical Congregations with 40,000 adherents. Since the Society's Bibles had much to do with the building up of these congregations, it was a happy thought which came to the British and Foreign Bible Society about this time leading it to offer to withdraw its Agent from Mexico, the American Bible Society taking over his stock of books at cost. The arrangement was very pleasantly made in 1879, and the question as to whether the Bible Society can do without an agent in Mexico has never since been raised.

Another of the fields where the Society had been distributing Bibles by the aid of missionaries and other friends during some forty years but without any permanent agent was Brazil. After the opening of the Presbyterian mission at Rio Janeiro and São Paulo, through Rev. Mr. Simonton and later Rev. Mr. Blackford, a considerable number of Scriptures were sent out each year from points where the Presbyterian mission established its outstations. In 1876 Mr. Blackford was appointed Agent of the Society. He travelled some 3,000 miles in the next year, visiting thirty-two cities and towns and putting in circulation several thousand volumes chiefly by sale.

Meanwhile Mr. Milne had visited the southern province of Brazil, reporting a great opportunity for Bible work and confirming the statement of Mr. Van Norden that new doors of usefulness were opening all over Brazil, since so soon as people receive the Bible and begin to read it they call for preachers to tell them what to do. Under the leadership of Mr. Milne an Auxiliary Bible Society was formed in Rio Janeiro which took up the supply of the city and vicinity with considerable enthusiasm. Members of this Society were for the most part European Protestant residents. Mr. Blackford resigned his position as Agent in 1880 and was succeeded by the Rev. William M. Brown, a young minister just graduated from Union Theological Seminary.

Rev. Mr. Brown did not long endure the strains of his undertaking. In 1886 he reported that changes in the social conditions of the people were hindering in some degree the progress of Bible distribution. Since the suppression of slavery in Brazil, German immigrants and Italian labourers had begun to pour into the country. Various other influences were at work to diminish the number of Scriptures distributed in Brazil. The Society's Agency seemed founded on sand. Some weight must be given to a curious incident. The Emperor Dom Pedro appeared, after the fashion of Haroun al Rashid, upon the platform of a village schoolhouse to criticise the teachers for slackness in failing to teach the children the Roman Catholic Catechism and in allowing a Protestant Bible on the desk. He made a definite statement that energetic measures would have to be taken to put an end to the Protestant propaganda. It so happened that for family reasons Mr. Brown withdrew from the field the same year. His successor as Agent, Rev. H. C. Tucker of the Methodist Episcopal Church, South, in 1889 wrote with a keen sense of a wonderful and comforting change: "Sending away the Emperor and establishing a republic in Brazil have greatly agitated the public mind. One act of the provisional government has already been to separate the church and state and to proclaim liberty to all religions." The permanence of the Brazil Agency coincided with the fall of the Empire.

The Central American republics had not received much attention from the Bible Society up to the year 1880, not because of lack of interest, but because of inaccessibility. The Panama Railroad had directed a steady stream of travel across the Isthmus and various missionary organisations had sought to care for the souls of the employees on the railroad and of the travellers passing across the Isthmus. At the beginning of this period Mr. W. L. Thompson at Panama was a correspondent of the Society, receiving small grants of Scriptures in Spanish as well as in English which he distributed as best he could. He was also in charge of a school at Panama for children of the people connected with the railroads. In 1873 he said: "My work is going on slowly, but steadily and surely, and I now hope by the grace of God to succeed. I must also state that I do believe the time is approaching for this people." But no Agency was yet in mind for Central America.

Closly adjoining the district of Panama are the mountainous regions of Colombia which were a challenge as well as an invitation to missionaries and to Bible Societies. There was very little possible in Colombia because of continual political disturbances, and, even after missionaries began to establish themselves in Guatemala and other points in Central America, it was years before an approach could be made to the interior of Colombia by any other route than the line of the Magdalena River.

Venezuela attracted the sympathy of the Society during this period by reason of the persistence of General Guzman Blanco, the President, in his sharp and liberalising controversies with the Roman Catholic hierarchy. In 1876 the Board sent Mr. Joaquin De Palma to Venezuela as a commissioner to open communication with the friendly members of the Government and to report upon the general aspect of affairs. General Guzman Blanco told Mr. De Palma that while personally interested in having the Bible or at least the New Testament introduced in the public schools as a text book, he was then approaching the end of his presidential term and did not feel disposed to make any radical changes which might embarrass his successor. Mr. De Palma waited until the new administration was installed and found plenty of encouragement in their courtesies. All this, however, seems to have amounted to very little in the way of Bible distribution. Ten years later Mr. Milne from Montevideo, with Mr. Penzotti, his assistant, visited Caracas and were shocked to discover no trace whatever of certain "Bible Committees" hopefully organised by Mr. De Palma. Mr. Milne and his companion lost about a month of precious time through allowing themselves to trust the empty promises of ministers of government. They appointed as colporteurs of the Society some members of the Presbyterian church, but insisted that Bible work in Venezuela could not be effectively pressed unless an energetic Agent was placed in charge. This urgent advice was heeded by the Board.

In 1887 the Rev. W. M. Patterson. D.D., of the Methodist Episcopal Mission in Mexico was appointed Agent for Venezuela. Dr. Patterson found the country more difficult as a field for Bible work than had been imagined. Men, women, and children had been carefully taught by the priests not only to resist offers of the Scriptures, but to answer the arguments of colporteurs who pressed Scriptures upon them. The case called for missionaries to be sent to Venezuela, at least to Caracas. Once more the Society suffered disappointment in its plans for this territory where so long it had sought an opening for its Bibles. Dr. Patterson officiated at the funeral of an acquaintance in Maracaibo. The man had died of yellow fever. After his return to Caracas, Dr. Patterson was attacked by the disease and died August 19th, 1889. But happily there was no disposition on the part of the Society to cease its efforts. In 1890 the Rev. Joseph Norwood, formerly a missionary in Peru, of the Methodist Episcopal Church South, was appointed Agent of the Society for Venezuela.

Curious problems in due course emerged in other countries where missionaries attended to the distribution of the Society's books, emphasising the need of some direct care of such work by the Board when missions grow. For years the Board had made liberal grants of money to American missions in Ceylon, in South India, in the Bombay Presidency and in some parts of North India. At the time of the opening of the American missions thus aided there was great need of help for Bible work. In fact, for a time the largest proportion of the money used in Ceylon by the Jaffna Auxiliary Society (British) came from the American Bible Society. Somewhat the same situation existed during the early years of the Madras Auxiliary of the British Society, for it was glad to get at least half of the money for certain publications from the grants made to American missionaries by the American Bible Society. Similar needs led to the grants to American Missions for printing in Marathi, and in Punjabi, Hindustani, etc. (in North India). The grants of money to American missions in India during this period amounted to $44,225.

But it came to pass during the present period of our story that the American missionaries in South India began to find colporteurs of the local British Auxiliaries so vigorously canvassing the American mission fields as to leave hardly any opportunity for missionaries to sell books. Similar word came from the region of the Punjab where a vigorous Auxiliary of the British and Foreign Bible Society had been formed. There, finally, about 1886 the British Auxiliary bought from the Presbyterian Lodiana mission the whole stock of Scriptures remaining in hand from those printed with the aid of the American Bible Society.

One of the missionaries put the case of the mission as to distribution of books in an entirely new light when he mentioned how great a relief it was to be delivered from the burden of book distribution which hitherto had rested heavily upon his shoulders, but which hereafter would be carried by the local Auxiliary of the British and Foreign Bible Society.

In each of these cases the question naturally arises whether it was wise on the part of the American Society to overburden missionaries already perplexed by the multiplicity of their cares — educational, pastoral, and evangelistic — in rapidly growing fields, merely for the sake of saving the sum which would have been necessary to provide an Agent capable of handling the enterprises which the Society had been so eager to initiate. However this may be, these experiences offered their own proof of the necessity of the appointment in every large field of a man able to see accurately, report clearly, and execute faithfully instructions from the Board — a man, in fact, whom the Board could fully trust as its envoy and ambassador. It was during this period, then, that decisions were finally taken which led to the establishment of the most of the Society's foreign Agencies.[1]

[1] In 1891 the foreign Agencies of the Society with the dates of their organisation were as follows:

Levant	1836	Mexico	1878
La Plata	1864	Persia	1880
Japan	1876	Cuba	1882
China	1876	Venezuela	1888
Brazil	1876	Siam	1890

CHAPTER XLV

THE CALL OF THE FAR EAST

THE decision of the Society to appoint an Agent to superintend Bible distribution in China was reached after several very urgent appeals from missionaries. The general missionary work was growing. It was beyond the strength of the missionaries to guide inquirers in their home station and also to press distribution of the Scriptures in outlying regions. In 1875 Rev. Dr. N. G. Clark, Secretary of the American Board of Missions, urged the Board of Managers to realise what might be accomplished at that stage of affairs if 500,000 copies of the Scriptures in Chinese could be put into circulation at once. Such a sowing of seed, he judged, could only be executed by Bible Society men, devoted entirely to the one work.

Partly because of this appeal, Rev. Luther H. Gulick, M.D., formerly a missionary of the American Board in Micronesia, was appointed Agent of the American Bible Society for Japan and China, and reached Yokohama early in 1876, full of interest in the project of increasing the circulation of the Scriptures in these two wonderful countries of the Far East. Dr. Gulick's first impression of Ningpo, China, was characteristic. "This city," said he, "was founded about the time of the prophet Isaiah and now, about twenty-six centuries later, the prophesies of Isaiah are only beginning to reach Ningpo."

At this time the Society had been giving grants in aid to American missions in China during some forty years. The missions were of eight denominations, besides the China Inland Mission which was international and interdenominational. The American Missions which had printing presses were the Methodist Episcopal at Fuchow, the Presbyterian mission at Shanghai (then unquestionably the finest printing house in China), and the American Board's mission in Northern China at Peking. At all of these places and many others the missions had important congregations. The American Protestant Episcopal mission at Shanghai had extended its work up the Yangtze River to Hankow. The American Board's mission at Peking, Tungchow and Tientsien, had reached out to the gateway of Mongolia at Kalgan, there supplying Arabic as well as Mongolian Scriptures to the people of the caravans from the desert. American missionaries had also reached out into West China as far as to Si Ngan fu, the outpost of ancient Nestorian missions; distributing large numbers of Scriptures by sale in the provinces of Shansi and Shensi, and everywhere being courteously received. The prospect for Bible distribution was inviting.

The missionaries had employed a few colporteurs at the expense of the Bible Society, but it was very difficult to find suitable men; men with really spiritual insight and able to understand thoroughly the object of the Gospel or other Portion which they were sent to sell to the people. Much of the work of the missionaries in the line of Bible distribution for this reason was as uncertain as the steering of a ship at sea in a fog. One satisfaction of the missionaries at this juncture was the fact that the Bible in some degree pre-empted the field of literature so far as the common people were concerned. In different parts of China the Holy Scriptures had been circulated in Chinese before any other work whatever brought from Western nations had been translated into Chinese.

By this time realisation had come to the most of the missions that in a country like China gratuitous circulation of Scriptures was not wise. To decide what proportion of the cost of the Scriptures should be fixed as the price of the books, then became a serious matter. In many cases the price was one-fifth, sometimes one-half of the actual cost of the books, and sometimes a merely nominal sum. Such a course is the only one practicable in countries where money is scarce or entirely absent. In Micronesia payment for Scriptures has been made in cocoanut fibre and oil.

Dr. Jacob Chamberlain on one tour in India accepted shells from the seashore instead of coin as payment for Bibles. In Western Africa Presbyterian missionaries have accepted fish, fowls, fruit, building materials, and anything that the people can give as payment for books. The two volumes of the Mpongwe Bible which cost in New York $4.50 were sold on the field for one dollar. But there was no dollar on the Gaboon. Four yards of print worth in America seven or eight cents a yard, were rated as a dollar. The cheapest edition of the Society's Mandarin Version of the Bible cost thirty-eight cents. The single Gospels in Chinese cost one and one-half cents apiece; but to the poor they were sold at half a cent each or less. Before the end of this period, when the number of Christians was multiplied, one edition of the Bible in Chinese was printed on foreign paper with elegant binding and was sold at two dollars a copy. The same book printed on Chinese paper in the Chinese style was sold at twenty-five cents a copy. In fixing prices for the Scriptures the general principle is that books are prized by those who pay something; but in dealing with poverty-stricken people those who circulate the Bible have to use great discretion, however large a draft the distribution may make upon charitable funds.

Greater than poverty as an obstacle to Bible distribution in China was the illiteracy of the people. The missionaries had found by experience a living hope for the country in the willingness of the people to learn to read, although there was no widespread ability to do so. A man would pass as "literary" who knew only a few Chinese characters. But such a one on getting a Gospel would proceed like a child with a picture puzzle. By persistently trying and asking, he could little by little master a whole line, and then a whole page; and by that time some idea of the subject of the book would encourage him to analyse still more of the unknown characters.

Two things took place in China upon the arrival of Dr. Gulick. In the first place a number of foreign colporteurs were engaged, men of ability and tested Christian character who would go into the field themselves to sell books and who would each take charge of a band of native colporteurs to whom they could impart something of the energy and hardihood necessary for the work. In the second place, the number of colporteurs working under the direction of missionaries was increased in different parts of the field. With this introduction of system also commenced a full and accurate accounting for all books distributed. Before long there had been organised a band of eight foreign colporteurs, each one of them superintending six or eight natives who steadily gained skill in Bible distribution. Dr. Gulick also employed fifty-two colporteurs supervised by American missionaries in different parts of the country. By these means the circulation of Scriptures in China increased six fold during the twelve years of Dr. Gulick's service.

The experiences of the colporteurs were varied, but their enthusiasm was always at a high point. One of these men, Mr. Gordon, went up the Yangtse River on a Bible Society house-boat named in Chinese, "The Glad-tidings Ship." His line of distribution was immediately along the shores of the river. He carried with him three months' supply of books, travelled more than a thousand miles and disposed of more than two thousand Gospels.

In 1887 Mr. Prothero, another colporteur, with six natives was the first successfully to distribute Scriptures in Changte, the capital of the fanatical province of Hunan. The province had many times previously been entered by missionaries and Bible Agents, who had been politely but speedily turned away. Mr. Prothero took six picked men into Hunan by way of the Tung Ting Lake and sent them to canvass the country. Three of the men sprinkled the city of Changte with a shower of Gospels before the authorities observed their presence. In the course of three months' work this expedition put into circulation in Hunan ten thousand Gospels and one hundred New Testaments, almost all of them sold and paid for. Mr. Copp, another of the Bible Society colporteurs, in 1886 marched westward to the confines of Thibet, leaving his family at Chungking in the province of Szechuan where were several other missionaries' families. When he came back from his adventurous tour it was to find his house and in fact all the missionary houses in Chungking looted and destroyed in one of those sudden and inexplicable outbreaks which are not rare in Chinese annals. Happily the inmates had escaped to Ichang.

In the province of Kansuh the colporteurs were rather disheartened by passing over districts where one might travel the whole day without seeing a man or a house. Mr. Thorne, another of the Society's colporteurs, gives a suggestion in regard to work in such places. He observes that the most forbidding looking people in the most wretched of places are sometimes just those whom God would not have the colporteur turn his back upon. Those who live off from the road, on the side of a higher hill, or deep below, where the hills divide; far enough away to make it an effort and loss of time to climb — the colporteur has to think of the possibility that just such a place is the one which he should visit.

Mr. Thorne was a rare character. He served the Bible Society nine years as a colporteur, Dr. Gulick having found him working in connection with the American Mission at Nanking. He had made a fortune in California and lost it, had been a merchant prince in Shanghai, where he lost another fortune. Finally he had attached himself to the mission station with the desire of doing something for the good of the Chinese, learning the language, and taking up with enthusiasm the distribution work which Dr. Gulick placed in his hands. In some of the villages along the canal in the region of Tsingho, the multitude of people in the street was such that no one could stop moving a moment without cries of protest from others whose way was blocked. Mr. Thorne was a tall, conspicuous figure and some of the people made it very disagreeable for him by taking small children and throwing them in his way in hope that he might stumble over them. One child who had fallen against his feet was crying. Mr. Thorne picked him up, and at the same instant another child used as a projectile was caromed from his side into a tub of fish. Happily, Mr. Thorne was able to see and catch the man who had thrown the second child, and him he presented to the fish-peddler. The altercation which followed between the two Chinamen left Mr. Thorne free to go his way unmolested. But his heart was deeply moved at the apparently sincere desire of the people to get his books. In one village, after he had left, having distributed all that he had, he heard a voice calling after him, "Oh, Foreign Devil; Foreign Devil! Please come back. More men are coming to get your books."

Another colporteur describes his sensations in going through the streets of the city jostled on one side by a small-pox patient and on the other by a poor creature white with leprosy. In such a crowd he might perhaps meet no adventure, but on the other hand a man inclined to trick foreigners might come up behind him, speaking over his left shoulder, and at the same time removing a good handful of "cash" from the colporteur's right hand pocket. Nevertheless, it was the universal testimony of the missionaries that foreigners could sell more readily than natives in those beginnings of the Society's China Agency. Dr. Fitch of Suchow said that native colporteurs were apt to be despised and railed at by the crowd, whereas a foreigner would be listened to and treated with more or less respect. Mr. Porter of the American Board's mission said that the mere fact of the foreigner's being able to talk Chinese was enough to win buyers. Native help, however, was always necessary to handle the money taken in, although the sum was often ridiculously small. A colporteur on a prosperous day will sell Scriptures for 3,000 "cash," paid five or ten cash at a time. Rev. Mr. Du Bose of Suchow notes that it commonly took his assistant two hours to count the receipts of such a day of book selling; the three thousand cash being worth about three dollars.

For this great undertaking the men chosen by the Society were always men of special ability, tested in missionary work, cultured, acquainted with the language, ready to turn to any branch of the service. Mr. James Ware employed in distribution by the Society for many years was valuable not only as a colporteur and as manager of the Society's office at Shanghai, but was a skilled translator of the Scriptures in one of the colloquial dialects.

Two acts of permanent importance marked the missionary history of this period. In 1877 the missions of all denominations working in China held a conference at Shang-

THE UNION MANDARIN REVISION COMMITTEE

hai. Including the Bible Societies, about twenty missionary bodies were represented in the conference. The mere ability to spend fourteen days in discussing aspirations and methods encouraged a spirit of fraternity, while the interchange of thought and the comparison of methods stimulated greater endeavour. The second of the two important missionary acts was another conference held at Shanghai in 1890. About 430 persons, men and women, coming from every part of China and representing forty-two missionary organisations, were members of the Conference. Such an act as the assembling of the conference was of great significance. The reports presented at this conference of 1890 showed a greater growth than was expected in the Chinese Christian community. The number of native communicants at 520 church centres was 37,287. The unanimous agreement of this body upon the question of unifying the Chinese versions favoured yet more rapid growth.

The range of the Society's work of Bible distribution was far greater than would at first appear. Every sale of a single Gospel in China might be deemed a step toward the conversion of the nation. From the widely distributed portions of Scriptures, thousands of people in all parts of the Empire learned the name of Jesus. An experienced Bible Society colporteur in China could reach places where a foreign missionary could not and a native preacher would not go. Those engaged in such distribution, though numbered by the hundred and the thousand, must each feel in that teeming population like a lone farmer undertaking to seed a section of 600 acres of land. How is it to be done? Who will care for its culture? Who will garner the fruit?

The seed of the word was often slow to show any green blade of promise. The case of Li of the province of Honan was a type of the long waiting that China imposes upon the missionary. He was unsettled in his mind, dissatisfied with the religious teachings of his ancestors; then he found at a wayside book shop a copy of the book of Acts which he carried home. It took him a year or two to find an intelligible or sane idea in the little book; but after seven years he had pieced together the various strange statements and found that he had a wonderful record of the teachings of Jesus Christ. His old mother was also interested in what he found in that book, and she finally told her son that he must go ask the foreigners at Hankow. He must make haste because she was growing old and must know more about this matter. The man travelled twenty days to Hankow. In some perplexity he was going along the street of the city when he came to a chapel where a preacher was setting forth the gospel. It did not take him very long to perceive that here was what he had come to find. In due time he was baptised. Provided with a Bible he tramped back the twenty days' journey to give his mother the news for which she longed about the "Jesus religion."

A colporteur from Peking travelling through the country stopped at a village inn and mentioned that he was selling books of the "Jesus religion." The inn-keeper said, "There is an old crank here in the village who will not bow down to idols and is all the time talking about Jesus." The colporteur sought the man out and found that he had possessed for twelve years some Christian literature. He did not know where to find any one that could inform him about it, but all alone, in that unsympathising, jeering crowd, he had done what he could to conform his life to the gospel teaching. As Rev. Mr. Du Bose of Suchow said: "Grant that a large number of these books will be destroyed, some burned, some unread, some laid aside on shelves and forgotten; it will not be so with all of them!"

It is worth noting just here that all the hindrances met by this work do not have their source in China. In 1890 one of the Vice-Presidents of the American Bible Society called the attention of the Board to the Chinese Exclusion Bill then pending in Congress which must necessarily have effect in limiting freedom of movement of Americans in China. In fact about the same time an American Bible Society colporteur found himself unable to sell any books in Hongkong because a boycott was declared against American goods when the Chinese Exclusion laws went into effect in the United States.

In 1881 the Agency was divided, Japan being assigned to Rev. Henry Loomis, while Dr. Gulick was transferred to

Shanghai to develop the China Agency. Dr. Gulick threw his whole strength into the work for China. It was barely seven years later that his health gave way. During his administration 2,000,000 volumes were issued by the Society in China, almost all of them being sold; and in each case with some acquaintance on the part of the purchaser with the Christian quality of the colporteur who sold them. Such acquaintance may be a vivid interpretation of the teachings of the book when a pagan cautiously inclines to buy it. In May 1889 Dr. Gulick escaped from China for a vacation rest; he resigned his commission as Agent in June 1890, and in March 1891 he passed to the better land. Mr. James Dalzell who had served as book-keeper in the office at Shanghai, took charge of the Agency until the appointment of Rev. L. L. Wheeler, D.D., in 1890 as successor to Dr. Gulick, but Mr. Dalzell died before Dr. Wheeler arrived, leaving Mr. James Ware and Mr. A. A. Copp to care for the Agency affairs.

The Southwestern frontier of China reaches down in an almost unknown loop to the borders of Burma and Siam, and the Laos people of Siam are near of kin to the mountaineers of those Chinese borders. In 1876 Siam was included in the field of the China Agency. The American Board had the initiative in work for Siam, but the mission later had been transferred to the Presbyterian Church. Missionaries freely went about the country, although travel was difficult. It used to be said that a longer time was required to go from Bangkok to the northern part of the Laos district than from Bangkok to New York. The extent of the country and the interest shown by the people, especially in its northern part led the Society in 1889 to constitute Siam a separate Agency. The Rev. John Carrington, pastor of a Presbyterian Church in San Francisco, was selected to be the Society's Agent. He had spent about six years as a missionary in Siam, submerged, as it were, in the masses until he had absorbed knowledge of the Siamese and of their tongue. He rendered important aid in printing the Scriptures in Siamese and in Laos; and his devotion to Bible distribution was a beautiful illustration of utter self-abnegation in the name of Christ.

The record of these Agencies, while showing growth as the missionary enterprise grew, cannot but emphasise the quality of the men supplied by the missions for the service of the Society. Through the consecration and efficiency of these men the Society was able to hear and heed the call of the far East.

CHAPTER XLVI

JAPAN AND KOREA

LONG before Dr. Gulick had finished his first year at Yokohama as Agent for the Society, he was chafing at the smallness of the trifles which occupied his time every day. He had arrived at Yokohama in January, 1876; and it seemed as if the whole year was occupied in getting his bearings, learning what he must not do, and in waiting for some clearly important work to occupy his time. As many others have done in similar circumstances, Dr. Gulick did whatever came to his hand, reassuring himself by reflecting that the seemingly futile activities of every day might have importance in the use made by them by his Divine Master. At the beginning of his work he learned the lesson of "waiting on the Lord."

One of the pleasant experiences of his first year was the printing by the Society of the Gospels of Matthew and Mark in the revised form prepared by the Committee of Missionaries. A part of the edition was furnished to the British and Foreign Bible Society and a part to the National Bible Society of Scotland; and it was noted in the report that the number of Japanese Scriptures stated as issued did not include 14,000 volumes sold to the British Societies.

The New Testament was published in four different forms: one to fit conservative classical scholars who loved the Chinese style; another for less cultured readers; a third for the lover of plain Japanese writing; and a fourth with the Roman letters for the benefit of Japanese who were newly learning to read and for foreigners newly learning the Japanese language. Rev. Dr. Davis of the American Board's Mission said that the publication by the Society of the New Testament in Japanese and of the whole Bible in "Kunten" Chinese[1] has made it possible at last for all

[1] This was the Chinese Bridgman-Culbertson Version, with Japanese diacritical marks to indicate the pronunciation and the order of words.

Christian workers in Japan to press on the work of preaching which they came out to do.

In May, 1877, the depository of the Society was opened in Yokohama. This step was approved by all the American missionaries, and the site selected was the very best possible in the whole city. Up to the first of January, 1880, Dr. Gulick reported that thousands of Chinese Testaments and hundreds of Bibles had been put in circulation in Japan, besides 100,000 New Testament portions.

The question of Bible circulation in Japan became important even before the Japanese New Testament was finished in 1880. The repeal of the anti-Christian laws in 1872 opened the way for Bible colportage. The first colporteur sent out by the Society was the Rev. J. Goble of the American Free Baptist Mission. Mr. Goble had translated into Japanese and published in 1871 the first version of the Gospel of St. Matthew in Japanese. Printing the Scriptures was a somewhat dangerous occupation in Japan at that time. Mr. Goble wrote of his experience: "I tried in Yokohama to get the blocks cut for printing, but all seemed afraid to undertake it. I was only able to get it done in Tokio by a man who, I think, *did not know the nature of the book upon which he was working.*"

When the books were printed Mr. Goble induced a few people to accept Gospels and he was happy. But his hopes were dashed. Every volume was carefully secured by the police authorities and returned to him with the injunction to refrain from circulating such books. The demand was even made that Christian Scriptures in Chinese belonging to the missionaries themselves should all be given up to the native authorities. But, with the assistance of the American Consul, that demand was successfully resisted.

During October and November, 1879, Mr. Goble made two tours for the Society, one of twenty-four days and one of eighteen, in regions to the north and east of Tokio. He had with him a Japanese convert well-known for his piety and Christian zeal. They went from town to town and village to village perched on the top of queer pack saddles, or riding in jinrickishas or making use of small river steamers whenever practicable. They made arrangements with 120 different parties, mainly book-sellers, to take Christian Scriptures on sale. Several times they were cheered by meeting little bands of Christians. "One day, while walking quietly along the dark road a number of farmers sprang up and almost frightened us by their eagerness to know who we were and what was our business. Before answering I asked, 'Who are you?' and they promptly replied 'We are Christians,' and when we told them our errand they seemed very much pleased." Only once did the colporteurs meet with any decided opposition, but they were sure that in due time that city, Mito, would become one of the most interesting mission fields.

It was a surprise to find that book-sellers were willing to keep the Scriptures in stock and that as the number of Christians in the country increased, they also aided the wide dissemination of the book which they loved. At Okayama the American mission had the New Testament for sale in its little book shop on a side street. Few purchasers appeared and some one suggested that perhaps a Japanese book-seller on the main street would be willing to handle the book. He was glad to try the experiment, took the New Testament at a venture, advertised it, and immediately began to sell considerable quantities. Few remember, when talking of Bible circulation in one of the missionary fields, that the vogue of the Scriptures is something like the growth of a snowball which the children roll until it becomes a splendid mass high as their heads. In the case of the Bible it is not only the missionaries and the colporteurs who circulate it in Japan. When the New Testament was published there were in the country 2,700 church members, besides considerable numbers of attendants at the mission services. There were 183 missionaries, men and women, in the country, of whom 140 were Americans. All of these people were possible disseminators of the Scriptures, in widely separated districts of Japan.

The Bible has begun to win a permanent place in any language when it is assimilated by many of the people. In Japan the man or the woman who is a self-seeker has precisely the same emotions toward other people (or the same lack of motions) as the self-seeking man or woman in

America. In either country, by the side of the self-interest which a materialist deems worthy as an aim, any champion of the duty of subordinating self to the interest of others is admired as wonderful for greatness and power. Something of this early began to be seen in Japan. Before ten years of free Bible circulation had passed, natives began to say that the Bible was exerting a notable effect in the development of Japanese intellectual life. Its ethical axioms and illustrations began to be used by Japanese writers. Before the end of this period Baron Ito, a member of the Japanese Imperial Privy Council, ventured to recommend to the Mikado some study of the principles and the theory of Christianity, pointing out that Bismarck and his Imperial master were believers. The fact was curious, and it illustrated the degree to which the Book was gaining a hold upon the minds of the people, even if this recommendation had little root and no after result.

An epoch in the history of missions in Japan then, dates from the time when the Bible began to take a place in the native literature of that country. The Japanese Mail in speaking of the translation of the New Testament into Japanese, said it was like the building of a railway through the national intellect. A good translation of Scripture does not veil its ideas, but lets the word unmarred, reach all. Dr. Verbeck spent seven years upon the book of Psalms in Japanese assisted by capable Japanese scholars. The result was that the book of Psalms was a gem. The standard form of the Japanese Bible was in the simplest style of the book language, and it resembled the English Bible in its fitness to suggest the happiest phrase to speaker or writer who is seeking expression.

As an instrument in opening the minds of men to spiritual aspirations, the Bible from the very first showed that it knows the way to Japanese hearts. In 1871 Captain James of the United States Army was engaged by a great Daimio (Prince) of Kumamoto to teach the young men of his retainers English — and the art of war. It so happened that Captain James was a warm-hearted Christian and his wife was a daughter of the Rev. H. M. Scudder, D.D. Neither had any knowledge of the Japanese language; and the

Japanese young men whom they were to teach had no knowledge whatever of English. About three years passed before they could communicate with any facility. But the Captain had meantime won the confidence of his pupils by his kindly deportment.

The young men of Kumamoto school had been taught to hate the very name of Christianity, but when Captain James suggested Bible readings they were glad to take them up for his sake. Captain James did not make personal application of the verses read, but after about a year of study of the Bible, several of the young men said that they felt obliged to follow its teachings. Only then did the Captain explain and urge the demands of the book upon all. In 1876 about forty students in the Daimio's school went to a neighbouring hill-top where they could be by themselves. There they made the momentous decision that having received a great blessing from God, it was their duty to make it known to their own people. The people of Kumamoto were horrified. Some wished to kill Captain James; some wished to kill the young men. The school was broken up and Captain James had to leave. But after study in Mr. Neesima's Christian Institute these young men became leaders in many departments of Christian work in Japan. The Kumamoto young men owed to the Bible alone, interpreted by the Spirit of God, their change from hate to eager service of Jesus Christ.

This story from Kumamoto suggests the influence which the Bible may exert upon a number of persons together. Let us also follow the influence of the Bible upon a single obscure individual, who fights his spiritual battles alone. In 1883 Rev. Dr. Ballagh described a curious incident of a Christian fellowship meeting in Japan. At the thanksgiving service a timorous man of some means confessed that for ten years he had been studying Christianity. He now wished publicly to declare himself a believer. He said that his testimony to the truth of the Christian religion was stronger because he was not a baptised person and no blind partisan of Christianity. He was a Buddhist. As a Buddhist he could bear testimony to the unsatisfactoriness and the untruthfulness of the Buddhist system. He had studied the Scriptures during ten years and was so thoroughly satisfied with the truth that he wished his testimony to the Bible to be practical. He then pledged himself to pay any amount up to the extent of his whole fortune to supply copies of the Scriptures to those who wished them and could not afford to buy them.

These two types, the solitary, silent man who absorbs nourishment for his soul and ponders the truth by himself, and on the other hand the associated group that cannot be still, but declares the truth far and wide — these two types might be cited in innumerable instances of the living power of the Bible then and since illustrated in Japan. There is neither room nor need for multiplied instances. There is need, however, to remind the reader that instances of bitter hostility also mark each chronicle of Bible work. During the year 1889 a reaction appeared in Japan against foreign influences. Patriots raised the slogan: "Japan for the Japanese!" There seemed to be at once a dampening of interest in the Holy Scriptures and for some time the influence of this popular outburst, encouraged in various ways by the Buddhists, was shown in a diminution in the circulation of the Bible. This falling off in the circulation was not by any means permanent nor did its symptoms excite alarm. It was simply a difficulty natural enough in such a country, and calling for an unlimited stock of patient endurance.

This falling off in circulation of the Bible was one element of a decision taken about this time for a better organisation of Bible work in Japan. A Committee of missionaries was formed belonging to different denominations, which the Agents of the three Bible Societies were invited to join, and the whole enterprise of printing and distributing the Scriptures in Japanese was placed under supervision of this committee. This experiment was the subject of correspondence between the three Bible Societies and the arrangement went into effect in July, 1890. In the new arrangement, since the Agency of the American Bible Society was the first to be housed in a Bible House of its own, and since Mr. Loomis' dwelling place was in the same building, it was agreed that the main depository of the General

Committee should be the American Bible Society's house in Yokohama. The care of the books and the plates belonging to the Society now passed under control of the Bible Committee, it being understood that of all expenses one-half should be paid by the American Bible Society, one-quarter by the British and Foreign Bible Society, and one-fourth by the National Bible Society of Scotland. In 1891 the Committee published its first year's report, full of hope for a more extended work in consequence of the coordination of all forces.

In 1882 the Rev. Henry Loomis began to take Korea within the sphere of his vision as Agent. The land could not as yet be visited by foreigners: in fact in 1883 the American Legation requested American missionaries not to attempt as yet to enter the country. The Korean Government, however, was beginning to show signs of willingness to be led by Japan.

The story of the opening of Korea to the Gospel can only be outlined at this point. But the outline would be incomplete without mention of a strange series of circumstances reported by Mr. Loomis about this time. At the great exposition at Vienna a gentleman named Tsuda was among the officials of high rank sent from Japan. Mr. Tsuda happened to have his attention called to an exhibit of one book which had been translated into two hundred different languages. The fact of these numerous translations was singular, not to say startling. Enquiry showed that the book was the Bible, and that it was translated, in part at least, into Japanese. When he returned to his own country study of the Bible led Mr. Tsuda to believe in Jesus Christ.

In 1881 an embassy from Korea arrived in Japan to study the new sciences and industries of that country. A member of this embassy was directed to Mr. Tsuda for information on scientific agriculture. On the wall of the room where Mr. Tsuda received the Korean official was a scroll written in Chinese containing the Sermon on the Mount. This the Korean read with profound interest. Mr. Tsuda explained to him that these were the words of Jesus Christ. The Korean dared not take the written scroll home with him, for at that time the death penalty was attached to acceptance of Christianity or of Christian documents. He told one of his friends in Seoul, however, who was about to be sent by the king of Korea on another mission to Japan, to go and see the scroll on the wall of the reception room of Mr. Tsuda. This second Korean official was named Rijutei. The result of his reading the scroll on the wall was ardent desire to know more; and finally, through Mr. Tsuda, he made the acquaintance of the Japanese pastor of a Presbyterian church, was baptised, and began an entirely new life.

The conversion of Rijutei was a link in a chain which cannot now be traced to its end. First there was Mr. Tsuda at the Vienna Exposition, then the Korean magnate in Mr. Tsuda's reception room, next the private information given to Rijutei in Seoul, and next the journey of Rijutei to Japan which led ultimately to his conversion. The first service that Rijutei undertook for the Lord Jesus Christ was the preparation of a New Testament in Chino-Korean and the translation into Korean of the Gospel of St. Mark. Meanwhile, in July, 1883, Rijutei wrote an impassioned appeal to the churches of America beseeching them to send missionaries to Korea.

The Korean Embassy to Japan was sent out in 1880. In 1883 Korea sent an embassy to the United States and following the appointment of the Embassy the American Presbyterian Board and the American Methodist Episcopal Church took steps to send missionaries into Korea so soon as the country was able to receive them. It was not until 1885 that it was considered safe for Americans to go to Seoul the capital of Korea. In that year Rev. Mr. Underwood of the Presbyterian Mission and Rev. Mr. Appenzeller and Dr. Scranton of the Methodist Episcopal Mission took up their abode in the Korean capital. The books which they could take with them were the Gospels translated by Rijutei and printed by the Society.

At this time but one other attempt had been made to translate the Scriptures into Korean. The Rev. John Ross of Manchuria in 1875, when Li Hung Chang abolished the "neutral strip" between Manchuria and Korea, travelled

SELLING BIBLES IN KOREA

in that region and met Koreans. With their aid he made a version of the New Testament which was printed in 1885 by the National Bible Society of Scotland. Unfortunately the dialect of Mr. Ross' teachers was not very intelligible as far south as the capital of Korea. At the beginning of the American mission in Korea, then, Rijutei's translation of the Gospels was used to the extent of several thousand copies. In 1887 the Scottish National Bible Society re-published the Gospel of Mark of this version with some improvements, but it was plain that the first duty of the missionaries must be to take from the original tongues an entirely new version of the Scriptures in Korean.

Mr. Loomis, the Society's Agent for Japan and Korea, spent two months of 1885 in Korea and returned to Japan full of enthusiasm for work in this new field. At this time there were only three missionaries in the Hermit Kingdom — all Americans. Three Bible Societies were also represented there: the American, which was first to visit Seoul, the Scottish National Bible Society, which arrived later, and finally the British and Foreign Society. A committee of the missionaries was soon formed to take up the work of Bible translation. It was quite impossible to do much in the way of Bible distribution, not only because of the slender stock of Scriptures on hand, but because the lack of trustworthy material for colporteurs as well as the stern laws of Korea made an almost insurmountable obstacle to Bible distribution. At the end of 1890 the chief feature of the story of the year for Korea was the fact that the translation of the New Testament under a competent Committee had begun in earnest and was steadily progressing. Here again the Japan Agency had to exercise that "waiting on the Lord" which the Bible so often sets forth as a means of strength.

CHAPTER XLVII

MEDIATING BETWEEN EUROPE AND ASIA

THE enterprise of the Society in the Levant resembled the work of a colonisation Socicty in a land whose people are backward in civilisation. The Bible Society, however, had but one colonist — the wonderful Book which had now gone into thousands of homes in the Levant. Some part of the story of this colonisation of the Bible will form the topic of this chapter. In actual fact it prepares a basis for mutual understanding between the West and the East.

In 1872 the Bible House in Constantinople was completed, marking an epoch in the history of Christian work in the Turkish capital. Formerly Bible and mission work had their separate centres in the European quarters of the city. Little by little the American Board's missionaries ventured to open book-rooms in Stamboul, the old city, and finally, about 1853, they experimented with residence there, in spite of the Turkish prejudices which had long excluded foreign residents from that part of Constantinople. The mission had an extensive publication work and its editorial rooms and sales rooms needed to be in Stamboul among the people for whom the books were intended, instead of being hidden away in the European quarters among the people with whom missionaries were classed. As the work grew the missionaries in consultation with the Agents of the two Bible Societies hired a large stone building near the Golden Horn, in which the mission and the Bible Societies had offices and storage rooms, and a salesroom jointly maintained.

The Bible House was built partly because this hired building was too small for the growing work, and partly because the unobtrusive quarters of the mission, changed when leases expired, were compared by the common people with the fine permanent buildings of Roman Catholic missions. People thought that the American missions had no permanent basis. The money for constructing the Bible House was raised chiefly in America by Rev. Dr. I. G. Bliss, Agent of the Society, with the approval of the Board of Managers, but without its assuming any responsibility in the matter.[1]

The building was one of the finest commercial buildings in the city, being four stories high with eighty feet front on one of the most important streets in old Stamboul. The American Board's mission with its publication department, which issued school books, weekly and monthly periodicals, religious books, commentaries and tracts in four or five languages, occupying the time of five or six missionaries, leased the larger portion of the building. The American Bible Society Agency with its storage-rooms was established on the second floor, and the British and Foreign Bible Society Agency with its store-rooms occupied a considerable portion of the third floor. One of the large shops fronting on the street was the salesroom jointly maintained by the mission and the two Bible Societies.

During the score of years of this period many attempts were made by the Turkish government to restrict the sale of Scriptures by colporteurs. It proposed to have the Scriptures marked "For Protestants only," in order to prevent Mohammedans from buying. Here a compromise was reached by the agreement of the Bible Societies to put upon the title page the words "Published by the American (or "the British") Bible Society." The wish to restrict these sales resulted in a law requiring every book to be specially licensed by the censor before being printed. Here, however, what was intended to be a hindrance favoured circulation, for thereafter every Bible printed in Turkey bore on its title page an official declaration that its publication was authorised by the Imperial Department of Public Instruction.

The reason why Turkish officials could not strike directly at the enterprises of the Bible House was the restraint put upon them by treaties of commerce. Any illegal interference with the book business of the mission or of the Bible

[1] It is owned by incorporated Trustees in New York who hold the property for Bible and mission work.

Societies was resented by both the British Embassy and the American Legation, for the business carefully conformed to the law. A year or two after the Bible House was opened, the Turkish police entered the sales room and undertook without process of law to seize the Turkish Bibles. By the time the Turkish government Ministers had got through hearing remarks on the case by Mr. George H. Boker, the United States Minister, they were willing to apologise, and to promise that such an outrage should not again be perpetrated.

Great was the progress which by this time the American Board's mission had made in Turkey. There were 195 preaching places scattered over the empire with an average Sunday attendance of 13,744 while the persons connected with these congregations numbered 19,660 registered Protestants. The mission maintained 225 schools with 7,623 scholars. This respectable little community constituted a fraternity of warm supporters of Bible work, since upon the Bible it was built up. That such a body existed at this time with its small groups in almost every province of European and Asiatic Turkey, accounts for the rapid development of Bible distribution during the period ending in 1891.

The field of the Agency in 1871 embraced the eastern half of Turkey in Europe, Turkey in Asia, Persia, Syria, Egypt, and Greece. The position of the Agent at Constantinople was, however, something such as would be that of a single Secretary planted at the Bible House at New York and instructed to supply the needs of the United States. Dr. Bliss had under his control at this time about thirty-five colporteurs, scattered through all of this immense territory. These men had to have in hand Scriptures in a score of languages.

This variety of tongues was pleasantly alluded to by Rev. Dr. Hogg of the American Mission in Egypt, in an address telling what the Bible does for the missionary. In the first place "it endows him with the gift of tongues." People come to the depository and get Scriptures in almost any language they ask for; immediately they assume that the missionary can speak and write all the languages; one of the

THE CONSTANTINOPLE BIBLE HOUSE

most wonderful things that they ever heard of. Then "the Bible gives the missionary a lodging and an audience" wherever he goes. As a stranger he arrives at a village where he wishes to pass the night. Looks are surly and suspicious but he announces that he has the word of God in his saddle bags. He is immediately conducted to the chief men of the village who treat him politely, if not cordially, and all the householders come together to hear what he has to say. Again "the Bible provides him with a text and gives him a hearing" among these people. The sleepy Christians of the old Oriental churches look with superciliousness upon a man from the New World of the West who wishes to talk to the hoary East about Christianity. But the Bibles taken from the saddle bags immediately provide a subject of conversation. The people are interested and the missionary can administer to them the kind of a sermon which they all need, while trying to sell them Scriptures. Finally "the Bible Society enables the missionary to leave preachers at each place" to which he goes. A single missionary is sent to a district perhaps as large as the state of Pennsylvania and as populous as Pennsylvania and New York taken together. He cannot provide preachers for the different towns, but by a little labour he can leave the book in hundreds of thousands of copies in all parts of this great field. It is in such ways that the Bible Society is an indispensable aid to the missionary.

Colporteurs of the Society sent out under supervision of missionaries travelled throughout this vast field; in most cases the colporteur being jointly sustained by the Bible Society and the mission. In this way the most distant portions of Asiatic Turkey were reached, even through Mesopotamia, eastward into Persia and southward as far as Bagdad. The Society maintained colporteurs in that distant city until about 1883 when the Church Missionary Society of England occupied Bagdad as a station, and it seemed proper to pass over the Bible work there to the British Society. In Northern Mesopotamia, at Mardin and Diarbekir, was a very eager demand for Bible distribution joyfully supplied by Rev. A. N. Andrus of the American Board's mission. In 1872 Mr. Andrus reported that the sales of Scriptures in

Mardin and vicinity had increased forty per cent. in four years. It was Mr. Andrus who took up the work of translating the New Testament into Kurdish, numbers of Kurds having won his sympathy in Northern Mesopotamia and on the borders of Persia. In such ways the splendid linguistic equipment of missionaries and Bible Agents furthered Bible distribution.

The Agent in Constantinople found it very difficult to make regular visits to the distant Persian field of the Society, there being no railroads and practically no wagon roads. In 1879 the Rev. W. L. Whipple was appointed Agent for Persia, that field being separated from the Levant Agency.

The period of which we treat in this Agency was a stormy, not to say dangerous period of clash between Asiatic and European ideas of the science of government. In 1875 an insurrection against the Turkish authority broke out in Herzegovina, and war followed with Montenegro and Servia. In the following spring took place terrible massacres of Bulgarians on the excuse that if left alive they might plan insurrection. The situation in Turkish government circles at this time was graphically outlined by Dr. Bliss in one of his reports. In 1876 two sultans were dethroned in rapid succession. "Men in and out of power played their games of chance with fiery energy. The hazards were desperate, and terrible the winnings — to most of the players, confusion, exile or death; to the lookers on — the people who bear the consequences — dismay, bankruptcy, ruin in every section of the land. Wars, famines, pestilences followed with their desolating trail." The war with Russia commenced in 1877 and ended with a triumphant Russian army inside of the fortifications of Constantinople, when Great Britain and other European Powers intervened to save the Ottoman Empire from destruction.

At such a time it seems a matter of wonder that any Scriptures could be sold, but those put in circulation in 1877 numbered 29,237 copies, and in 1878, 39,183. The account of issues for this last year contains the item, "Sixty-nine volumes stolen from and lost by colporteurs." This item reveals the strict accountability to which the colporteurs were held. On the whole, this war time permitted a wonderful distribution. Some thousands of the books were gratuitously circulated among prisoners of war and soldiers, both Russian and Turkish.

At the end of the period (1891) the Levant Agency had in the field about one hundred colporteurs, some in European Turkey among the Bulgarians, some in Egypt, some in Syria; but the greater portion in that immense field of Asiatic Turkey where the American Board's missionaries have so long been working to bring the ideas of Bible Christianity from the West into the slow and listless East.

The colporteurs in all this Levant region did a work trying to body and mind. The fatigues of travel were greater than Americans can well imagine, and fanatical religionists often stirred the people to attack the Bible men, so that, like St. Paul and his friends in some of their journeyings in pagan Asia Minor, they had to escape as best they might. In one of the villages of Sivas, Turkey, a colporteur was thrown down stairs, dragged out of the village and severely beaten. The memory of this cruelty remained in the mind of the ringleader until it became an appeal to conscience of such force that the man went out of his way to find a colporteur who could supply him with a New Testament. Before many years had passed the man and his wife had both revolutionised their ideas of life and joined the Evangelical Church.

The work of the Agency was not merely the difficult work of Bible distribution. It included a continual labour in Bible translation or revision. Rev. Dr. Riggs was at work on the Bulgarian version and on the large Armenian Reference Bible; Rev. Dr. Schauffler was building up a new Turkish version, and Rev. Dr. Christie of the Scottish mission to the Jews was revising for the Society the Hebrew-Spanish Bible. His work was arrested, by the way, for some months by a curious quarantine inside of the city against cholera. This entirely cut off his compositors from access to the Bible House presses.

In 1871 efforts were made to revise the Armeno-Turkish Version of the Bible, translated by Dr. Goodell many years before. A question which continually thrust itself forward was whether it would not be possible to unify the Turkish versions. For now the Turkish language was changing so as to tolerate the substitution of many Turkish for Arabic and Persian words in literary work. The Rev. A. T. Pratt, M.D., with a competent native assistant, experimented in this direction, consulting with Rev. Dr. Elias Riggs and Rev. Dr. George F. Herrick. After Dr. Pratt's death in 1872 a committee was formed to carry on the work of revision of the Turkish version with the idea of striving to make a version intelligible to the common people, and yet acceptable to educated Turks. The committee commenced its work in June, 1873. It was composed of Rev. William G. Schauffler, D.D., Rev. Elias Riggs, D.D., Rev. R. H. Weakley, of the Church Missionary Society (of London), and Rev. G. F. Herrick, D.D. Dr. Schauffler was not able to meet with the committee regularly and to the great disappointment of his colleagues, as well as of the British and American Bible Societies who jointly met the expenses of this work, he resigned. The work was then carried to completion by the other three members, assisted by Armenian and Mohammedan literary men. To meet with this Bible revision committee brought a thrill to the heart. The Mohammedan masters of Turkish expression joined heartily and reverently with their "Amen" in the prayer for the guidance of the Holy Spirit with which every session was opened. The work was finished in 1878 and with some slight additional revision to make the book more clear to the uneducated reader, this has become the Union version in Turkish.

We have said nothing about the office staff of this great agency. Rev. I. G. Bliss, D.D., became Agent in December, 1857. In October, 1872, his son, Rev. E. M. Bliss, was appointed Assistant Agent. Prof. Porter took charge of distribution in the Syrian field, and Rev. Mr. Alexander or at times some other of the missionaries of the American United Presbyterian Church in Egypt acted as sub-Agent of the Society for that great section of the field. The burden was too great for Dr. Bliss' health and early in 1888, when Mr. E. M. Bliss was obliged to resign on account of the failure of his wife's health, the Society lost no time in appointing the Rev. Marcellus Bowen of Hartford, Conn., Asso-

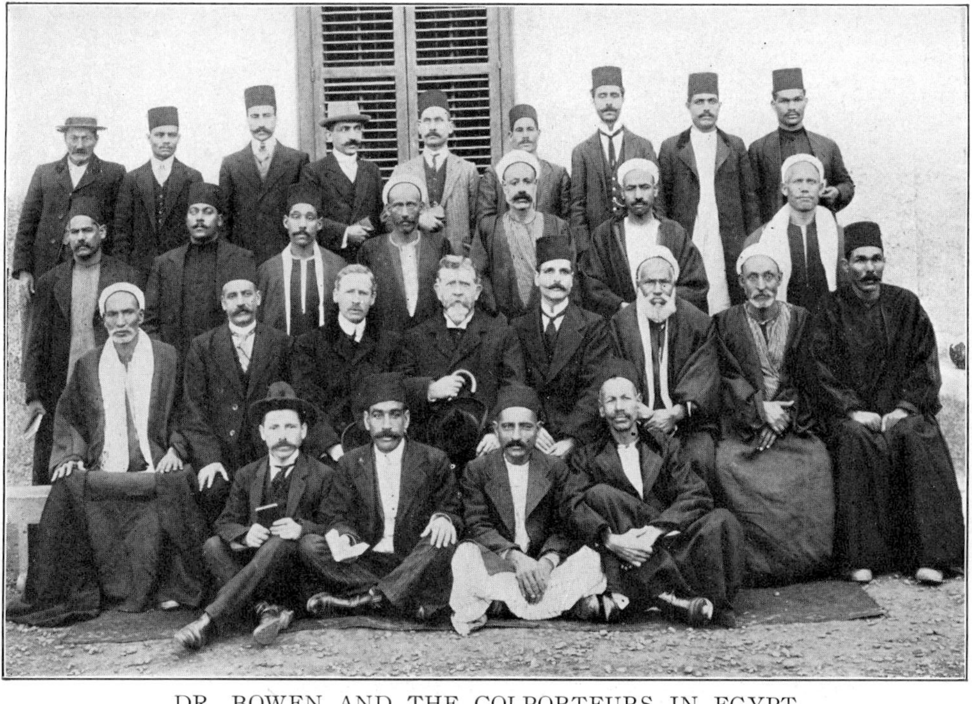

DR. BOWEN AND THE COLPORTEURS IN EGYPT

ciate Agent for the Levant. Mr. Bowen had been for some years a missionary of the American Board in the region of the "Seven Churches of Asia" and had a good knowledge of Turkish. Reaching Constantinople in September, 1888, he immediately took up the Agent's burden by making a journey of some months through Asiatic Turkey to inspect and animate the work of distribution.

Upon the American missions, the Society, and the newly appointed Associate Agent, Mr. Bowen, deep sorrow fell when Rev. Dr. I. G. Bliss, while making a tour of upper Egypt, sickened and died at Assiout in February, 1889. He had been thirty-two years the devoted, unresting and successful representative of the American Bible Society in the great field which during more than a quarter of a century received fully one half, and even at the time of his death one third, of all moneys appropriated by the Society for foreign work.[1] During the thirty-two years of Dr. Bliss' service the Agency under his charge put into circulation 875,849 volumes of Scripture in some thirty different languages. It had been a great privilege to Dr. Bliss to throw all of his powers into the work of sowing seed, but it was characteristic that he never claimed achievement for himself. He believed that the Bible work in Turkey was given to him as his life work, and that any man called of God to do a work has strength, not his own, for its performance. In his view whatever was done by the Agency was done by the Divine help. Results belonged entirely to the Master who protected and fostered the work.

Among the Greeks of Turkey the clergy objected to the circulation of the Bible more strenuously than did the Armenian clergy. A large proportion of the Greek subjects of the Sultan lived in the central part of Asia Minor and had lost entirely the use of the Greek language. In those parts of Asia Minor the Seljoukian Turkish sultans who ruled from the eleventh to the thirteenth century had stamped out all languages excepting the Turkish. The memory of this piece of savagery was perpetuated among

[1] The sum expended on the foreign agencies in the year ending March 31, 1891 was $134,918.25. Of this amount the sum expended in the Levant Agency was $45,156.92.

Armenians and Greeks of the region by those curious literary cenotaphs known as Armeno-Turkish and Greco-Turkish writings. A considerable Greek population along the coasts of Asia Minor and of European Turkey bordering on the Egean Sea used the Greek language, and Scriptures in Greek were circulated among them to some extent.

The mission Board of the Presbyterian Church in the United States (South) had established a mission to the Greeks in Athens, Volo, and Salonica. Much was done by the missionary, Rev. Mr. Sampson, in introducing the Scriptures in the Greek schools in the neighbourhood of Salonica. An interest in the pure gospel which was full of promise was shown by the remark of a prominent member of a Greek school board: "I have ordered the New Testament to be read regularly, and have strictly forbidden all observations or interpretations. *This will cut the root of all false traditional teaching which I have found it so hard to free myself from,* while the truth will be left to do its proper work."

This period was also a time of wide circulation of the Bulgarian Scriptures. The usual fruit from sowing the Bible appeared in every part of Bulgaria. It seemed particularly suited to hold and shape the lives of some people in every town or village. One of the labourers in the American Methodist Episcopal mission said: "If I can sell one copy of the Scriptures in a Bulgarian village I can see moral improvement in the whole village within six months." In 1886 there was war between Servia and Bulgaria in which the Servians were defeated. In the Bulgarian Army the usages of what is styled "civilised warfare" were observed, but not in the Servian Army. This difference was so marked that the missionaries were inclined to attribute it to the circulation of the Bible in Bulgaria. Its circulation had not been permitted in Servia.

From the Koran Mohammedans of Turkey derive some true notions of God. It is one of their favourite exercises to repeat audibly God's "beautiful" and "terrible" attributes. These, however, are so diluted in interpretation that a common weakness with Mohammedans is to say, "Lord! Lord!" but to omit doing the things which the Lord has said. The habit of thinking worshipful thoughts of God forms a basis, however, in the Mohammedan mind for interest in the Bible. During the whole of this period some thousands of copies of Scripture in Turkish (written with Arabic letters and used, in general, by Mohammedans only), were sold every year. It became quite common for colporteurs to meet Mohammedans who were interested in Bible instruction. Here and there throughout the country were men who came like Nicodemus, secretly, to learn more about Christianity. Some of these ceased coming after a time, finding the demands of the Bible too hard for their easy-going morality, or perhaps finding the pressure of relatives or of the police too fierce to be braved.

At the same time there were Mohammedans in Turkey, Syria, Egypt, and Persia who cordially adopted the Christian faith. For example, an officer in the Turkish army suffered imprisonment for a year for insubordination. His disobedience was a refusal to obey the command of his superior to cease reading the New Testament. At the end of the year the officer was released and allowed to resign, and he lost no time in escaping for his life to a foreign land. The lot of any Turkish Mohammedan convert to Christianity was bitter. Even if the government regarded his case as too trivial to be taken up, fanatics might consider it a duty to God to slay the apostate; or at best his relatives would fret his soul with perpetual menaces. The number of such converts during this period was comparatively small and yet there were sufficient in all ranks of society to show the overwhelming influence of the word of God interpreted by the Holy Spirit.

The case of one of the Mohammedan converts is peculiarly interesting because he became acquainted with the New Testament through his desire to refute its teachings. He lived not far from an American mission station in a town in the eastern part of Turkey where he was the *imam* (or pastor, as we might say), of a Mohammedan parish. The New Testament taught him many things, with the result that he had to believe on Jesus Christ. As soon as the change in his views became known, men banded together to kill him and he fled across the Russian frontier. This man, when he was baptised in a Christian church in Turkey, selected for himself the name which he would take. The name was "John, Son of the Gospel," or in Armenian, "Hohannes Avederanian." At Tiflis in Russia the fleeing convert fell in with some Swedish missionaries, was sent to Sweden, received a theological education, and went forth as a missionary to Mohammedans in Central Asia. He has proved the reality of his conversion to Jesus Christ by many years of service in Eastern and Western Asia and among Mohammedans in Bulgaria (after the independence of that country made it safe for him to return to work among his own people).

In the Levant, as in all other fields of the Society, uncounted instances prove that the Bible as a colonist or messenger for Christ is both suited to men of every race, and powerful to enlighten their consciences; it brings together even those who have been too far apart to tolerate each other.

CHAPTER XLVIII

SEVENTY-FIVE YEARS OF SERVICE

WITH gratitude for life, for success, for memories of a past that has left no lasting pain, and for inspiring hopes for the future, people gather to celebrate any anniversary. Whether at an anniversary of birthday greeting, of appreciation toward a faithful worker, or of general thanksgiving and benediction these elements enter into it. Such was the celebration of the seventy-fifth anniversary of the American Bible Society, held on the 13th day of May, 1891.

There was an assembly in the afternoon of that Thursday at the Bible House, the Hon. J. L. Chamberlain of Maine, Vice-President of the Society, presiding. In warm and graceful terms greetings were presented to the Society from the American Board of Missions by its President, Rev. R. S. Storrs, Jr., D.D.; from the Mission Board of the Reformed Church by Rev. Dr. J. M. Ferris; from the Missionary Society of the Protestant Episcopal Church by Rev. J. Kimber; from the Missionary Society of the Methodist Episcopal Church by Rev. Dr. J. O. Peck; from the American Tract Society and the American Sunday School Union by Rev. Dr. J. M. Stevenson and Rev. Dr. M. H. Williams.

The evening session was held in Chickering Hall, President E. L. Fancher in the chair. After a formal report of the progress of seventy-five years by Secretary Alexander McLean, an eloquent and powerful address on the "Vitality of the Bible" was made by the Rev. Dr. Phillips Brooks of Boston. Addresses of greeting followed by the Rev. T. Aston-Binns, from the British and Foreign Bible Society, Rev. James Stalker from the National Bible Society of Scotland, and the Rev. J. Burton, B.D., from the Upper Canada Bible Society. These addresses pleasantly emphasised the singleness of purpose which unites different denominations and different nationalities in the Bible cause, belittling the differences which might hinder union.

The record of the third quarter of a century of the Bible Society's labours was one that quickened faith. The men of the Society had worked under pressure; they had suffered disappointment in the support given by the home churches, but they had also been carried to heights from which the outlook gave them enthusiasm for labours to come. In the home field two general efforts to supply the destitute had occupied the minds of the Board; the first being the completion of the Supply ordered in 1866 and the other having been commenced in 1882. These were the third and fourth occasions when the Society threw its strength into supply of those destitute throughout the United States who would accept the Scriptures. In the third supply 5,454,778 families were visited, and in the fourth supply 6,309,628 families were visited and furnished books whenever they were willing to buy or to accept them.

Great numbers of immigrants had landed upon our shores, and the Society was obliged to keep in stock Scriptures in thirty languages for use in the United States, and to grope for means of putting them in the hands of the new-comers. It was a time of steady work for the Board, the Secretaries, and the twenty district superintendents. In looking back over the period one seemed to perceive a great depression which was a hindrance if not a barrier. The nature of this barrier, as due apparently to the Christians of the homeland themselves, was brought to light on examining statistics of contributions to the Society as noted in detail in the 39th Chapter. The total receipts of the Society in seventy-five years from all sources were $20,864,962, but on analysing the receipts an extraordinary fact appeared. The field of the Society's operations had been extending but there had been no corresponding increase in contributions for this work. The gifts from Auxiliary Societies and from churches in the third quarter century amounted to $1,378,-000 and $353,000 respectively. These amounts were practically the same as those from these two sources in the Society's second quarter century. Gifts from individuals in the third quarter century ($594,575) were actually less than those from the same source in the second ($655,643).

Yet the number of books issued in the third quarter of the century was 32,448,136 volumes. This was nearly 15,-000,000 volumes more than the number issued in the second quarter century. In the 39th Chapter it was shown that legacies carried the Treasury over the troubles of this period. This fact, however, did not make the failure of contributions from the living any less serious as a feature of the Society's history. There is nothing to be said in criticism of the decisions of Christians as to the amount which Bible work requires them to give for its support. It is necessary, however, for every Christian to bear in mind each year that gifts to the Bible cause must increase in due proportion to the growth of Christian missions throughout the world. After what has been written in past chapters, argument on this truth is superfluous.

Mention of Christian missions carries the thoughts back to the chapters on the work of the Society abroad. The retrospect suggests one extraordinary feature of that work during this period. The history of current events abroad embraces catastrophes, wars, revolutions, and famines like that in China in 1878 where people were starved to death by millions. Monarchs were dethroned like the sultans of Turkey, and like the Emperor of Brazil, and hereditary heirs to vacant thrones were sometimes expelled by the people. During ten years from 1876 to 1886 there seemed to be a continuous record of bloodshed and fighting in different parts of the Society's Levant Agency, ranging from the insurrection in Herzegovina and the Bulgarian massacres and the war with Russia, to the Egyptian revolt against European methods, and the attempt of the Mahdi of the Soudan to make the sword of Mohammed again a terror to Europe. The marvel is that these events which affected a considerable portion of Asia and large sections of Africa did not anywhere permanently block the extension of Bible circulation. Distribution was checked, the men engaged in it were often placed in danger, but such disturbances were only temporary, and no impassable barriers were built up.

All these great events concerned the home churches as

well as the Bible Society. They represented the throes of nations seeking to find themselves, and Christians cannot refuse sympathy to such. Contact of the Society with such convulsions and with missions passing through similar experiences interpreted it to the missions, and also gave a better understanding of the missions to the Society. In the quiet of the afterglow it appears that these experiences brought the Society into the fullest fellowship with all American missions which it aided. The relation of the ten foreign agents with the missionaries was that of trusted and beloved co-labourers under God. To all kindred Societies the American Bible Society was a coadjutor, ready to work by gifts, by prayers, and by toils, as well as by striving in virtue of the special object of its existence to make the Bible everywhere the most easily obtained and the cheapest of all books.

We have rapidly recounted the means by which the Society sought to increase knowledge of Jesus Christ and His Gospel in many communities in Europe. We have told how the " seals have been broken " from the Bible among many nations speaking many tongues. We have delighted in the growth of Christian ideas and in the revelation of the power of the cross of Christ in the vast pagan realms of China, Korea and Japan. Glimpses of the influence exerted by the Bible in the great Mohammedan Empire have rejoiced our hearts. It is a blessed thing to know that those who by the Scriptures are lifted up and united in the knowledge of Jesus Christ are of every colour and every race found in any part of the world.

The minds of the speakers at the Anniversary meeting were much occupied with the great lesson of past experiences; namely, that the faith of the founders of the Society has been justified by the results of distribution of the Bible in many lands. Indelibly should this truth be impressed on the minds of all supporters of the Society and of bystanders in Christian churches. None can afford to be without knowledge of how the Bible has taken hold of all races. Three instances must suffice to illustrate the significance of this part of the story.

In 1879 a colporteur in his journeyings reached the town

of Guarapuava in the Brazilian province of Parana. He had no particular success in finding purchasers for his Bibles and Testaments. Men did not care for such books. A merchant in that town seeing that they were cheap, finally took all the books, thinking he would make money in selling them. When customers came in he would open the Bible and read a little to show them that the book was good. He sold the books for three or four times what they cost, and Scriptures were thus scattered throughout the region. Five years later Rev. Robert Leamington made an evangelistic tour through the province and in Guarapuava many people came to hear him, among them this merchant, without showing particular interest in the gospel. Afterwards colporteurs and other Christian labourers stopped at this town several times, and finally that merchant, as though he had bathed in some pool of Siloam began to see the Bible for the first time. He shut up his shop on Sundays; he spent the day in reading the Scriptures, first by himself, but later to people who could not read, for he thought they ought to know these beautiful truths. Out of this custom grew an evangelical reading club. Finally in April, 1888, the Rev. G. A. Landes found more than seventy persons in Guarapuava who wished to make a profession of faith in Jesus Christ as their Saviour. Fifty-three of them seemed to be fit to be received into the church and when at the end of two weeks he left the place, he left as many more studying the Scriptures and looking forward to his next visit as a time for making public profession of their faith. The Bible had broken down old superstitions and lifted the whole group to a higher level of spiritual understanding and aspiration. In the providence of God the beginning of the movement was the merchant made as by a galvanic shock to see the crucified One in the Bible and then to feel drawn to fraternal interest in others who ought to see the light.

Let us turn from Brazil to its antipodes. One day in January, 1883, a ship bound for Japan sighted a canoe riding easily upon the surface of the ocean. It was curiously decorated after the fashion of the islanders of the South Seas. In the canoe were five dark-skinned men who lay at the point of death from starvation. Not unfrequently a canoe passing between two islands of the Pacific is blown out of sight of land by some storm and becomes lost on the trackless ocean. These poor fellows were rescued by the sailors, and kindly nursed back to life.

As soon as the islanders were able to move about, they knelt on the deck together and offered prayer, evidently of thanksgiving. The sailors were astonished; still more did they wonder on seeing that among the few things saved from the canoe were books, from which these men read every morning and evening in their strange language. To rescue Pacific islanders always classed with savages and cannibals, and to see them piously praying together every day was to the sailors like being witnesses of a miracle!

When the ship reached Yokohama the remarkable five men were found to be Gilbert Islanders who when picked up at sea were five hundred miles to the westward of their island of Apemama. The Scriptures which they had were the fruit of the life labour of Dr. Hiram Bingham, printed by the American Bible Society; and the naturalness and satisfaction with which these men used the Bible in their daily worship was a sure token that the gospel was rooted in their hearts. In their canoe, buffeted by the waves, starving, hopeless and about to die, those men showed themselves as stubborn in the faith as Job, who said, "Though He slay me yet will I trust in Him." Here again the effect of this faith drawn from the Bible was to lift them into fellowship with all of us who believe. Far from home these Gilbert Islands' waifs in the Christian circles of Yokohama were still in the fraternity to which they belonged!

Let us give another incident which occurred during this same period, in Persia. In the city of Hamadan, the reputed home of Esther and Mordecai, some Armenian women in 1885 heard the story of Rijutei of Korea and of his earnest appeal for missionaries and for Scriptures in Korean. These women in far off Hamadan had received Armenian Bibles supplied to the missionaries in Persia by the Society's Levant Agency. They well knew how precious a possession the Bible is and how destitute those are who have it not. Their hearts ached for the people of Korea; they put their pennies together and so they sent a donation of twelve dollars and sixty cents to the Society in New York to help give Bibles to the Koreans.

It is some 15,000 miles from the province of Parana in Brazil, by way of the Gilbert Islands, to Hamadan in Persia. A Persian Armenian, a South Sea islander, and a Brazilian merchant have neither aim nor environment approximating one another. Yet these far separated and widely differing people by means of the Bible were brought into a fraternity whose members are slowly becoming conformed to the image of the Son of God! There is no conceivable service more glorious than that for which the Bible Society was formed and by God's grace performs.

The successes of the Society were not, however, a subject chiefly to be celebrated at its seventy-fifth anniversary. It had issued in seventy-five years 54,233,712 volumes of Scripture. The fact was to be borne in mind, but the great subject of thanksgiving and praise to God at such festivals of the Society is the fact which these incidents and thousands of the same nature attest; namely, the power of the Bible to win people of all races to permanent union in Jesus Christ. At the end of a Marathon race the winner, if he has recovered the power of speech, tells of the bursts of speed by which he was able to overcome his competitors at different parts of the course. But no spirit of rivalry is possible in the labours of a Bible Society. The Society tells in its reports what it has been called to do and in what places; but this is no ground for boasting. Its reports have nothing resembling the spirit of the man in the temple who thanked God because he was so good. What fills the thought of the officers and Agents and colporteurs of the Society at such a time of accounting is wonder at the changes which the Bible is bringing about in all parts of the world. From all parts of the United States, from all parts of Latin America, from Asia, from Africa, from the islands of the Pacific, has come evidence in literally uncounted sheets that the Bible can move men everywhere, and that the object of its existence is to win men to faith in Jesus Christ and Him crucified.

The universal living ministry of this book was beautifully unfolded by Rev. Dr. Brooks in his address at the Anniversary celebration. Referring to the varied company which had been blessed with the word of God in the seventy-five years, he said: "With what various colours of bright and dusky skin, with what various voices and tongues, and various words, would they speak in your ears the words of gratitude for what they and their friends have received through the ministry of this great Society!

. . . "It is possible for us, as we look back over those seventy-five years, to see in them the representation of the great life stories of years in which the Bible has been dear to the hearts of men and doing its beneficent work, in every age and nation. We look back into the past, and can seem to see the Bible almost as if it were a great majestic person walking through the history of human life. We can seem to see it going up and down, doing its blessed work everywhere, with outstretched hands, and a blessing dropping out of those hands, in every age through which it walked, looking at this life of ours in all its richness and misery, and greatness and sin, and everywhere giving it inspiration and hope. That great being which we think of as the Bible has come to us through these years, has come to us through the long history of the human race, and at the heart and soul there is that great spirit of hope for mankind, that great belief in human nature, which comes from every association with our human race.

"And so, as it stands to-day, this Bible, bearing, as it has moved on through the past, this thought, has been full of promise, anticipation, and hope. . . . The works that are done for the progress of humanity are ever changing their form, but are ever the same, and therefore it is impossible to understand, on a jubilee evening, and think what the Bible has done as it has been spread abroad by our Society and other Societies, without looking forward into the future and asking ourselves, as men who belong more to the future than to the past, what the Bible has to do in the future? If human life is to go on, if man is to be the same great living creature, with more and more vitality in his existence, then surely our Bible, which is the Book of Life, has a great work to do in the future, and the time shall never come, until the vitality of our humanity shall be completely finished, in which the Bible shall not have its work to do, and they who can put the Bible into any hands that have not received it, or spread it before any eyes that have not read it, shall not have their great inspiration and duty before them."

What the Society rejoiced in at this seventy-fifth anniversary, then, was that it had a story to tell of how it had been used by Almighty God to place this book in the hands of millions who had to be reached in accord with the gracious plans of God Himself.

SEVENTH PERIOD 1891–1916

CHAPTER XLIX

AT THE BIBLE HOUSE

THE end of a year often brings serious and perhaps mournful reflections. The end of a century may be expected to recall and emphasise numbers of sad occurrances. The end of the nineteenth century brought to the men at the Bible House a sense of calamity almost overwhelming. During the three last years of the century, the President, three Corresponding Secretaries and the General Agent died. This distressing loss, unusual in the history of any institution, had to be entered upon the last page of the Bible Society's record of the nineteenth century.

On the 19th of March, 1898, Rev. Alexander McLean, D.D., was taken from this life, after twenty-four years of service as Secretary of the Society. Dr. McLean was called in 1874 to the office of Corresponding Secretary. At first he had oversight of the District Superintendents and the colporteurs of the Society in the West and South, and later was given charge of the correspondence of four important foreign Agencies. He was a man of generous sympathies, and easily won the love of his associates and the esteem of the members of the Board. His familiarity with methods and procedure in ecclesiastical bodies, his methodical habits as well as his energy eminently fitted him for an office so full of perplexing details. His death left a vacancy which seemed to his associates most appalling.

In September, 1898, Rev. A. S. Hunt, D.D., Corresponding Secretary, passed away, having served the Society with devotion during twenty years. Dr. Hunt had served on committees of the Society during twelve years before this, so that his high abilities were well known. On the resignation of Secretary Holdich in 1878 Dr. Hunt, then pastor of St. James' Methodist Episcopal Church in Brooklyn, was called to the vacant post. His literary taste and power of expression made him a most welcome representative of the

Society at conferences, synods, and other public gatherings, while his tact and wisdom and his unsullied life made him an honour to the Society which he loved.

A year later, in November, 1899, Mr. Caleb T. Rowe, for forty-four years General Agent of the Society, finished his long and useful career. In 1854 he came to the manufacturing department at the Bible House from the publishing business in New York City. His conscientiousness and close attention to detail made him a most valuable officer of the Society. During his long period of service 42,000,000 volumes of Scripture went forth from the Bible House. Upon the death of Mr. Rowe his larger duties were passed over to the Treasurer, Mr. William Foulke.

Three months later, in February, 1900, President Enoch L. Fancher finished his earthly career. The work of the Bible Society had been familiar to him for more than forty years, since he became a member of the Board of Managers in 1859. In only one instance has a President served the Society longer than the fifteen years allotted by Providence to Judge Fancher. His Presidency, through his influence in the community, his large legal knowledge and experience, and his warm love for the Bible was of great benefit to the Society.

In December, 1900, Rev. Edward Gilman, D.D., Corresponding Secretary of the Society for almost thirty years, passed away. Dr. Gilman had acquired repute as a pastor in the Congregational denomination, his last charge, as already mentioned, having been the Congregational Church in Stonington, Conn. On removal to the Bible House he revealed rare fitness for the office of Secretary. All of the foreign Agencies, excepting the one in the Levant and the one in the La Plata region, were developed under his supervision. He wrote a large part of every annual report during the whole term of his service. With rare linguistic ability he closely watched over the versions which the Society took up, and his love for literary pursuits made tender care of the Biblical Library an essential part of his duties. Twice Dr. Gilman represented the Society at important gatherings in Europe, and papers prepared by him for promoting the interests of the Bible cause and for special public occasions in the United States brought honour to the Society as well as to himself.

As we have said, these afflictions smote heavily the men at the Bible House and in fact they were felt as bereavements not only in the United States but in its Agencies and among its correspondents in Europe, Asia, and Africa. To many of these old and tried friends it seemed as if the old order of things must change when these great leaders were stricken. It is always the case, however, in a work which is dear to our Master that a vacancy among leaders is quickly and thoroughly filled. Upon the death of Dr. McLean the Rev. John Fox, D.D., pastor of the Second Presbyterian Church of Brooklyn, was elected Corresponding Secretary, and to the vacant chair of Dr. Hunt the Rev. William I. Haven, D.D., was called from St. Mark's Methodist Episcopal Church in Brookline, Mass. To the place left by Dr. Gilman the Rev. E. P. Ingersoll, D.D., pastor of Immanuel Congregational Church in Brooklyn, was invited. In his early years he became a lawyer, but after an inward struggle, he later decided to study theology and enter the ministry. For years he had been well known in the Board as a member of the Committee on Agencies. His courtesy and tact and broad-minded way of dealing with affairs won him the respect and affection of all his associates. In 1904, Dr. Ingersoll represented the Society at the Centennial Celebration in London of the British and Foreign Bible Society. The state of his health soon gave concern to his associates, and at the end of 1906 he resigned his office after five years' service, feeling that he could no longer do justice to its demands. Two months later in February, 1907, his days on earth came to an end, to the profound regret of his colleagues.

The choice of a new President for the Bible Society is a serious duty, and it was not until 1903 that the Board elected Dr. Daniel Coit Gilman, one of the Vice-Presidents of the Society, to the office of President. Dr. Gilman's fame was national. His brilliant career included a professorship at Yale, the Presidency of the University of California, and afterwards, for twenty-five years the Presidency of Johns Hopkins University in Baltimore; and when he stepped from his throne at Johns Hopkins he had become the first President of the Carnegie Foundation at Washington. He was also President of the American Oriental Society and had been deeply interested in Bible work for many years as a member of the Board of Managers of the Maryland Bible Society. Dr. Gilman's tenure of office was cut short at the end of five years. His death in October, 1908, was very sudden and unexpected.

In May, 1909, Mr. Theophilus Anthony Brouwer was elected to succeed Dr. Daniel Gilman as President of the Society. Mr. Brouwer was of an old Dutch family whose records run back to 1626. He belonged to the Dutch Reformed Church, being Treasurer of the Collegiate Church of New York City. For sixty years he had been connected with Bible work in the city, eighteen years as Manager of the Young Men's New York Bible Society and its President after it became the New York Bible Society, and for forty-two years a member of the Board of Managers, and twenty-three years a Vice-President of the American Bible Society. The Society was bereaved by the death of Mr. Brouwer in June, 1911.

In November of the same year Vice-President James Wood was elected President of the Society. He had been at that time for fifteen years closely connected with the administration of the Society's affairs; and for many years President of the Westchester County (N. Y.) Bible Society. He occupies the highest official position in the Society of Friends, being chairman of the Five Years Meeting, and for many years he has been the presiding officer of the New York yearly meeting of that Society.

Among the Vice-Presidents taken from the Society by death were Ex-Presidents Rutherford B. Hayes (d. 1893) and Benjamin Harrison (d. 1901). Hon. David J. Brewer, Associate Justice of the Supreme Court, died in 1909. He inherited the missionary spirit which kept warm his interest in the Society from his father, an early missionary in Turkey. In 1909 also died Major-General O. O. Howard, a Vice-President during thirty-eight years, and a thorough Christian gentleman. Vice-President J. H. Taft (d. 1905) was a man of systematic benevolence and spotless character and was for thirty years a member of the Board. Vice-President Robert C. Winthrop, pupil and successor in statesmanship and oratory of Daniel Webster, died in 1894. He was for thirty years Vice-President of the Society and was also President of the Massachusetts Bible Society. In 1896, Hon. G. G. Wright passed away, the "Patriarch Statesman" of Iowa, and during twenty-five years a Vice-President. Vice-President Elbert A. Brinckerhoff died in 1913, after a long and valued service as member of the Committee on Finance. Another member of the Committee on Finance was Vice-President E. B. Tuttle (d. 1914), an influential member of the Methodist Episcopal Church and twenty years a Manager of the Society. In the same year the Hon. S. B. Capen, President of the American Board of Missions, died at Shanghai, China, in the midst of a visitation to the missions abroad. In the same year, too, died the Hon. J. L. Chamberlain of Maine, forty-three years Vice-President of the Society which he loved, who during the Civil War was promoted on the battlefield by General U. S. Grant for distinguished service. John L. Williams, Esq., warmly interested in Bible work, having been during forty-one years a Manager of the Virginia Auxiliary Bible Society, died in 1914. He was of unique personality and great in his Christian influence.

Among the Managers taken away by death during this period we ought to name A. D. F. Randolph, Esq. (d. 1897), whose long experience as a publisher made him a very valuable member of the Committee on Publication. In 1904 F. Wolcott Jackson, Esq., died, for twenty-five years member of the Board of Managers. He was a descendant of Oliver Wolcott, a signer of the Declaration of Independence. In 1908 the Board of Managers lost three valuable members: Dr. H. D. Nicoll, an eminent surgeon, Chairman of the Committee on raising the Endowment under Mrs. Russell Sage's offer; J. S. Pierson, Esq., for twenty-one years a member of the Board, deeply interested in the welfare of sailors, having served the New York Bible Society effectively in its marine department, and also the New York Port Society; and G. E. Sterry, Esq., a successful merchant, for seventeen years a member of the Board and of its Distribution Committee, a man of strong influence and wise in counsel. In 1911 the Society lost Frederick Sturges, Esq., for thirty-six years a member of the Board, a banker most valuable in the Finance Committee, and W. T. Booth, Esq., one of the last of the older group of Managers, who had been for thirty-six years a member of the Committee on Distribution. E. P. Tenney, Esq., died in 1912, greatly valued in the Committee on Agencies during fourteen years. T. G. Sellew, Esq., a prosperous business man, for twenty-four years a member of the Board, died in 1913. Alexander E. Orr, for thirty years a member of the Board, eminent in financial circles in New York City, died in 1914. The same year James A. Punderford, Esq., for twenty-six years a member of the Board, finished his useful service on earth.

Appointments to the staff of the Society were Rev. H. O. Dwight, LL.D., for thirty-two years a missionary of the American Board in Turkey, who was elected Recording Secretary in 1907; and in preparation of the Centenary of the Society, Dr. Dwight having been set apart to prepare a history of its operations, the Rev. Henry J. Scudder, B.D., of the Arcot Mission of the Reformed Church in America, at home on furlough, was elected in 1914 Acting Recording Secretary of the Society. In 1915, as the work increased of preparing a proper celebration of the Centennial, the Rev. L. B. Chamberlain, M.A., also of the Arcot Mission of the Reformed Church in America, and a son of the Rev. Dr. Jacob Chamberlain, long a correspondent of the Society in India, was elected Assistant Corresponding Secretary.

Early in 1896 an arrangement was made with the New York Public Library by which the Society's collection of books and manuscripts was transferred to the custody of that institution as a special deposit. At the Bible House were retained only those books which are necessary for reference in the ordinary work of the Society. The object of the Board in proposing this arrangement was in the first place the protection of this precious collection from danger of fire, and secondly, the convenience of access by scholars and the public to its accumulated treasures. The collection, which consists of between 5,000 and 6,000 volumes, will continue to be known as the Library of the American Bible Society.

By far the larger part of the Biblical Library consists of Scriptures in many languages, beginning with English Bibles antedating the Authorized Version, as well as issues of 1611 and subsequent reprints. Histories of the Bible, of Bible translation and of Bible Societies, and biographies or memorials of men of renown in Bible work, especially of those connected with the American Bible Society, are also found among these treasures.

The Secretaries of the Society perform one important service of which the difficulty is rarely appreciated by those who profit thereby. This is the preparation and distribution through the country of literature of information. Some 30,000 life directors and life members of the Society, and literally thousands of churches are thus supplied with little documents showing the story of the Society in the making. There are between twenty and thirty of such leaflets or booklets, always fresh from fields in which any particular pastor or church is interested. What is known as the "Story of the American Bible Society" tells, mainly by incidents, about the Society's work each year. The Annual Report is a great book of over five hundred pages containing details and statistics from the home and foreign fields. This is sent at the cost of postage on request to members of the Society, to libraries, and to pastors and other individuals who wish to keep up with the march of progress. Besides all this literature the Bible Society Record, an illustrated monthly, goes to the members of the Society and to friends and subscribers who pay a merely nominal price to cover postage.

The work of printing at the Bible House is always interesting. One of its new features is the steady increase in the number of Scriptures in the English language absorbed by the United States. The report of 1891 stated this number as 850,139, and that of 1915 as 1,862,754 volumes. In 1904 the Society at its annual meeting adopted a modification of the Constitution by which the revisions of the Authorized Version of the English Bible as well as that version can hereafter be issued by the Society. With this permission an arrangement was made with owners of the copyright by which certain editions of the American Standard Revision were added to the Society's list of English Bibles.

From the Bible House constantly issue strange tongues. If the books could speak aloud as they go forth it would seem to the multitude like chattering magpies. During this period the African languages, Mpongwe, Benga, Tonga, Bulu, Sheetswa and Zulu have been jostling each other in the press rooms and have gone forth to the different parts of Africa where the languages are spoken; the Sheetswa and the Zulu including the whole Bible, and the others going out in portions as the translation proceeds. By far the greatest circulation attained by African Scriptures of the Society is that of the Zulu. During the period from 1891 to 1915 covered by the statistics in hand, Zulu Scriptures printed at the Bible House were shipped to Africa to the amount of 220, 179 volumes.

For the American Indians the Muskogee Bible translated for the main part by Mrs. A. E. W. Robertson, has been printed, and sent out to the Indians anxiously awaiting it. Other new Indian versions were the Arapahoe, of which the Gospel of Luke was prepared by the Rev. Mr. Roberts, printed in 1902, and the Navaho of which some portions prepared in co-operation with the Presbyterian Board of Home Missions, were printed in 1911.

All of these versions are the result of consecrated talents. The names of many missionaries engaged in translation or revision will be found in the appendix. That the work of these missionaries is not improperly called a work of genius is clear when one considers the difficulties of a task successfully completed. The words, " I am the bread of life," seem to form one of the easiest of sentences to translate; but what shall be done in Micronesia or in Korea where there is no bread? It requires much thought to discover a way of reproducing with exactness in the translations the force and the life of the words of Scripture.

An interesting incident of the supply of the Micronesian Islands was the aid given by the Society to the publication of the New Testament in the language of the Island of Nauru (Pleasant Island), if that lonely pile of rocks may be considered a part of the Micronesian field. Mr. P. A. Delaporte, missionary of the American Board, made the translation. The Hawaiian Missionary Society gave him a printing press; the Nauru Islanders connected with the mission school did the typesetting; the translator's salary was paid by the Central Church in Honolulu, while the binding of the book, as well as the cost of the paper was supplied by the Society. This new book began its work in 1907 among the Nauru people. Another language of the islanders of the Pacific was placed upon the Society's list in 1908. The Island of Guam which seems to be an appanage of the Navy of the United States, was occupied as a mission station by the American Board, and Rev. Mr. Price, the missionary, translated the Psalms, the four Gospels, and the Acts into the Chamorro language spoken in that Island. These also were issued from the Bible House.

An inspirational story is connected with the translation of the Bible into the language of the Gilbert Islands. This was the life work of the Rev. Hiram Bingham, Jr., D.D. Dr. Bingham's missionary life in Micronesia began in 1857, when he and his wife from the little boat of a sailing vessel were landed like marooned sailors on an island just below the Equator. They had come to teach the islanders the gospel. Neither of them knew a word of the language spoken on that island, and of course the islanders knew no English. By the familiar method of taking hold of something and getting the people to tell its name, a vocabulary was built up. As soon as possible Dr. Bingham followed the charge given to him at ordination by his father: "Acquire the language of the people to whom you go; reduce it to writing; translate the Scriptures." Thirty-four years after that lonely couple was left on that island Dr. Bingham completed the translation of the Bible into the Gilbert Islands language. Dr. Bingham tried to print the first Gospel which he translated at his little palm-clad island 5,000 miles from San Francisco. A printing press, type, and material had been sent to him from the United States, but he could not make it work. The two American exiles were almost despairing, when a small boat appeared at the lagoon bringing shipwrecked sailors who had rowed a thousand miles in search of land and at last found this island. One of these sailors had been a printer. He readily consented to stay and show the missionary how to set up and use the printing

A GREAT WORK WELL DONE

press. In that strange way the Gilbert Islanders received their first glimpse of the Gospels.

A very pleasant circumstance was the completion of the printing of the Bible in New York. On the 11th of April, 1893, Dr. Bingham and his wife, the Secretary of the American Board, with the Secretaries of the Bible Society, and others, gathered in the composing room on the sixth floor of the Bible House. There a short service of prayer was held. Then the composer put in type the last verse of the book of Revelation. Dr. Bingham read the proof to see that all was right; the page was taken down to the press room and the last pages of the first complete Bible in the Gilbert Islands language were printed. In October, 1908, this arduous but noble and joyous life came to an end; not, however, until the painstaking missionary had watched over the issue of eight editions of the Bible to the preparation of which he had given his heart and his whole strength.

In 1897 the American Board of Commissioners for Foreign Missions, which had occupied quarters in the Bible House during forty-three years, decided to remove its offices to Twenty-Second Street. Sacred memories cling to the rooms which this Society so long occupied. Perhaps the most of the 2,000 missionaries sent out by the American Board since its organisation had been welcomed there as they returned for rest after years and years of toil, or as they newly went out to the field.

The assembling in New York of delegates of missionary Societies from the whole Protestant world was an event of the year 1900 in which the Society was deeply concerned. Ex-President Benjamin Harrison, a Vice-President of the American Bible Society, was honourary chairman of the Conference. Secretary Gilman made a telling address on the Bible Cause entitled "The Gift of the Nineteenth Century to the Twentieth," and Secretary Fox and Secretary Haven were members of Committees and otherwise contributed to the success of the Conference. The British and Foreign Bible Society was nobly represented both in the persons of its delegates and in their utterances. The meetings were held in Carnegie Hall and in several neighbouring churches during ten days and created a profound impression. Including many other addresses on the Bible cause, besides those just mentioned, six hundred and fifty-one addresses were made during the conference. It is needless to add, the Bible Societies stood in this great meeting as a symbol of the unity of Protestant denominatons throughout the world. One result of this great missionary conference was the formation of what is known as the Foreign Missions Conference of the United States and Canada, composed of representatives of more than forty different missionary Societies, including the American Bible Society, which meets annually to consider the means of securing greater efficiency by united action throughout the world.

The year 1903 was the one hundredth year of the British and Foreign Bible Society, and, on the suggestion of that Society, its American co-labourers secured the observance of March 6th, 1904, throughout the United States as Bible day. At the Centenary Meeting in London, May, 1904, the Hon. Joseph Choate, a life Director of the Society and Ambassador of the United States, and Secretary Ingersoll were the representatives of the American Society, both making addresses which were enthusiastically received by the audience.

In 1911 a celebration of the three hundredth anniversary of the publication of the King James Version of the Bible was promoted in the United States by the Society. Celebrations were held in different parts of the country culminating in a great meeting at Carnegie Hall in New York, when letters of greeting were read from the President of the United States and the King of Great Britain, and addresses from distinguished men on different phases of the influence of the Bible upon the English speaking world held the attention of a great audience until a late hour.

One of the salient features of the period was the organisation of special Home Agencies of distribution intended to do a work of supply of the destitute which the increase of population made it impossible for the Society to achieve by the old method of periodical efforts at general supply. Nine of these Home Agencies have been established which are more fully described in another chapter.

CHAPTER L

CHANGES IN THE AUXILIARY SYSTEM

ALL of the great cities of this country give constant illustration of the processes of reconstruction going forward without serious interruption to the use of ancient methods. New terminals are erected and trains are kept on schedule time. Subways are dug beneath great avenues without any apparent diminution of the ceaseless traffic on those thoroughfares. This is true the world around.

It seems characteristic of human nature to rebuild its shell. As the Bible Society is an intensely human institution it is not strange that this characteristic should reveal itself in its history.

The story of the Auxiliary Societies has been recounted in these pages. The Society was founded by Societies, many of whom became its Auxiliaries. Some abide in strength to this day. The spirit of the beginnings spread all over the republic until every state was dotted with local Bible Societies.

The record of the achievement of these Societies would be a notable contribution to American History. In our growing cities and towns the most influential men were Presidents and Vice-Presidents and Secretaries and Treasurers of these Societies. The list of these well known and well beloved men and women (for the Deborahs and the Hannahs and the Marys have had their part in this local work as conspicuously as the judges and the rulers of the land) would prove a veritable " Who's Who " through the decades.

A local Bible Society meeting was for years one of the events of the year in these communities. Friends would drive in from the surrounding country. Some local church would provide an entertainment, and a bounteous feast it would be. The election of officers and the report would be the feature of the morning and then would come the social hour in which neighbours of different communions and of different communities would mingle as at some high festival, and later a preacher of distinction would exalt the place of the Bible in the life of the people. A New England town meeting, a Southern barbecue was not more democratic or a better centre for the neighbourhood interest than the County Bible Society Annual Meeting.

When one realises that at one time there were more than two thousand of these Auxiliaries, each with their retinue of memorable names in the laity and the ministry, one realises what a power they were. Would that the golden age could be repeated!

Nearly two decades ago the Board of Managers awakened to the fact that the spirit of the times had changed; that many of these Societies were like the Church at Laodicea which had a name to live and was dead. In 1893 out of 2000 Auxiliaries only 107 reported as conducting canvasses of their communities. In 1895 only 116 Auxiliaries supported workers in their field. In 1900 out of nearly 2000 Auxiliaries only 113 reported any general operations and in 1902 only 46. A printed blank was annually sent from the national office to each of these Auxiliaries with columns prepared in which to report the general operations in the canvassing of the local field. One of these returned bore this significant message, "These things are not done here."

A part of the explanation of the somewhat rapid dissolution of many of these local Societies which often existed in one person alone or in some local store where a few Bibles were kept for sale; sometimes a meat shop; sometimes a millinery store; sometimes as by the following advertisement: "The Legget Store on Main Street has been receiving necessary repairs, decorations and general cleaning up, in anticipation of its being opened by José Gallardo. Gallardo will continue to carry on the hair-dressing and shaving business, and in addition the manufacture of the hair and sale of the works of The American Bible Society"— lies in the removal of the staff of workers known as District Superintendents.

The work of these representatives of the Society has already been explained. Their main function was to assist the local officers in the care of their accounts; the handling of their books and in general to keep them in vigour where possible. The cost of these superintendents became a noticeable burden on the Society's funds as compared with the income from the Auxiliaries. The expense of these District Superintendents was between $50,000 and $60,000 a year. It had been reduced to $30,000, but the outlay had not been met by satisfactory results even in Bible circulation, to say nothing of the collection of funds.

Twenty-one District Superintendents represented the Society during the year ending March 31st, 1898. Gradually these Superintendents had been given the care of colporteurs which were supported not by the Auxiliaries, but by the national Society. In 1894 the Society employed thirty such colporteurs. In 1895 twenty-seven colporteurs in twelve states and two territories carried forward their work under the supervision of the District Superintendents. The District Superintendents in the latter years were instructed to direct their energies also to the collection of money from churches which the Auxiliaries failed to reach. It was clear that this method had failed owing to the changed conditions. A general notice, therefore, was sent out to all the Auxiliary Societies in 1897 that no District Superintendent would be commissioned for the fiscal year opening April 1, 1898. For seventy-five years a devoted body of men had performed the duties of this office. With this prop gone the whole structure collapsed as a continental organisation for meeting the needs of Bible distribution in this great country.

Many notable illustrations of continued vitality existed and still exist. Certain Welsh Societies, born out of the enthusiasm which made Thomas Charles of Bala and Joseph Hughes the creators of the British and Foreign Bible Society; here and there Female Bible Societies in which granddaughters kept alive the memory of their grandmothers, gracious ladies of an earlier day; and certain County Societies blessed with the leadership of families that had continued their homesteads, generation after generation, on the same acres or in the same cities; together with a few State

Societies; were fruitful in advancing years locally, and liberal, according to their resources, to the national Society. As a system the machinery had ceased to turn because its popular support had failed.

Facing this situation and realising that the Society had been created to meet the needs of this great nation, the Board of Managers decided in 1899 to call a conference of the Auxiliaries. Already a special circular had been sent requesting these local Societies to enter into closer relations with the Secretaries of the national Society after the discontinuance of the District Superintendents and a special arrangement had been entered into with the Brooklyn Bible Society and the New York Bible Society in which the offerings were to be taken in both communities in the name of both Societies and a definite proportion guaranteed for the local work whch should equal the average income for a number of preceding years. October 10, 1900, this Conference of Auxiliaries was held at the Bible House, New York. Representatives came from regions widely enough scattered to make it a genuinely representative gathering.

The following series of resolutions were adopted which the Board of Managers of the American Bible Society were requested to present to the Annual Meeting of the Society to be held the following spring. In view of the consequences of the action of this Conference, this series of resolutions is presented as adopted entire:

1. Resolved, That we recognise the fact that the system of transacting business between the American Bible Society and the local Societies throughout the country, while it has worked successfully in the past, owing to the changes that have taken place, has become unsuited to the present requirements; and this Conference asks the American Bible Society to carefully consider the whole question of its relation to the Auxiliary Societies, and to formulate and present to the Annual Meeting of the American Bible Society such plans as may appear best suited to existing conditions.

2. Resolved, That we recognise that correct business methods should be observed in the transaction of business between the American Bible Society and the Auxiliary Societies, and in the judgment of this Conference all books

shipped by the national Society to the local Societies should be distinctly under the heads *of gift* or *of sale,* and that the ownership of, and responsibility for, such shipments are, and must be, with the local Societies.

3. RESOLVED, That special communities and exceptional populations throughout the country should be supplied with the Scriptures by the local organisations if there are such, but where there are no local Societies, or where such Societies are unable to do the work required, the business should be undertaken by the national Society.

4. RESOLVED, That the Conference recognises the identity of interest of the Bible cause, whether promoted by national or local agencies, and that every district of our country should contribute to both these agencies. Each has a right to solicit for its support, the local Society in its territory, and the national Society everywhere. In this work there should be entire harmony of action.

5. RESOLVED, That in the judgment of this Conference the depositories through the country should be much reduced in number and continued only in those places where the judgment of the local Societies deems them required.

6. RESOLVED, That the Auxiliary Societies should endeavour to induce all the churches in their territory to devote one service in the year to the presentation of the Bible cause, and that the closest relations between the churches and the Bible Societies should be fostered by every practicable means.

7. RESOLVED, That we recognise that the foreign mission work of the American Bible Society is among the great and efficient agencies for the spread of the Gospel throughout the world, and that the missions of all the churches are greatly aided thereby. The importance of this work should appeal to the Christian people of our country and should have universal support. In the judgment of this Conference this feature of the work should be presented by the local Societies and in the churches everywhere.

8. RESOLVED, That, as representatives of Auxiliaries of the American Bible Society, in Conference assembled, we gratefully acknowledge the cordial reception given us by the representatives of the Parent Society, and we hereby re-

assure the Society of our cordial sympathy and readiness to co-operate in all departments of its great work to the extent of our ability.

The whole Conference was a most cordial and satisfactory gathering. At the Annual Meeting of the Society in May, 1901, the resolutions were unanimously adopted.

At this time the following provision was made for the revision of the roll of the Auxiliaries. Where local Societies sent no report of their activities for three years to the national office, or forwarded no contribution for the general work of the Society, it was decided that they should cease to be regarded as Auxiliaries. Here and there a local Society might continue to buy books from the Bible House, but this was not a sufficient nexus. If no contributions were made to the world-wide interests of the national Society and there was not sufficient life to report local activities, it seemed to the Society that the local institutions could not properly be considered auxiliary.

Under the operations of this new arrangement, the total of Societies reported very soon fell from the thousands to the hundreds. In the year, 1904, 804 Auxiliaries were removed from the list because they had either ceased to be living Societies, or at least had failed to have any part in the work of the American Bible Society. In every case communications had been sent to these Societies and they had been urged to take on new life. "The smoking flax He did not quench," was the text of the Society in these relations with its Auxiliaries. In too many instances there was neither fire nor smoke, and in very many cases the letters sent out to the Auxiliary officers came back like Noah's dove to the ark.

Various reasons had brought this about. The immense changes in transportation which had united the whole country into one big community so that the local isolation that gave a "raison d'être" for the local Society in the earlier days had passed away. The development of the use of the mail; the distribution effected by great department stores and mail order establishments; the change in the character of American communities, where the permanent ministry that had given strength to any local Societies existed no longer, the pastorate of thirty and forty years being as extinct as the stage coach; the moving about from place to place of families so that the old-fashioned homestead remained chiefly in story books; the demands upon the churches for the support of new enterprises; and the spirit of the times in which the thing that was new appealed more than that which was old, all worked together to bring about the new condition of things.

There was nothing to be done but return thanks for all the years and look forward to the new day. We would not, however, in drawing this picture, fail to recognise the distinguished Societies which abide and in their loyalty support the general Society, not only in its work of meeting the necessities of this nation, but in its greater work of ministering to the world. The Society now has 206 Auxiliaries.

In one year, namely 1909, The Massachusetts Bible Society, the Connecticut Bible Society and the Bible Society of Maine each held its Centennial. In 1912 the New Hampshire Bible Society had its Centennial. In 1913 the Rhode Island Bible Society had its Centennial. Earlier in its organisation than any of these, the Pennsylvania Bible Society in 1908 celebrated its Centennial. Certain of these Societies are not Auxiliary to the American Bible Society, but are intimate and effective co-labourers. In two or three instances the Auxiliary relationship has been terminated. That of the Connecticut Bible Society in 1900 and the New York Bible Society in 1913. Mention should also be made of certain illustrious County Societies that still abide in strength as those in Westchester, Orange and Rockland Counties in New York; Sussex, Hunterdon, Cumberland and Somerset Counties in New Jersey.

The office of District Superintendent did not cease altogether with the discontinuance of the District Superintendents in 1898. The Society recognised that it was necessary that it should have some representatives in the field, who could visit the churches and assist the Corresponding Secretaries in informing the people as to the importance and necessity of its work. Two of the District Superintendents were continued as Field Agents, the Rev. Dr. Thomas H. Law of Spartanburg, South Carolina, and the Rev. Dr. George

French of Morristown, Tennessee. Dr. Law was a member of the Southern Presbyterian Church and Dr. French a Southern Methodist. To these there were added three others — The Rev. Dr. Henderson, a member of the Presbyterian Church, with headquarters in Chicago; the Rev. Dr. John Pearson of Cincinnati, Ohio, of the Methodist Episcopal Church; and the Rev. Dr. Dickinson of St. Paul, Minnesota, a Congregationalist. Two other officers were added at this time: One, a Financial Agent for Greater New York, the Rev. Frederick D. Greene, the son of a veteran missionary of the American Board in Turkey; and the Rev. A. E. Colton for Massachusetts, by an arrangement of courtesy with the Massachusetts Bible Society. Later both of these gentlemen became Field Agents, and for a number of years Mr. Colton throughout all New England, Mr. Greene throughout New York City and State, Dr. Law in the South Atlantic region, Dr. French in the Mississippi Valley, Dr. Pearson and Dr. Henderson throughout the Central States, and Dr. Dickinson in the Northwest, visited church gatherings, represented the Society on association and conference and synod platforms, held "Bible Days" in all the more important centres at which large gatherings of people were attracted to listen to papers or addresses by various representative ministers on "The Bible in the Home," "The Bible as a Comfort in Sorrow," "The Bible as a Support for National Ideals," etc., in an afternoon session; and then in the evening to the presentation of the general cause, showing the needs throughout the nation and in the great mission lands. Through the efforts of one of these workers, Dr. Law, a Permanent Committee on the Bible Cause was appointed by the General Assembly of the Presbyterian Church in the United States. By the initiative of another, Dr. French, each Annual Conference of the Methodist Episcopal Church, South, created a Bible Board to represent the Society at District gatherings.

This field-agency plan, however, was only tentative, and when the Board of Managers recognised that the work of distribution in the United States must be cared for by the General Society, as well as the task of informing and educating the people in Bible Society matters, and the new Home Agencies were established, the office of Field Agent ceased to exist. In 1907 all of the Field Agents were retired and this chapter in the Society's work concluded.

CHAPTER LI

NEW METHODS AT HOME

FOLLOWING the methods that had proven so effective in foreign lands, the Society determined to meet the needs of this country by establishing, as opportunities might open, large agencies covering many states. It was expected that the agent would study the field assigned to him, present an estimate of its needs to the Board of Managers, and under the appropriation given him carry forward the work of the distribution of the Scriptures according to the need. This would require that he should employ a staff of colporteurs and arrange with correspondents who could give only a portion of their time to this work and come in touch with all volunteer distributors wherever he could discover them. Each agency was to have its headquarters to which books would be sent from the Bible House in New York and from which they would be distributed throughout the agent's field. It was also expected that these new representatives of the Society would carry forward the function of the field agents in visiting preachers' meetings, conferences, synods, presbyteries, associations and all sorts of gatherings wherever they might obtain a hearing. It was believed that with the story of work accomplished locally they would be given a hearing that would be particularly acceptable, and from the description of local work they could very easily lead their hearers to an interest in the world activities of the Society.

The special Agency among the Coloured People of the South had proven so satisfactory in reaching this needy population that it encouraged the Society in the formation of other similar agencies.

In November, 1906, after continued conference with the Chicago Bible Society that organisation became the nucleus of the new Northwestern Agency which included the states of Illinois, Indiana, Michigan, Wisconsin, Minnesota, Iowa, Nebraska, North and South Dakota. The Secretary of the

CARRYING BIBLES TO AN ISOLATED SOUTH DAKOTA FARM

Chicago Bible Society was appointed as the Secretary of the new Agency. The two states of Dakota which were in this field had enjoyed their statehood less than ten years. Hundreds of thousands of new citizens, coming through the great portal at New York, had found their way to these wide prairies. Forty-three languages were represented in the distribution in this field. The Rev. J. F. Horton, the Agency Secretary, employed nineteen colporteurs who, taken together, spoke more than twenty different languages. One of these colporteurs, an Italian, named De Luca, found an Italian colony at Ladd, Bureau Co., Ill., interested to read the Bible in their own language and he succeeded in establishing a night school for Italians in connection with the Presbyterian Church. He then went on to Spring Valley where he found similar opportunities for instructing the Italians, and the Congregational Church there asked Mr. Horton to allow Mr. De Luca to remain for some months to build up an Italian work in connection with that church. A successful mission was soon established and when Mr. De Luca left Spring Valley, after five months, the Presbyterian and Congregational Churches had permanent Italian Missions with Italian missionaries to carry on the work in Bureau and adjacent counties, all this the outgrowth of one Bible Society colporteur.

In January, 1907, in co-operation with the Virginia Bible Society, one of the oldest and most distinguished of the State Societies, the South Atlantic Agency was organised, covering the states of Virginia, West Virginia, North and South Carolina, Georgia, and Florida. The Rev. M. B. Porter, a Southern Presbyterian minister became Agency Secretary in September and during the balance of that year put into circulation 11,824 volumes.

The same year, the Western Agency was created in the vast empire embracing Missouri, Kansas, Arizona, Colorado, Idaho, Montana, Wyoming, Utah and New Mexico. The Rev. S. H. Kirkbride, D.D., was placed in charge and reported in five months a circulation of 3,678 volumes. His comment was only too true a statement of the facts, "The Bible Society is unknown to churches and people. It must be put on the map."

On the Pacific Coast from the first days of the settlements there, Bible work had gone forward which had been organised into the California Bible Society. In co-operation with the trustees of this Society, the Pacific Agency was opened late in 1907. Its field was the states of California, Nevada, Oregon, and Washington. The Rev. G. A. Miller, who had had charge of the work in the Philippines for a year or two, was fortunately in California and became the Agency Secretary temporarily. He reports, "There are more Chinese, Japanese and Koreans in this field than in any other part of the United States and thousands of Mexicans, Portuguese and Italians."

Toward the close of the year 1907 another Agency covering a most extended region, was organised in the Southwest, with headquarters at Dallas, Texas. The states of Louisiana, Arkansas, Texas, and Oklahoma, "the Beautiful Land" which had been purchased by the government from the Indians and opened to settlement less than ten years, formed this new field. Here were large Spanish speaking populations and those who used French and Italian. The Indian dialects were still in use in Oklahoma. The Rev. Glenn Flinn, a minister of the Methodist Episcopal Church, South, was made the Agency Secretary.

In the following year the Eastern Agency was organised to minister to New York State and adjacent states where the field was not supplied by Auxiliary Bible Societies. The Rev. W. S. Elliott, at home on furlough from his subagency in China, was appointed Agency Secretary.

The Central Agency, covering the states of Ohio, Kentucky, Tennessee, Mississippi, and Alabama, with headquarters in Cincinnati, was organised in co-operation with the Young Men's Bible Society of Cincinnati, in 1909, and the Rev. George S. J. Browne, D.D., was appointed Agency Secretary.

On the 2nd of December, 1909, in co-operation with the Pennsylvania Bible Society, the oldest of the existing Bible Societies, the Atlantic Agency was established, embracing the states of Pennsylvania, Delaware and New Jersey. The Rev. Leighton W. Eckard, D.D., Secretary of the Pennsylvania Bible Society, became the Agency Secretary.

In 1910 the Rev. S. H. Kirkbride, D.D., was transferred from the Western Agency to the Northwestern Agency to take the place of Mr. Horton, resigned; and the Rev. George E. Farnam, a Congregational minister, was appointed Secretary of the Western Agency.

The Brooklyn Bible Society, in 1910, became a part of the Eastern Agency, and its General Secretary, Rev. W. H. Hendrickson, was appointed Agency Secretary, Rev. Mr. Elliott having gone back to China. That same year Mr. Flinn resigned to enter the pastorate in Texas, and the Rev. J. J. Morgan, formerly the President of Wesley College, Terrell, Texas, was appointed in his place.

On the Pacific coast, the Rev. A. Wesley Mell, who had had charge of the English-speaking Methodist Episcopal Church in Bombay, India, became Secretary in 1908.

Mr. Farnam, of the Western Agency, died November 2, 1912, and on the first of April, 1913, the Rev. Arthur F. Ragatz, D.D., was appointed Secretary.

The Rev. W. H. Tower succeeded the Rev. Mr. Hendrickson in charge of the Eastern Agency in 1911.

This is the outline of the organisation of these nine (9) Home Agencies.

Peculiar conditions prevailed in the United States at this time owing to the unexampled increase in immigration and the character of it. A student of these problems has said, "A striking fact is the close sympathy between immigration and the industrial prosperity and depression of this country. Indeed, so close is the connection that many who comment on this matter have held that immigration during the past century has been strictly an industrial or economic phenomenon, and that the religious and political causes which stimulated early immigration no longer held good."[1] We think there are very great exceptions to this fact, however true it may be as a general proposition.

"Between 1820 and 1906," the latter date being about the time of the creation of the Home Agencies, he goes on to say, "there entered our ports more than 5,200,000 Germans, while Ireland was sending 4,000,000. Beside the Germans

[1] "Races and Immigrants in America," by John R. Commons, pages 67 and 69 and 70.

and the Irish, the largest numbers of immigrants during the middle years of the nineteenth century were English and Scandinavians. About this period, however, a great change occurred. In 1882, Western Europe furnished 80% of the immigrants and in 1902 only 22%, while the share of Southeastern Europe and Asiatic Turkey increased from 13% in 1882 to 78% in 1902. During twenty years the immigration of Western races most nearly related to those which fashioned American institutions declined more than 75%, while the immigration of Eastern and Southern races, untrained in self-government, increased nearly six fold. For the year 1906 the proportions remain the same, although in the four years the total immigration had increased two-thirds."

By 1909, the immigration records show that more than 6,000,000 immigrants had come to the United States in the preceding seven years, the vast majority never trained to read the Bible.

New languages became familiar on the streets of our great cities, but there were no Scriptures in these languages in the Bible House. In June, 1907, however, the Rev. R. M. De Castello, who had been in the service of the Society in the Northwestern Agency, was sent to visit all these European countries from which these "new citizens" had come, to see what publishing houses there were that could publish Scriptures for the Society and at what prices; what it would cost to buy plates; to see if there were Bibles in European languages about which the Society did not know, and to find out about all places where the different Bibles were published, especially in the Southern languages. Mr. De Castello went thoroughly over the field and presented a long and elaborate report. Upon the basis of this report the Society entered into negotiations with the British and Foreign Bible Society and their European Agencies with German and other Bible Societies, and so developed its importations that where it had been carrying on its list thirty of these European languages, it now has in its depository and distributed throughout its Home Agencies all over the Republic, the Scriptures in forty-two European languages. Counting with these the American Indian and Far

Eastern and other dialects and tongues, the total circulation of the Society at the close of its one hundred years embraces ninety-two languages in the United States alone. Little could the fathers have foreseen such a polyglot circulation in this country.

Nearly all of the Home Agencies are caring for this problem, though the language distribution differs a little in each. The problem of Home Missions within the last decade has been the problem of contact with these peoples of strange speech. The Bible Society has helped to solve this problem. Of the thirty-four colporteurs employed in the Northwestern Agency in the year 1909, thirty-one were assigned to duty among the people of foreign speech. These spoke twenty-four languages and were able to sell Bibles in forty languages. Twenty flourishing missions belonging to different denominations had sprung up in this territory all directly the result of colporteur work.

In the South Atlantic Agency, in old Virginia and the neighbouring states, Scriptures were circulated in thirty-four foreign languages.

In the Western Agency eleven colporteurs gave their time exclusively to immigrants.

In California sixty-five nationalities were encountered, even Hindus coming by the hundreds, and Scriptures in Bengali and Urdu and Hindi, never before required in the United States, were added to the catalogue of the American Bible Society.

In the Atlantic Agency one of the colporteurs spoke seven languages and another five. One of these was shot and seriously injured by a Russian who thought he was doing God's service. Another was knocked down and left senseless by a blow from a club wielded by a Roman Catholic who thought it necessary to prevent Bible distribution.

In the Southwestern Agency Scriptures are distributed in forty-two languages and the colporteurs speak seventeen different languages.

Quietly and efficiently the seed of the Kingdom is being sown in these new homes and the way opened for new churches. If the great revival was necessary to save England in the eighteenth century, a great spiritual awakening among these new members of the family in this nation is necessary in this twentieth century to create a homogeneous God loving people.

It is a fact, however, that the colporteur traversing the rural regions of this country has found an extraordinary number of homes of people, of what we call the old American stock, who have utterly neglected religious worship and who have no Bibles in their homes. Some of the reports of our Home Agencies would make Samuel Mills astonished as they describe the destitution of the Scriptures found in our great cities, in country communities and the lonely cabins of the new settlements. In the Central Agency in one year 3,169 homes were found without Bibles or Testaments. In the Ozark Mountains of North Arkansas at least half of the families visited in 1909 were found without the Bible. The Secretary reports that between 30 and 40% of the English-speaking people in certain of his fields in the Southwest were in the same condition. The same year in Western Oregon 900 towns and villages were found without religious services and the majority of the homes without the Bible. In the Northwestern Agency in the following year 11,100 homes were found without the Scriptures, and a colporteur writes: "I have seen a lot of this world, but I have never seen the need of God's Word in the homes of the American people as I now do. I never would have believed that Christian America had so many homes without God's Word as I find in this region." In the Eastern Agency similar conditions prevail. One of the most picturesque features of its service is among the throngs of merry-makers of all nations and races crowding the sands at Coney Island in the summer time.

During the years since the establishment of these Agencies, the circulation has increased phenomenally. Dr. Wragg among the coloured people, during fourteen years has circulated 44,123 volumes. Just what this means may be illustrated by one incident where one of these colporteurs among the coloured people met with a woman who had a Bible that she said she would not part with for all the Bibles he had. He says, "I saw it was one of our 50-cent Bibles. So I said to her, 'that is only a cheap Bible.' She said,

'Yes, but I would not take $25 for it. I know it is a cheap binding, but a man brought it to my door when my husband was very sick and we bought it and he read it through. He was converted before he died. I would not part with this blessed book.'"

This is the story all over this Republic.

In Texas one colporteur met an old Bohemian. He was without the Bible and had taught all his children that there is no God. Moreover, he had suffered in his children the evil results of such teaching. When he heard the colporteur tell of the Bible, he said to him, with deep feeling: "Oh, my son, go to all the world and tell all men that we have a living God who rewards right and punishes sin. I wish that all men might read this book of God!" In contrast to this glad acceptance of the Bible was an example of the bitter fruit of life without it. In the same state another colporteur met two Bohemian farmers who said: "The Bible points to heaven. It is far off. We prefer to go to hell which is nearer."

At a County Fair, in the Eastern Agency, a colporteur opened a Testament to the words, "The wages of sin is death," and showed it to a young man. "What kind of business is this?" he asked. It was explained to him what sort of business it was, and the meaning of the text, when he responded, "I had a mother once who read and believed the Bible, but I have wandered far from her teachings." Then he told how he had come to the fair "to have a big bust and go the limit." But after a little further conversation he said he guessed he would go home and find mother's Bible and see if there was any way by which he might escape "the wages of sin."

All sorts of excuses are brought up to the colporteur revealing the thoughts that go through the minds of the people of this country. Here are a few samples: "No money." "Bibles are only for Christians." A Socialist said, "No church, no Bible for me." One woman would not buy one because she "swore too much." One coloured person said "It is the white man's book." "I don't believe in the Protestant Bible." "The Bible makes me feel my sins too much." "I will put my money into a good time instead of a Bible." "My priest would take it away, as he did my other one, and excommunicate me." "My priest says your book is a bad book." In contrast to these it was refreshing to read of one poor man who bought a book saying, "I have absolutely nothing in this world, and the Bible promises a new heaven and a new earth."

The gross materialism of some of the people is unbelievable. When a Croatian was asked by a colporteur about his God, taking a quarter out of his pocket he said, "That is my god!" An Italian opening an oven door and pointing to a cooking roast of meat said, "This is my only book!" These people are breaking with their state churches. Socialistic workers are constantly among them. Some one must go to them with the open Bible and the real teachings of Jesus.

Humorous things happen here and there that show that some homes have been familiar with the Bible. One of our workers found a family where there were two children, named "Alpha" and "Omega," but they were neither the first nor the last. The mother simply liked the names because they were Bible names!

Many Roman Catholics love the Bible, in spite of the opposition of their priests. One woman said, "I cannot help it if the priest will not bless it. The reading of this Book makes me feel good in my soul." Polish priests especially refuse to allow their people to read any Bible. One woman was ordered by her priest to burn the two Testaments she had. The priest told her "If she read the Bible, she would get too smart and would get like God."

The power of it all is revealed in the following experience: "One young German woman invited me very kindly to her home. When she found out that I sold Bibles she said: 'Oh, what a wonderful book this is — every letter is golden. I received a Bible as a present, but did not read it for a long time. Once when I started to read the Lord appeared to me and opened my eyes and heart and I found out what a big sinner I was. Since I read the Bible I am a new creature; all is different with me. I have five little children, but the Lord strengthens me every day with new power.'"

These are but fragments from the daily life of a company of over five hundred workers threading their way through the streets of our great cities, journeying out on the far prairies, sleeping by the wayside, living humbly, and yet carrying the Light into the dark places of this land.

In the year closing December 31, 1916, 1,185,297 volumes of Scriptures were distributed through the instrumentality of these Home Agencies. This is not by any means the total distribution of the Society in the United States, but it shows the effectiveness of this new instrument in its service.

CHAPTER LII

LATIN AMERICA

THE migrations of peoples over the face of the earth in general follow the apparent path of the sun. Not universally but with remarkable frequency they are from East to West. Whatever may be the theory as to the location of the Garden of Eden, and even if the original movements of the human race were from the North to the South, for many centuries it is indisputably the fact that the people seeking new homes have journeyed toward the sunset.

It is not strange then that the South American Republics have felt the influence of Southern Europe more than that of North America or Northern Europe. The Spanish conquistadores opened up these new lands for gold and the Cross, and the Portuguese adventurers had the same purpose, and in the opening of the last quarter of the Society's century, these Latin-American lands are noticeably the product of the old Mediterranean civilisations of Europe. The new environment and the example of the great Republic have had their influence and all of them, with slight exceptions, have broken off their allegiance to European countries and have become independent republics. But their social life, their language and their religious ideals are permeated with the spirit of the old world. At the beginning of this period, the American Bible Society is established permanently in Mexico, Central America, Venezuela and Colombia, Brazil, and in all the rest of South America, which it entitles the "La Plata Agency" from the great river that waters so many of the nations included in this field.

The West Indies have also long been a field for the Society's labours. Wars, revolutions and the difficulties of transportation have made constant changes in the handling of the West Indies. At one time Cuba was a separate field, at another Porto Rico, at another these islands were grouped and together with them, San Domingo, Hayti and the French

Islands. Again Porto Rico is added to Venezuela because local lines of steamships make communication more convenient. It would be unprofitable to give the detail of all these changes. Most recently it has been found desirable to administer the whole region from New York City because, strange as it may seem, the agent could more quickly travel from Cuba to San Domingo or even from Cuba to Porto Rico by way of New York than directly.

The last year of record shows the high water mark of over 33,000 volumes.[1]

Mexico continued to be an open field for the Society's work. It was remarkable the number of places in Mexico where the people were ready to be organised into churches originating in Bible distribution. The proportion of sales to donations increased every year and the construction of new railroads facilitated the transportation of the books. In spite of the liberality of the government intense fanaticism reigned in certain sections. Perhaps the climax was reached in the announcement of one Mexican priest that "He who kills a Protestant will not have to go through purgatory." More than once our colporteurs fell into the hands of bandits, who stole their mules from them and all their books. They were shot at, they were tumbled down precipices and left for dead, but they kept on, the agent reporting real eagerness on the part of many people in Mexico to own a Bible.

After the war with Spain, when the friars were driven

[1] Rev. A. J. McKim resigned in Cuba in 1894 and was appointed to Porto Rico in December, 1898. Rev. F. G. Penzotti administered in Cuba in 1899. Rev. J. M. Lopez-Guillen was appointed agent in 1900. Secretary Fox visited the islands in 1901. Rev. Dr. Donald McLaren took charge of Porto Rico, January, 1902. Mr. Joseph Lamb followed Dr. McLaren in 1904. Rev. J. M. Lopez-Guillen retired 1905 and Mr. Lamb resigned. Rev. Dr. McLaren took charge of both Cuba and Porto Rico 1906. Rev. Pedro Rioseco followed Dr. McLaren in Cuba and Mr. Bailly of Venezuela cared for Porto Rico. Rev. W. F. Jordan succeeded Mr. Rioseco in October, 1908. In 1909 Rev. H. C. Thompson had charge of Porto Rico. Later Mr. Jordan superintended the whole field including San Domingo, Hayti, Martinique, and Guadeloupe, assisted by Mr. Williams and Mr. Neblitt in Cuba, and Fernand Cattelain in Hayti. Rev. David Cole later took Mr. Neblitt's place in Cuba, Rev. E. L. Humphrey assisting.

out from the Philippines, they came and settled on the west coast of Mexico, stirring up new fires of opposition.

August 20, 1905, Rev. Hiram P. Hamilton died. From the time of his leaving the Theological Seminary, for more than twenty-six years, his entire ministry had been given to this work of circulating the Scriptures in Mexico. Twenty to thirty Mexican colporteurs looked up unto him as a father in the gospel. He knew all their movements over the mountains and into the valleys of all the different states in that Republic. During the last few years of his life his wife had assisted him in the care of the Agency and was peculiarly well qualified for its management.

Secretary Haven visited the field in the winter of 1906 and found that it would be agreeable to the missionary body if Mrs. Hamilton was appointed agent to succeed her husband. No woman had ever before been placed in charge of an agency of any of the Bible Societies, but Mrs. Hamilton's perfect knowledge of the language, her sympathetic acquaintance with all the colporteurs and their families and their needs, her standing in the missionary body and her business ability all caused the Board of Managers to place her permanently in charge of this field. Faithfully she administered her trust. Over her desk in her office in Mexico City hung a large map of the Republic. On it were little marks showing the position of every one of her colporteurs. As they moved from place to place, these marks were changed, and daily by name she followed these heroes of the faith in prayer that they might be given courage and patience for their work. She travelled over the Republic, visiting the missionary gatherings. As the Centennial of the Mexican Republic approached a special edition of the Four Gospels and the Book of Proverbs was prepared in paper covers bearing the Mexican colours. Sixty-six thousand of these little volumes were circulated in that year, which, added to the 23,328 volumes of the normal circulation, brought the total up to 86,610 volumes.

Then followed, after this brilliant day, the night! Diaz was overthrown. Madero came to the Presidency — and we need not tell the story of calamity of these last years. It all wore upon Mrs. Hamilton. Again and again the Board of Managers asked her to withdraw, and at last, finally commanded her to leave Mexico, which she did in April, 1914. Through all the fiercest fighting in the city, even when the flying bullets stirred the skirt of her gown, as she sat at work in her home, she did not lose her nerve. Her heart was with the Mexican people and of a broken heart she died, suddenly, at the Bible House, on the 5th of June, 1915. A rare and precious spirit, sincerely loved and widely mourned throughout all the Christian communities of the Republic.

The Society was fortunate in having at hand one used to difficulties and successful in overcoming them, and in December, 1914, it requested the Rev. W. F. Jordan to do what he could for Mexico in addition to his care of the West Indies Agency. In spite of all the turmoil he reports during the last year of the Society's Centennial a circulation of 68,818 volumes in that troubled land, making a grand total of 919,223 Scriptures, as the circulation of the Society in Mexico.

Three brief facts concerning versions should be mentioned. In 1905 a Spanish Gospel of St. John in Braille type for the blind was published by the Society. The type was set by a blind woman in Mexico. In 1912 the Gospel of St. John was published in Zapotec for the Indians of Southern Mexico. The movement for the revision of the Spanish Scriptures, to which fuller reference will be made, also took its rise in Mexico, in a missionary conference in 1897.

In 1894 the Brazilian State of Rio Grande do Sul was transferred from the La Plata to the Brazil Agency. The year before there were larger sales in Brazil than in any previous time in the history of the agency. This year revolutionary movements limited colportage, and, curiously enough, the largest sales were to Italians. A Bible salesroom was opened in the centre of Rio Janeiro. Out of the twenty states of the Republic of Brazil, it was possible two years later to report that nineteen (19) had been entered by the Society. The circulation at the close of 1897 amounted to 40,195 volumes, the larger portion was handled by missionary correspondents. The same flaming out of fanaticism of the friars who were expelled from the Philippines that we have noted in Mexico appears also in Brazil, where these newcomers particularly opposed Bible distribution. As the Bible entered their land, as recorded in our Philippine story, they are entering other lands to attempt to arrest its progress. The result of it all, however, appeared to be an increase in Bible readers, for the circulation in 1902 amounted to 70,113 volumes.

Brazil is laid out in states like a checker board. In order to avoid undue rivalry and competition, an arrangement was entered into between the agent of the British and Foreign Bible Society and Mr. Tucker, the agent of the American Bible Society, for a division of this territory and on the plan of each Society taking three or four states adjacent to each other, arranged curiously like the knight's move on the chess board. In this way the larger settled portion of the Republic was so adjusted between the two Societies as to make large colportage districts in touch with each other and yet give each Society a separate field. Almost as the result of this economy of energy Mr. Tucker toured a thousand miles into the interior to see that no territory was left without investigation. In 1894 the missionaries in Brazil united in urging the need of a revised Portuguese Bible. Later the British and Foreign Bible Society brought out an improved edition to which the American Bible Society decided to conform its version, but this was not satisfactory, and in 1901 a committee for thoroughly revising the Portuguese version was formed. The expenses of this committee, and the expense of the publication of the version were arranged for by the American Bible Society and the British and Foreign Bible Society conjointly. In 1903 two Gospels were published for criticism. In 1910 the final revision of the New Testament was printed and ready for circulation on the field and steady progress is now being made in the revision of the Old Testament. It is a notable fact that during the early part of this revision work the Roman Catholic Congress at Bahia, Brazil, decided to issue New Testament Portions for the common people, and we are happy to record that in 1908 the Archbishop of Rio exhorted his people to study the Gospels, and in his address speaks of "Our separated brethren, the Protestants." Two years previous to this the Hon. Elihu Root made a visit to Brazil in his journey about South America which very profoundly impressed the Brazilian people. Missions are extending their work into the interior and many people enlightened and converted through the reading of the Scriptures are being discovered as these missionaries follow the trail of the colporteur.

The almost universal story as to the relation between the circulation of the Scriptures and the beginnings of new churches formed of groups of believers who have never seen or heard a missionary is as true in all the great states forming the La Plata Agency as in Mexico or Brazil, or for that matter in the heathen world. Any one at all skeptical as to the divine power of the Bible would find his skepticism utterly dissipated after listening to the actual records in the correspondence of the Society of minds illuminated and natures quickened and whole neighbourhoods changed by the influence of the Spirit upon humble people reading by themselves or together the Holy Scriptures.

Mr. Milne, of the La Plata Agency, in 1891, writes that he could mention immediately half a dozen churches in that field which had originated with the work of Bible colporteurs. The following year he intensifies this statement by saying that in his field fifty places of worship were opened by colportage, seven of the ministers having formerly been the Society's colporteurs. In 1905 he visited Punta Arenas on the Straits of Magellan. Many years before a humble colporteur stopped at this spot with a few Bibles; subsequently a church of 47 members was started. At this visit 289 church members welcomed Mr. Milne and one of his former colporteurs was the pastor.

Before the end of the nineteenth century Ecuador adopted a new constitution giving liberty of worship, and all restrictions of the sale of Bibles were done away. Even in Peru at the instance of Mr. Milne, obstacles interposed by the Custom House at Callao against the importation of Bibles, were removed, and yet only three or four years before one of our colporteurs in Ayachucho was attacked by a mob of infuriated Indians led by monks and priests and he had to escape by the roof, the mob contenting itself by taking his clothes and his box of Bibles and burning them in the public plaza.

In this period, by arrangement with the Valparaiso Bible Society, Chile was added to the field of the La Plata Agency. In 1902 even Bolivia, hitherto closed against Bible distribution, now under more liberal laws, became accessible to colporteurs who obtained permits from the government.

The year 1903 is a notable one, as it is the fortieth year of Mr. Milne's service for the Society. During this time he has seen the work of the Agency established from the Equator to Cape Horn. He has had the privilege of directing the circulation of over 700,000 copies of the Scriptures. The very oldest copy of the Spanish Scriptures that he ever met with in South America, he says, "is the New Testament of the American Bible Society of 1819," published three years after the founding of the Society.

The great desires of his heart have been answered. Everywhere the field is open. New missionaries have been coming to organise and develop the new churches of these lands. The government imposts and Custom House burdens have been removed, a new and attractive sales room has been opened on one of the central streets in Buenos Aires, and best of all, a gifted lady, Madam Clorinda Matto de Turner, has undertaken to translate the Gospels into the language of the Quechua Indians. The ignorance and superstition and need of these Indian tribes in Peru, and Ecuador, and Bolivia had long weighed upon the heart of Mr. Milne. A song of rejoicing goes up when he is assured of the purpose of this earnest woman. Before her death she translated the Gospels of Matthew, Mark, Luke, and John, the Acts of the Apostles and the Epistle to the Romans into the Quechua, and these Scriptures were published by the American Bible Society. Certain of the Gospels were later published in parallel columns, one column in Quechua, and the other in Spanish.

Curiously enough a Roman Catholic friar who had persecuted the colporteurs, rendered unconscious assistance to this lady in her translation by preparing, with government assistants, a vocabulary of the Quechua language defining some 12,000 words.

QUECHUA INDIANS OF BOLIVIA

Within the last few years it has been deemed wise to bring out jointly with the British and Foreign Bible Society a translation of the Gospels into a form of Quechua especially adapted to the Indians of Bolivia. So far work has been carried forward by the Rev. George Allan, and these books will also be issued in diglot editions with the Spanish.

In 1906 occurred the memorable visit of the Honourable Elihu Root, Secretary of State. Mr. Milne was among those who met him in Buenos Aires and presented to him a statement of the work of the Society.

On the 20th of August, 1907, after forty-three years of service, Mr. Milne passed to his reward. No one will be able to write the history of Christianity in Latin-America without giving a noticeable place to the work of this consecrated man who was instrumental in putting into circulation nearly one million volumes of the Scriptures. He saw the daylight of a pure Christianity breaking in these great republics.

By a natural succession the Rev. F. G. Penzotti, an Italian Swiss who had emigrated to South America, and who was converted by reading a Gospel of St. John put in his hands by Mr. Milne, and who for many years had served under Mr. Milne on the West coast of South America, suffering imprisonment in Peru, as has been narrated, was transferred from the care of the Society's work in the Central American Republics to this larger field. The circulation has risen year by year until in the last year of the Society's century it reached 86,000 volumes, making a total in the La Plata Agency of 1,464,674 volumes.

Venezuela, to which reference has already been made, had been visited more than once as a part of the La Plata Agency and later the Southern part of Colombia was included in the same Agency, though the Northern portion was associated with the Central America field.

In spite of persecution in 1894, in both Venezuela and Colombia, Mr. Norwood reported a circulation of 6,916 volumes. The next year he transferred his central depot to Baranquilla, in Colombia. He visited many towns and cities for the first time. The authorities professed to guarantee religious liberty.

In the year 1898, ten years after the establishment of the Agency, Mr. Norwood became engaged in a law suit because of the attempt of the Roman Catholic clergy to prevent Bible distribution. After a long and expensive contest a decision was given at Bogota entirely denying the claims of the priests to exercise censorship over literature. The following year civil war again interrupted the work of Mr. Norwood. The agent was so shut off by the armies that it was extremely difficult for him to have any communication with the Bible House in New York. Government officials refused to allow Bible distribution to the soldiers, but in the liberal army colporteurs were permitted to enter the barracks and to offer a copy to every soldier who promised to read it. The following year work was again interrupted by revolution, and practically no circulation took place. Mr. Norwood was unable even to communicate with New York or with Mr. Bailly, his co-labourer in Venezuela. Shut up in Bucaramanga, his work was merely nominal.

In the year 1903, Mr. Norwood was obliged to leave Colombia, and when he went back after the establishment of the Republic of Panama, he found so strong an antipathy against all Americans that he advised the discontinuance of Bible work there and was recalled. He continued his interest in Spanish speaking people and was engaged in mission work in the United States until his death. The fields of the Agency were then divided between adjacent Agencies and have been so continued.

Out of Colombia came one of the most important versions on the Society's list. For some time there had existed in the new Protestant Churches in Latin America a desire for a more faithful translation of the original Hebrew Old Testament and the Greek New Testament into Spanish than in the opinion of scholars was represented in the Valera version, which some claimed to have been made largely from the Vulgate.

Dr. H. B. Pratt, a Presbyterian missionary at Bogota, and a thorough student in the languages of the Bible, was commissioned by the Society to bring out a new version. After seven years of work, on the 28th of February, 1893, he completed his translation of the Bible into Spanish. It was called the Version Moderna and at once met with a very favourable reception. Dr. Pratt did not feel entirely satisfied with his translation of the New Testament, on the preparation of which he felt that he had been hurried, and he was requested by the Society to give such time and strength as he had to its revision. He was able to complete the work on the Gospels before his death, which occurred on the 11th of December, 1912, at Hackensack, New Jersey. His name is on the roll of honour of the missionary translators of the Bible.

Mr. Norwood, of the Colombia and Venezuela Agency, and Mr. Penzotti, of the La Plata Agency, visited five republics of Central America in the early nineties, exploring as far as the Isthmus of Panama. In the year 1892 the Rev. F. G. Penzotti was appointed agent for Central America and Panama. The circulation averaged seven or eight thousand volumes a year. It was a difficult field, the people scattered in six different republics. When the Agency was established the only evangelistic work in any of the five republics was conducted by the Presbyterian mission in Guatemala. Guatemala City was made the headquarters of the Agency. Nine or ten colporteurs were employed continuously. In 1903 the circulation reached a total of 16,673 volumes.

All at once the Agency assumed new importance. With the securing of the Canal Zone by the United States from the new Republic of Panama and the gigantic operations undertaken to open a canal from ocean to ocean, the attention of the world was called to this region.

Filled with zeal and enthusiasm, Mr. Penzotti recognised the importance of these movements and asked for means to double his force of colporteurs. A few years later there was to be a population of 50,000 in the Canal Zone and the Society employed twenty men in the six republics who visited in one year 2,211 towns and villages.

On the appointment of Mr. Penzotti to the post in the La Plata field made vacant by the death of Mr. Milne, the Rev. James Hayter, a Baptist missionary, and a co-labourer with Mr. Penzotti, was appointed Agent for Central America.

On his furlough in 1913 Mr. Hayter was requested to

visit the depot of the British and Foreign Bible Society at Port Said that he might particularly acquaint himself with the methods employed in reaching the ships that pass through the Suez canal.

An arrangement was entered into by which the American Bible Society transferred to the British and Foreign Bible Society all of its work and good will in Persia and in return the British and Foreign Bible Society turned over to the American Bible Society the work which it had had in Central America, recognising that it was peculiarly the province of the American Society to minister to the opportunities opened by the construction of this new great highway between the oceans. In the celebrations connected with the opening of the Canal, Mr. James Wood, the President of the Society, visited Panama and arrangements were at once entered into for the erection of a Bible House at Cristobal which it is hoped will prove a beacon light to many and many a traveller for generations to come.

The requests of many missionaries for a new revision of the Spanish Scriptures were echoed by certain religious bodies in Argentina, in particular the Conference of the Methodist Episcopal Church. It having proved impracticable to arrange at this time a joint committee with the British and Foreign Bible Society, in 1909 a special committee consisting of the Rev. Henry C. Thomson, of Mexico; the Rev. Charles W. Drees, of Argentina; the Rev. John Howland, of Mexico; the Rev. Francisco Diez, of Chile, and the Rev. Victoriano D. Baez, of Mexico, was organised in the Bible House in New York City. For seven months this committee met daily having before them not only the original Greek but all of the existing Spanish versions to prepare a new revised Spanish version. With the completion of the Four Gospels in 1910 the committee was discontinued in order that their work might be tested on the field. On his way to the World's Missionary Conference in Edinburgh, in 1901, Secretary Haven, taking with him the new version of the Four Gospels, visited the Spanish peninsula and conferred with the committee in Madrid at work upon a revision of the Valera, and later with the Committee of the British and Foreign Bible Society in London.

The project of a joint translation was taken up, and in 1912 three representatives of the American Bible Society, the Rev. H. C. Thomson, Rev. Dr. Charles W. Drees, and the Rev. Victoriano D. Baez, were sent to Spain to meet with three representatives of the British Society. Faithfully this joint committee has been at work, and the approaching Centennial will be celebrated by the completion of their version of the New Testament for the ninety millions of Spanish speaking people in the world. As the Centennial approaches the Latin-American Congress is meeting at Panama, which may prove a significant turning point in the development of Christian work in all these countries where the Society has been a pioneer, and there could be no more fitting moment for the publication of a revised version of the Spanish Scriptures, and the recounting of these years of missionary labour, sowing the good seed over these vast regions.

CHAPTER LIII

OPENING DOORS OF THE FAR EAST

This waterfall's melodius voice—
Was famed both far and near;
Although it long has ceased to flow,
Yet still with memory's ear,
Its genial splash I hear.

In this Japanese poem of the tenth century is stated the deathlessness of influences that have been set in motion even when conditions have changed. The days of the beginning of the introduction of the Scriptures into Japan have passed but the impression made by the early translators and the effect of the early translation continues. Korea, at the beginning of this period a separate nation, is inextricably entwined with the affairs of the Japanese Empire. In the mind of the Society, the two fields are one and Mr. Loomis administered the work in the peninsula of Korea from Yokohama, as he did the work in all the islands of Japan. There is this difference, however, that translation work in the early nineties was just beginning in Korea. In 1894 a translation committee was finally chosen by the missionaries and the Society agreed to participate in the expense of the work. Five thousand copies of Rijutei's St. Mark, printed for the Society, with certain changes in orthography, were sent to Korea and a new supply of Korean Gospels written with Chinese characters.

In 1895 the Japanese Government undertook the reconstruction of the Korean administration. The Japanese Minister of Home Affairs, sent to supervise the work, took with him as associates two Christian Japanese. The result was that on January 1, 1895, all religious restrictions were removed in Korea and Sunday was proclaimed a day of rest by an Imperial edict. The excitement of the war between Japan and China disturbed evangelistic work, but it left free those engaged in the work of translation. The following year Mr. Loomis visited Korea and made arrangements for the publishing of the new version and for Bible distribution, but it was not until 1899 that the translation committee decided to print the whole New Testament without waiting for a full revision of it.

The great success following the use of the Scriptures by the missionaries in Korea led them to this step. One of the Methodist missionaries at this time said: "Nine-tenths of our successes are the result of Bible work." A Presbyterian missionary said: "Nearly every encouraging case brought to our notice shows some influence of the Bible colporteur." The first Sunday in May was set apart as Bible Sunday. It was not, however, until September, 1900, that the completion of the translation in Korean was celebrated, and two years later the Society was informed that the native Christians were eager for the translation of the whole Bible.

In Japan Bible distribution through this period was entrusted to a committee. Three of the committee were the agents of the American Bible Society, the British and Foreign Bible Society, and the National Bible Society of Scotland. Six missionaries were appointed by the American Bible Society and four by the British and Foreign Bible Society. This arrangement was entered into at the request of the misssionaries of Japan in order to bring about harmony between the Societies operating in the Empire. All possibility of rivalry or competition was by this means removed, but the circulation was less than was expected. In 1894 the committee gave up the premises in Yokohama that had been occupied by the American Bible Society for fifteen years and transferred the headquarters to a place more convenient to the foreign residents, although more distant from the Japanese quarters. The following year the Bible House in Yokohama burned and floods and drought brought difficulties. The great war with China absorbed attention and there was a shortage of books. On the other hand the Commander-in-Chief of the Japanese army gave his hearty approval for the distribution of the Scriptures among the soldiers and expressed his thanks for the same. The circulation for this year was less than

100,000 volumes. In 1895, however, 257,578 volumes were put into circulation, but the following year again the circulation dropped to just a little over 100,000 and three-fourths of these were free grants. The changes produced by the war and various disasters in different parts of Japan accounted for the demand for gratuitous distribution. Two hundred and fifty thousand people were estimated as receiving government relief at this time.

An interesting attempt to minister to the ancient people of the northern islands was the publication, in 1896, of an Ainu version of the Psalms prepared by Rev. John Bachellor, of the Church Missionary Society. Two years later the complete New Testament in this language was published by the committee. The same year, 1898, the Roman Catholic Mission brought out an edition of the Four Gospels with notes, in two volumes, at a price a good deal higher than the books of the Bible Societies.

For a number of years the circulation averaged about 100,000 copies. This did not seem satisfactory, and in 1904 by a mutual agreement between the agents of the Societies and the missionaries, the Bible committee was dissolved and the Japanese field was divided, the American Bible Society taking the Northern portion of the Empire, with its headquarters in Yokohama, and the British Societies operating together, taking the Southern portion of the Empire, with their headquarters at Kobe. It was agreed that the same editions should be used by both agencies, and at the same prices.

Interestingly enough, at the very time when the committee was given up in Japan, arrangements were made at the suggestion of the British and Foreign Bible Society for a joint agency in Korea. Translation work has proceeded slowly in Korea and the American Bible Society had deemed it wise to wait until that work had approached completion before developing a separate agency in that country. The British and Foreign Bible Society had entered the country from its North China and Manchurian Agency, with a subagent in Korea. The American Bible Society had continued care for that part of its field through its agent in Yokohama.

During the year 1901 the Rev. D. A. Bunker acted as

Superintendent of the Society's work in Korea. Hitherto it had been difficult to get colporteurs. This year certain native Christians were selected who seemed to learn the work quite easily.

The joint Agency did not go into effect until the first of January, 1904. The Rev. Alexander Kenmure, who had been the agent of the British and Foreign Bible Society and the National Bible Society of Scotland, was chosen as the joint agent of the three Societies. In his report he says, "The joint Agency is a striking fact, and yet, why should it be in any way remarkable? There is one Lord, one faith, one baptism, why not one Bible Society circulating the Word?"

This year the Korean version of the New Testament was at last finished and ready to go to press. The extension of the influence of this version is seen in the fact that Korean labourers began to emigrate to Hawaii, Western Mexico, California, and even Yucatan.

The following year Mr. Kenmure returned to England in ill health and Mr. Hugh Miller, who had been assistant agent, was appointed to the care of the joint Agency. Fifty-three colporteurs and fifteen Bible women were employed, and the agent reports "The Korean is awakening out of the sleep of ages with a hungering for better things and a willingness to buy Christian books and investigate the truths which they set forth." Four sentences seem to cover the facts of the year—"Work going on. Blessings coming down. Converts coming in. Praise going up."

At the request of the British and Foreign Bible Society, the joint Agency was given up at the close of the year 1907. This year the Emperor of Korea abdicated in favour of his son, and the Japanese officials sent the son to Japan to be educated, in the meantime taking over the whole administration of the Korean government. At the request of the American Bible Society, the Rev. D. A. Bunker, of the Methodist Episcopal Mission, agreed to take charge of the Society's interests on the first of January, 1908. He engaged twenty or more colporteurs and sent them forth into districts where foreign missionaries had never been seen. That year 24,206 volumes were circulated, and the following year 70,187 volumes, an increase of more than 100%; over 1,000 villages had been visited and thirteen new churches sprung from this work.

Interesting work was carried on among the Japanese in Korea, a Japanese colporteur being employed.

In 1911 the Rev. S. A. Beck, of University City, Nebraska, who had been for a number of years a missionary of the Methodist Episcopal Church in Korea, and who was acquainted with the language, was chosen as the agent for the Society to succeed the Rev. Mr. Bunker, who had returned home on furlough. In 1910 the Korean Old Testament, long in making, was at last finished. The type favoured by the people was so large that this Bible was brought out in two volumes. The translation of the Scriptures into Korean was accomplished by a faithful band of missionaries so burdened with other tasks in the development of that wonderful field that it had been impossible to give themselves wholly to translation. Two of this group had entered Korea in 1885 together, one the Rev. H. G. Underwood, now a veteran missionary of the Presbyterian Church in Seoul, the other the Rev. H. G. Appenzeller, of the Methodist Episcopal Mission. On the 11th of June, 1902, Mr. Appenzeller took passage on a steamer to attend a meeting of the Bible Committee. The same night, in collision with another steamer, Mr. Appenzeller's ship sank with all on board. The influence of his life remains not only in many Korean converts who revere his memory, but in the New Testament, in the translation of which he bore a most important part.[1]

In 1912, the Board of Translators changed their name to the Board of Revisers. It was not sufficient to have the Scriptures in Korean. It was necessary for them to be brought out in what is called the Mixed Script, in which Chinese characters are used. This work is still going forward and with it the revision and the perfecting also of reference versions. The circulation has advanced remarkably. In 1913 it totalled 176,880 volumes. In 1914 it reached a total of 458,694 volumes. Nowhere in the world

[1] Missionaries who have had a part in this Korean Version are named in the Appendix.

is there a more intense Bible loving Christian church than in this country known only a few years ago as "the Hermit Nation."

There perhaps was never a more startling event outside of the present almost unimaginable conflict in Europe, than the war between Japan and Russia. No one dreamed that the little island empire would dare to attack the Colossus of the Snows. The provocation was of ten years' standing. When at the conclusion of its war with China, Japan found its fruits of victory taken from it and Russia occupying Port Arthur, the iron entered into its soul. In one of the hidden villages of the empire years after, a traveller was told by the simple villagers that they had heard the voices of the spirits of the soldiers who had died in the Chinese war calling them to be ready for the war with Russia. It broke in all its fury in 1904 and in the swift months that followed Japan emerged onto the world stage as one of the mighty nations of the earth. It is sad to reflect, as one of its own nobles said, "that all it had wrought in painting, and sculpture, and delicate artistry in precious metals, and all of its courtesies and kindly manners had failed to give it the world recognition that it received from its feats of arms." The Society recognised in this hour of the nation's intense patriotism an opportunity that comes rarely. Mr. Loomis, in most intimate relations with many of the leaders of the Japanese Empire, secured at once a welcome for the Society's Scriptures in the navy and received from one of the Japanese Admirals a most cordial letter of thanks. Tens of thousands of Japanese Gospels were placed in the comfort bags which the Japanese women prepared for the out-going troops; but perhaps the most blessed ministry of all was the going from cot to cot in the military hospitals and placing in the hands of the sufferers the Holy Scriptures. Numerous instances are on record of the light from the face of Jesus Christ breaking in upon the hearts of those who read these Scriptures to the great joy of these young soldiers. One wrote, "I was sent to Oiwake to recover from my sickness, and while there I learned about the narrow way, and by God's help I was able to enter into the gate of life." Even Count Okuma is quoted as saying, "As you read the

Bible, you may think it is antiquated. The words it contains may so appear, but the noble life which it holds up to admiration is something that will never be out of date."

One of the immediate results of the war was the great influx of students into Japan. In 1906 there were 800 Korean students and about 17,000 Chinese students studying in Japan. The Society at once attempted to reach these students with the Scriptures. The following year 7,000 volumes in European languages were purchased by the students of Japan in the pursuit of their studies. The knowledge of the Bible has so permeated the nation that the words of the prophets, and apostles, and many of the sayings of Jesus are quoted in the daily newspapers.

In the year 1910 Mr. Loomis retired. The circulation had advanced to 201,190 volumes in the Northern part of the Empire alone. The following year Mr. Loomis resigned after thirty years in the service of the Society. He had the respect and confidence of all the missionary body and the esteem of the growing Japanese Church. Courteous in his manners, acquainted with the best in the Empire, thoroughly believing in the purposes of the Japanese people, he made friends innumerable for the Society.

In his illness Dr. Herbert W. Schwartz, of the Methodist Episcopal Mission, attended him and also relieved him of the burden of the cares of the agency; so that it was a pleasure to the Society to appoint Dr. Schwartz as Acting Agent and later as its Agent for its work in Japan. Through his skill, his knowledge of Japanese, his intimate acquaintance with the Japan Church, the circulation has advanced year by year until it reached the total in 1914 of 643,799 volumes circulated during the year.

All the astonishing changes taking place in this country were reflected in their language. The speech of man is a fluid-flowing medium. It is only fixed when the language is dead.

The very satisfactory work of the translators, recognised by the Emperor of Japan in presenting to Dr. Hepburn on his ninetieth birthday the "Jewelled Order of the Rising Sun," could not, however, be permanent. For a number of years a desire for a revision was manifested here and there, and in 1906 the Japan Evangelical Alliance proposed to the agents of the Bible Societies that steps be taken for a revision of the Japanese Bible, published in its completed form twenty years before. Four years later a Committee of Japanese scholars and missionaries, four of each, was appointed to undertake this revision, the Bible Societies agreeing to meet the expenses of the Committee.[1] The work has made commendable progress, and it is anticipated that the revised New Testament will be published during the year 1916.

In Yokohama, in the heart of the city, is one of the most interesting industrial plants of the Far East. It is a purely Japanese printing establishment. Its founder and present manager, Mr. Muruoka, is a member of the Christian Church and an honorary life-member of the American Bible Society. From small beginnings this firm bearing the name " Fukien or Gospel Printing Company " has developed and enlarged until it serves not only the Christian communities of Japan and Korea, but the great churches in China, and the Philippines and even Siam.

The American Bible Society has long made use of its accurate and careful workmanship and has brought out editions from its presses in all the languages of the Far East. The other Bible Societies operating in these lands have also found it a most dependable establishment. It is a pharos illuminating the coast and sending its rays of light far into the adjacent lands of Asia.

How little could Gutenberg have dreamed when he printed the Latin Bible on the first printing press on the Rhine, that the day would come when a great plant for the printing of the Scriptures would rival his own on the shores of the Pacific!

An American orator has said that " the Far East is like a great ship and Japan is its rudder." If this be even partially true, what reasons for thanksgiving there are that the Bible has so widely entered into the life of this dominant people.

[1] The names of the Missionary members of this Committee will be found in the Appendix. The Japanese members of the Committee are Prof. U. Bessho, Prof. T. Fujii, Rev. M. Kawazoe, and Prof. T. Matsuyama.

CHAPTER LIV

THE WHITE ELEPHANT AND THE DRAGON

SUDDENLY and swiftly events come to a climax, startling the world, for which quiet and unseen forces have long been working. Under the waters of Hellgate at the entrance of New York Harbour, in the dangerous rocks that made the channel narrow and perilous, engineers had been working for years cutting corridors here and there and planting mines. In a moment when all was ready, by simple electric contact, in a vast upheaval, the whole barrier of centuries was swept away and a new entrance to the great harbour free for all the argosies of commerce and friendly intercourse with the nations of the earth was opened.

For years upon years earnest Christians offered prayer for the opening of the Far East to their spiritual messengers. Now suddenly it is all open and there are no closed lands.

Two nations, one Siam, a liberal monarchy; the other ancient China, in a convulsion changed from reactionary Imperialism to the outward forms and much of the spirit of a Democracy, are lands in which the circulation of the Scriptures has played a large part in the influencing of public opinion.

We have recounted the early labours of Mr. Carrington. We have seen him busy in the translation of the Scriptures into Siamese; seeing their publication through the press of the Presbyterian Mission at Bangkok and in self-denying journeying going about as a colporteur distributing these Scriptures among the people. In 1896 he brings out an experimental Version of the Gospel of St. Luke in Cambodian in order that a region where no evangelistic work has been attempted may be opened up. In 1899 he brings out the Book of Genesis in the Laos language prepared by the Reverend Jonathan Wilson. In 1905 approval is

BINDING SCRIPTURES FOR THE AMERICAN BIBLE SOCIETY IN YOKOHAMA

granted for the transliteration of the Siamese Scriptures into the Laos dialect to temporarily supply the Laos people until books are ready in their own tongue. Three years before three books of the New Testament and Isaiah were translated into this language. Later when Mr. Carrington is on furlough, Mr. Cameron temporarily in care of the Agency pressed out into the Northern mountain region of Siam among tribesmen known as "Yao men," whom he found very eager to have the Bible. Just over the border are Chinese who are called "Miao" for whom Scriptures have been prepared which has led some vain reviewer to intimate that the Bible Societies are not content to minister to all the strange tongues of human speech, but are even preparing the Scriptures for the cats.

Everywhere Mr. Carrington found doors wide open, opportunities as he says, "limited only by the strength of workers to go forward." One of his great difficulties is in securing colporteurs. Government officers and foreigners in business in Siam are so quick to offer high salaries to any one who is competent, that when a faithful man is trained to be a good colporteur, he finds himself in great demand; so the Agent depends on the widely scattered forces of missionaries of the American Presbyterian Board, the American Baptist Missionary Union and the Plymouth Brethren from England on the Western side of the Malay Peninsula, together with five colporteurs and his own personal labours. In the year 1905 the Agent himself sold 16,249 books. The field is difficult because of lack of rapid travelling. It takes as long to go from Bangkok to Cheng Mai in Northwestern Siam as it does from Bangkok to San Francisco. One of his journeys to the West Coast occupied four months. Weary and lonely Mr. Carrington often was, but he writes to the Bible House in New York, "We are willing to be let down into the dark here because we know that the rope is held by your hands with a loving, firm, constant grip, and that you will not let go."

In 1903 Mr. Carrington asked for a boat, which was granted to him, with which he was able to visit large areas of population living on the banks of rivers and canals accessible in this way from Bangkok.

That which gives courage and strengthens the faith of such a man is an incident he relates of a Chinaman receiving a Chinese New Testament on the West Coast of the Gulf of Siam. Some time after this man, thoroughly converted by reading the New Testament, decided to declare himself a Christian. He invited a missionary to visit him and help him clear his house of idols. The idols and altars were all taken out in front of the house and publicly burned.

In 1908 Mr. Carrington came home on a well earned furlough. The first translation of the Bible into Siamese, a very large portion of which had been the work of Mr. Carrington himself, was completed. The whole was in process of revision. Beginnings had been made in Cambodian and Laos. At the Commencement of Princeton University in the spring of 1908, in recognition of the scholarly labours of all these years and of the distinguished services of this man, who had the good faith of the common people and the friendship of the highest officials in Siam, he was given the title of Doctor of Divinity.

On his return to Siam, having the advantage of an Assistant Agent, the Rev. Robert Irwin, formerly a member of the Presbyterian Mission to the Laos, he is able to report an increase of more than 30,000 in the circulation. In 1913 he reports the New Testament in Laos completed and some advance in the translation of the Old Testament.

Suddenly on October 11th, 1912, Dr. Carrington ceased from his labours. On October 13th he was buried in the Siam that he loved. He was a significant figure in the missionary annals of the Far East, universally respected and greatly beloved. His funeral cortege vied in numbers and distinction with that of two other great Americans, Stroebel and Hamilton King, the American Minister to Siam.

The Rev. Robert Irwin entered upon his labours and after the close of twenty-five years since the creation of the Siam Agency, the Society reports, in addition to the service rendered in the translation and publication of the Scriptures in the language of this nation, the circulation of 1,194,819 volumes among the people.

In the Empire to the North of this Southern Kingdom this period begins with the great popularity of the new issue of the Bible in Foochow colloquial all over the Fukien Province, where the missions of the Methodist Episcopal Church started their first work in China and where the American Board had developed important interests in the city of Foochow. Colporteurs were sent to work in Formosa. The Canton colloquial, many years in preparation, was now ready for the press to meet the needs of the American Presbyterian and Baptist missionaries in Canton, one of the most characteristic cities in the Far East.

Perhaps the most notable event for the Society in these years, approaching the close of the nineteenth century, was the appointment on November 1st, 1893, of the Rev. Dr. John R. Hykes, of the Methodist Episcopal mission of Kiukiang, China, as the Agent of the American Bible Society for China. The first church opened in this city, four hundred miles up the Yangtse, was ministered to by one who had been a colporteur of the Society. He was the first Chinese minister of the Methodist Episcopal Church in these regions. His daughter is known the world around as Dr. Mary Stone, and her hospital at Kiukiang is a Mecca for all who love to see how the ministry of healing can be made a ministry also of salvation. From this mission on the Yangtse, founded in the circulation of the Scriptures, it was natural that an Agent should be chosen to whom it should be given to see the most wonderful changes in China of all its long, long history, and to have a part in a circulation of the Scriptures passing from a total in the year that his predecessor, Dr. Wheeler, died, April 20th, 1893, of 192,215 volumes to a total for the last year, ending December 31st, 1915, of 2,244,746 volumes. Little could he have dreamed at his appointment of this vast expansion of the work before him. He was peculiarly adapted to take up this work by his almost perfect knowledge of Chinese, so that he could talk freely with the people, and his business sagacity, as well as his sincere love for the Scriptures and belief in their power as an evangelising agency.

The world is familiar with the events of these two decades. The war with Japan; in 1897 the seizure of Kiaochow by the Germans, the occupation of Port Arthur by the Russians and the demands of France in the South in

1898; the decrees of the young Emperor in 1899 abolishing the essay system of examinations; establishing a University, introducing the study of Western sciences, officially undertaking the translation into Chinese of books of Western learning and the sending of young Chinese abroad for study.

The forces of darkness swiftly gathered. On the 22nd of September by *coup d'état* the Empress Dowager deposed the Emperor and took over again the Regency of the Empire. Six days later, without trial, six martyrs to reform were executed at Peking. Before he died T'an Sz T'ung said: "If my death will save my country I do not regret it. For every head cut off this day a thousand men will arise to carry on the work of reform." In 1900 the terrible Boxer massacre broke out all over the Chinese Empire in which 183 Protestant missionaries, including 60 men, 75 women, and 48 children, were killed, the native Christians were cruelly persecuted, their crops destroyed, their property looted, their houses burned, and in numberless instances they were tortured and put to death. The movement starting in the Province of Shangtung spread into the Province of Chihli, and its path was marked by pillage, murder and nameless cruelties. On June 11th the Chancellor of the Japanese Legation was killed on the streets of Peking by Imperial soldiers, and on the 20th, the German Minister while on his way to the Foreign Office was murdered on the streets by a military Mandarin in full uniform. The foreigners took refuge in the Legations, where they were besieged for two months by the Boxers and Imperial troops, until after breathless suspense all over the world they were finally relieved by the troops of the allied powers on the 15th of August. An Edict went forth in June from the Empress Dowager ordering the extermination of all foreigners in China. The rage, as Dr. Hykes says, of the infuriated Boxers was "directed equally against diplomat, merchant, traveller, and missionary, so that the movement cannot be truthfully said to have been solely anti-missionary."

After the arrival of the allies with the first year of the new century, Reform Edicts were issued by the Empress Dowager. In 1905 the startling war between Japan and Russia stirred China through and through. Three years later the Empress Dowager died and her nephew the Emperor Kwang-hsu also. In another three years, after agitations and transformations in which the campaign against the vice of opium smoking must not be forgotten, came the establishment of the Republic and the overthrow of the Manchu Dynasty. Floods and plagues accompanied these events, and now as we close our century, the Republic so suddenly erected is ancient history and Yuan Shih Kai the one great outstanding figure in China has ascended the Imperial throne, though his coronation is deferred.

The part of the Bible and the Bible Society in all this is not so well known. The young Emperor Kwang-hsu was a devout Bible lover and frequently retired to a quiet place in his Palace to pray. It is recorded that one of the eunuchs of the Palace visited Dr. T. J. N. Gatrell, then in charge of our work in North China, at his book-store, carrying a slip of paper on which was written, "One Old Testament, One New Testament." One Wang Yu Chou, the helper at the store, an educated fellow, was struck by the uncommon look of the characters and was led to ask who had written them. The eunuch replied, "The Emperor." "Indeed," said Wang, "to-day the women of the Christian Church in China have presented the Empress Dowager with a copy of the New Testament." "Yes," answered the eunuch, "the Emperor has seen it, and now wishes to see copies of the books of the Jesus religion." When the books were got ready and were paid for, Wang secretly took the slip of paper and laid it away on one of the shelves, but the eunuch soon missed it and he was in a great state until it was returned to him, when he said, "It will never do for me to lose the Emperor's order."

The approach of the storm was also felt before it broke by the Society's colporteurs. In 1899 some of our men were beaten and robbed by rowdies in Shantung. In West China, at a river mart on the borders of the Kansuh and Shensi provinces, three of our men were tied up by their thumbs to trees and beaten with sticks while the crowd gathered and called out to them that Jesus was crucified on a tree and they were going to do the same with them. Our Superintendent in West China wrote: "After they had beaten them till their bodies were covered all over with marks and wounds, and their wrists and ankles were cut and lacerated with the ropes that bound them to the trees, they were allowed to hang under the scorching heat of a July sun until the darkness came when they were eventually taken down by the inn-keeper, who got a few friends to intercede with the mob to release them. One of them, a young converted Taoist priest, was not able to speak until the next day; he was so overcome." This was before the outbreak. During the Boxer rebellion our Agent visited Peking to investigate, and after consultation with the American Minister decided, acting on his advice, that our men should go out as usual on their book-selling tours, but that they should be warned to keep away from the disturbed district. The Agent writes: "They were warned of the risk they were running, but not a man of the noble band of eighteen flinched. Their reply was, 'We go. God's will be done.' Only four of the eighteen returned. We shall probably never know how some of them obtained the martyr's crown, but we are sure that they died 'witnessing a good confession,' and that they were worthy of a place among those who were 'slain for the word of God, and for the testimony which they held.' So far as can be ascertained, the homes of these martyrs were looted and burned and their families exterminated. Those who survived escaped to the mountains, where they suffered terrible privations. One of them, Mr. Wang, was chased by the Boxers and so badly injured that it took him months to recover. Another, Mr. Wen, had his wife and two children killed. Of the colporteurs under missionary supervision, not one escaped. Some of our men, knowing where the native Christians were living, heroically went out of their way to warn them of the impending danger." It is also an interesting fact that the guide of the allied troops from Tientsin to Peking that relieved the besieged legations was Mr. C. F. Gammon, the Sub-Agent of the Society in North China.

During all this time the work of translation went forward undisturbed by famines, floods or revolution. Three revision committees called for by the Missionary Conference of 1890 were selected and organised. Colloquial translations were added to and perfected. The whole Bible was brought out in the Canton colloquial. The Shanghai colloquial New Testament was revised. The Hinghua colloquial was brought out in Roman letters. Certain of the Gospels were published in the Shantung colloquial. The Gospels were translated into the Sam kiong colloquial by Miss Eleanor Chestnut, M.D., one of the martyrs who was massacred at Lienchow. Work was also forwarded in the Soochow colloquial and, sixty years after the first book was finished, the translation of the whole Bible into the Shanghai colloquial was finished on the 6th of August, 1906. These colloquials serve a great purpose, the language in the different provinces of China varying almost as much as in the various countries of Europe.

The three revision committees were at work, however, on the Mandarin, the High Wenli and the Easy Wenli, the literary and more universal languages of the nation. At the great Missionary Conference in 1907 in which was celebrated the completion of the centennial of Protestant missionary effort in China, to which Conference the Rev. Dr. Fox, one of the Corresponding Secretaries of the Society, was sent as a delegate, it was unanimously decided to unite the High Wenli and the Easy Wenli and make provision for only one Wenli version. Now as our century draws to its close, the Union revision committees in which the three Bible Societies: the British and Foreign, the National Bible Society of Scotland, and the American Society, are approaching the end of their work. It is expected that both revisions will be completed in 1916.[1]

Separate and distinct from the colloquial versions and the Committee versions stands out the work of Bishop Schereschewsky. It is one of the distinctions of the American Bible Society that it has had fellowship with this remarkable man. Samuel Isaac Joseph Schereschewsky was born May 23rd, 1831, in the town of Tauroggen, in Russian Lithuania. His parents were Jews. He must have been a very precocious child, for at the age of seventeen he was engaged as tutor in a Russian family and at eighteen he wrote poetry in

[1] We have placed in the Appendix the complete list of the Missionary scholars who have accomplished these tasks.

Hebrew. About this time he left Russia and spent a number of years in Europe, principally in study. In 1854 he came to the United States, where he embraced Christianity and became a student at the General Theological Seminary in New York. On graduation he was asked if he would accept a Professorship in the Seminary, a position for which he was peculiarly qualified. He replied that he would not and said that he intended to go to China as a missionary. His friends much surprised said, "What! Do you prefer to go to that country and bury your talents?" The answer was, "I want to go to China to translate the Bible." He was appointed a missionary to China and arrived in Shanghai in company with the venerable Archdeacon Thomson in 1859. During the long voyage from New York the new missionaries studied Chinese under Senior Bishop Boone, who was returning to China, and Mr. Schereschewsky's progress was so marked and rapid, that not one could keep pace with him. When he arrived in Shanghai he astonished the native teachers by being able to write good classical composition. He remained in Shanghai two years, studied the Shanghai colloquial, Mandarin and classic Chinese, and then moved to Peking. In 1875 he returned to the United States on furlough. In the autumn of the same year he was appointed by the House of Bishops to the Bishopric of Shanghai, but declined. He was again appointed in 1876, and after much doubt and hesitation finally accepted and was consecrated in Grace Church, New York, October 3rd, 1877.

For forty years until his coronation on the 15th of September, 1908, in his seventy-seventh year, he devoted himself almost exclusively to Bible translation. All of his work he did for the American Bible Society. He translated the Book of Genesis into Mandarin as early as 1866. He was one of the Committee which translated the Mandarin New Testament first published in 1872. He translated the whole of the Old Testament into Mandarin, and this version has had no rival for forty-one years. He produced the first version of the whole Bible in Easy Wenli, and to him belongs the honour of making the first reference Bibles — Mandarin and Easy Wenli — in the Chinese language.

BISHOP SCHERESCHEWSKI

Eight years of the Bishop's life he spent in the United States in making the simple or Easy Wenli translations and revised his Mandarin Old Testament. He had no Chinese assistant, and though quite capable of writing Chinese characters himself, he was unable to hold a pen in his partially paralysed fingers. He, therefore, wrote the entire text of his Wenli Bible and the notes for his revision of the Mandarin Old Testament in the Roman letter on a typewriter, using only the middle finger of each hand. He often facetiously refers to this Easy Wenli as "a Two Finger Bible."

It seems to us as though the record of heaven will be that he was a living martyr to the great cause of Bible translation. The story of his life is one of the romances of the history of the Bible.

What of the circulation of the Scriptures all through this turbulent period? Strangely enough, it is almost a commonplace in the history of the Society, that wars and rumours of wars and tumults and revolutions do not seriously set back the sowing of the good seed of the Kingdom. They seem, however, to be like divine ploughshares opening up the soil for the reception of the seed.

In 1894 there was a great distribution of the Scriptures among the students of Nanking gathered for their triennial examinations. Four thousand New Testaments and 25,000 Portions were distributed among these men; three Bible Societies uniting in the work at the request of the Nanking missionaries. Two years later the Agent writes—"the demand is without precedent." The entire circulation amounted to 400,916 volumes, 98 per cent. of which were sold; at prices, however, less than the cost of manufacture. In 1898 he writes, for the first time in the history of the Agency, more than half a million copies have been issued in one year in thirty-three different languages or dialects and they have been circulated in almost every one of the eighteen Provinces. The *coup d'état* of the Empress in 1898 materially checked the sales of the Scriptures, but after the Boxer rebellion the demand increased and new applications came to the depositories for the Scriptures. In 1901 a Chinese professor in a Government School wrote for fifty English Bibles for the use of his students. In his letter he says: "The school is one of those established by the Chinese Government for educating young men in Western knowledge to be employed in its service in after life. It has been in existence over thirty years and I have been in charge of the English Department for the last twenty-seven years. My old scholars are now scattered all over the world in the Government service in the capacity of translators, interpreters, and teachers in English, but in one respect I have often felt that I have not done my duty to them, their religious training. When I speak of God, honesty, patriotism, etc., to my scholars, their eyes sparkle. Yes, there is hope for China and it lies in the young. The Bible has done good for every country and it will do good for China. I have thought upon the present condition of poor China over and over again and always have come to the conclusion that we need the Bible more than anything;—guns, machinery, and what not; so I have made application to you and you have responded in true American style. I need say no more except to beg you to convey to the Bible Society my most heart-felt thanks for the gift and to inform you that this gift will be greatly appreciated by the recipients, who actually begged me to get the Bible for them. It is the greatest book. It is the miracle of the world."

So vast a field as China could not be administered from the headquarters in Shanghai alone. Dr. Hykes has been assisted in his work by sub-agents resident, one in the capitol at Peking, now in charge of the Rev. W. S. Strong, to whom was granted the unique privilege on New Year's Day, 1913, of selling the Scriptures on the balcony of the Temple of Heaven, directly opposite the main entrance. This was the first time any one had official permission to sell Bibles or preach the gospel from this sacred place. At one of the great fairs in Peking Mr. Strong sold on an average more than 1,000 copies a day for twelve days. In Nanking Rev. James Moyes superintends work in two provinces. Further up the River of the Yangtse the Rev. F. C. Crouse, of Kiukiang, to which reference has already been made, has charge of colportage in parts of two provinces. At Hankow, the manufacturing centre of China, the Rev. Godfrey Hirst looks after distribution through three provinces. Further on up this wonderful river at Changsha, the Rev. W. S. Elliott has charge of the Hunan province, and above the rapids in Szechuan, the Rev. W. C. Hooker is stationed at Chungking, and the Rev. Thomas Torrance is stationed at Chengtu. In the South, at Canton, the Rev. Alfred Alf cares for two provinces and has a very interesting work among the immense boat population of that most characteristic Chinese city.

During Dr. Hykes first furlough in the United States in 1903, the Rev. H. V. S. Myers, assistant to the Agent, had charge of the Society's affairs; Mr. Charles F. Gammon, who had been Superintendent of colporteurs in North China, assisted Mr. Myers. Rev. W. W. Cameron, to whose work in Siam we have already referred, has also had care of the Society's affairs once or twice when Dr. Hykes was out of China and is now helping at the headquarters in Shanghai.

A notable feature of the present is the large number of Scriptures sold by voluntary Christian workers. In all there were 462 different men engaged in this voluntary distribution during the year 1914 under strict and efficient supervision, some devoting a few days or weeks and others a longer time to this work. This is a new departure and has helped to relieve the embarrassment occasioned by reduced appropriations. In addition to these voluntary workers the Society has eighty-seven paid native colporteurs directly under the Sub-Agents and forty-eight under the oversight of missionaries in their respective fields, besides forty-one under missionaries reporting direct to the Agency, a total of 176 native colporteurs, in addition to the 462 voluntary workers. Some idea of this service may be gained from the statement that the colporteurs spent altogether 42,694 days in one year in distributing the Scriptures; travelled 225,258 miles, and visited 28,453 different towns and villages.

In the first forty-two years, when the work was under the care and direction of the missionaries, the circulation amounted to 1,300,500 books. During the first eighteen years under the Agency the distribution was 3,052,688 copies, or over twice the number in three-sevenths of the time. In the twenty-one years since the appointment of

Dr. Hykes, the Agency distributed 14,318,127 volumes,[1] more than three times the entire distribution of the previous sixty years. It is also suggestive as showing the wonderful transformation which has taken place since 1908, that the circulation for the past six years (1909 to 1914 inclusive) was just double the total distribution of the first sixty years and the sales for 1914 were 50 per cent. more than the entire distribution for the forty years under the missionaries. And now the statement comes as this chapter is going through the press that the circulation for 1915 reaches the amazing total of 2,244,746 volumes.

Altogether the Society has published fourteen versions which were made for it and has assisted in the translation of five others. It has circulated 20,916,061 volumes.

As Dr. Hykes says in the close of his review of eighty-two years, "the value of its work cannot be over-estimated. It certainly has been one of the potent factors in bringing about the transformation in this ancient country, which has astonished the world. It will continue to scatter the leaves which are for its healing until the Chinese Church has its own Bible Society, produces new and improved versions of the Scriptures and circulates them among their own people."

[1] If we add the figures for 1915, just received, this should be 16,562,873 in 22 years.

CHAPTER LV

AMERICA IN THE ORIENT

THE lure of islands is, we believe, as old as the human race. There is something about a body of land all surrounded by water that is irresistible. Sancho Panza's statement to his wife is true of nations as well as individuals: "Troth, wife," quoth Sancho, "were I not in hopes to see myself ere long governor of an island, on my conscience I should not stir one inch from my own home." In the war with Spain, undertaken for the rescue of the liberties of one island, the United States not only secured another in the Atlantic, but, to its great astonishment, a whole archipelago in the distant waters of the Pacific.

The thunder of Dewey's guns in Manila Bay had not died away before the Bible Society, alert and eager, cabled to the Rev. Dr. Hykes, its Agent in China, May 14th, 1898, to improve any opportunity that should offer for sending Scriptures to the Islands. In September of the same year he was instructed to visit Manila for the sake of preliminary inquiries about any possible opening there for the distribution of Scriptures.

Dr. Hykes' report is a classic. It gave a graphic survey of the social and religious conditions in those Islands eighteen years ago. It was circulated very widely throughout the United States. It was received with unusual interest by the Senate and House of Representatives and by other leaders of the Government in Washington. We cannot do better than present here brief quotations from Dr. Hykes' report: "As soon as the ship came to anchor in Manila Bay we were made aware that we were in an American port and that it was under military rule. An army surgeon boarded the ship as health officer, and the customs official was a soldier in uniform. I secured the last room in the Hotel de Oriente, a commodious and fairly comfortable

Spanish hotel. This is the hotel in which Lallave, a colporteur sent to Manila in 1889 by the British and Foreign Bible Society, was poisoned shortly after his arrival.

"The Philippine group consists of more than 1400 islands,[1] the majority of which are mere islets or rocks projecting out of the sea. The total area is about equal to that of New England, New York, New Jersey, Delaware, and Maryland. The population is variously estimated at from 8,000,000 to 10,000,000, of which number about one-half are domesticated natives. The remainder is made up of independent hill tribes, Mestizos, Spaniards, and a few Europeans and Americans.

"Before the war there were 60,000 Spanish officials, friars, and soldiers in the islands. The Spanish half-breeds and creoles form a distinct class as well as an influential one. Among the native population the Tagals are the principal tribe in Luzon and the Visayans in the southern islands. In the mountains of nearly every one of the inhabited islands native races are to be met which are supposed to be the aboriginal inhabitants. The Negritos are to be found in most of the islands. The Igorrotes are the chief mountain tribe in Luzon. They are perhaps the best of the aboriginal races."

Dr. Hykes describes in detail, which it is not possible to reproduce here, the effect "of more than three centuries of Spanish rule in civilising and enlightening the native races." He talked with men of all classes, some of whom had been in the Philippines for more than twenty-five years, and he was convinced that "*sacerdotal despotism* and *official rapacity* were alone responsible for the rebellion." The governors monopolised the trade of their districts, they fixed their own purchasing price and sold at current market rates. No conscience was shown by any officer in his rigorous exactions from the natives. Men and women were arrested merely on a suspicion expressed by a single individual, thrown into prison without even the formality of a hearing, and allowed to remain there for years without a trial. There was no such thing as trial by jury, no writ of habeas corpus, no right of appeal. When the United States troops took

[1] Now said to be 3000.

Manila there were 2900 prisoners in the jails. An investigation was instituted, and the result was 1100 were released. The clerical and secular rivalries formed one of the disgraceful pages in the history of the Islands. The friars often usurped civil authority and openly defied the civil governors.

"The exactions and iniquities of the friars are the subjects of common conversation. Every event in a man's life is made an excuse for getting a fee. The fees in one cemetery amounted to more than $50,000 every five years. The fees of the church near the hotel at which I was stopping amounted to $100,000 per annum. It is not pleasant to write these things, but it is necessary that you may understand the conditions in these islands. I am sure that the Roman Catholics in the United States would be as much shocked as anybody at the immorality of these friars. The mass of the people are painfully ignorant in religious matters. I think it would be difficult to find a more needy field. The people are and have been without the Bible. They know there is such a book, and that is about all.

"Under Spanish rule it was impossible for the Bible Societies to do any work in the Philippines. An attempt was made in 1889 by the British and Foreign Bible Society, which in March of that year sent two colporteurs, M. Alonzo Lallave and F. deP. Castells, to Manila to try and distribute the Word of God. Shortly after their arrival and after distributing a few copies of Scriptures they were poisoned in the Hotel de Oriente, at which they were stopping. While I was in Manila I met an old resident who told me he knew Lallave, who had formerly been a Roman Catholic priest in the Philippines, and he spoke in the highest terms of his sterling character. This gentleman also told me that the hatred of the priests toward Lallave was so bitter that his body was refused burial and lay for several days in the cemetery until it was in an advanced stage of decomposition. Castells did not die from the effects of his poisoning, but was thrown into prison, at the instigation of the priests, and afterward banished from the islands."

This report was so startling that the Society immediately determined upon the appointment of an agent for this new field.

In 1822, as has been already stated in a previous chapter, Scriptures had been sent out by the Society to the Philippines through ships sailing around Cape Horn, and had been circulated in the harbours of the southern islands. Little was it imagined at that time that an agency for the translation and publication and circulation of the Scriptures would be established in these lands.

The Rev. J. C. Goodrich, B.D., just graduated from the Drew Theological Seminary, Madison, New Jersey, was chosen for this field. Under appointment of the Society, in the late summer, he left New York with his wife, via London and the Suez canal, for his new home. He arrived in Manila November 26th, 1899, and at once entered upon his labours.

The British and Foreign Bible Society had been no less active in seizing the opportunity of the opening of the Philippines to carry forward the high purposes with which they had sent out their colporteurs ten years before. They appointed a representative who went from Singapore and opened an office in Manila.

Our agent and their representative, realising the magnitude of the work before them, agreed upon a programme of co-operation which was supported by the offices in New York and London. One of the peculiar problems that faced Mr. Goodrich and his co-labourer was that of reaching the people in their native tongues. Some years before, a traveller, leisurely enjoying days in Spain, came in old Valladolid to a quiet ecclesiastical establishment that was the Mission House for the Philippines. In a conversation with the ecclesiastic in charge that benignant gentleman told the traveller that their missionaries had "taught the Filipinos Castilian and the adoration of the Virgin, and that ought to content any people." Our Agent found, however, that only a trifling percentage of the people of these islands knew Castilian and, if any real progress was to be made in reaching them with the story of the gospel, it would have to be put into their native dialects.

Here was a difficulty. There were no missionaries in the islands who had been there long resident and had acquired a knowledge of these dialects and who were also familiar with the Scriptures in their original tongues. It had been the general rule of the Society, under the advice of the Committee on Versions, to approve for publication and distribution only such versions as were made, in the New Testament from the Greek, and in the Old Testament from the Hebrew, and made by scholars capable of conveying these originals into the new dialects. To meet the exigency, which was a very real one, the Society departed from its custom and authorised its Agent to secure the best possible translations of the Gospels, in particular, into the principal dialects, using as the original either the Spanish version or the English Bible, especially the American Standard Revised version, which had just been issued and was recognised as an unusually faithful translation of the originals.

The number of dialects needing time to be brought into subjection to the gospel were many. There were said to be upward of seventy-five dialects in the islands, which could be reasonably grouped into twelve or thirteen families of languages. Instructions were given to begin work in the more important, and in order to economise energy a temporary arrangement was made with the British and Foreign Bible Society by which the American Bible Society should take certain of the dialects and that Society others.

Already by an unusual Providence portions of the New Testament had been translated by the Rev. Eric Lund, a Baptist missionary working in Spain, with the assistance of a Filipino convert; and Lallave had translated the Gospel of St. Luke into Pangasinan. Certain of these Scriptures were at Singapore and were immediately available. In the mutual adjustment the British and Foreign Bible Society continued its work, already begun, and became responsible for the following languages: Tagalog, the principal dialect of the islands, Pangasinan, and Bicol. And the American Bible Society undertook its work in the following: Pampangan, Visayan (Visayan de Iloilo, later called Panayan), Cebuan (Visayan de Cebu), Zambal, and Ilocano.

The conquest of these languages has gone on, and now, after nearly twenty years, the whole Bible has been translated and printed in the following languages: Tagalog, Pangasinan, Bicol, Ilocano, Pampangan, Panayan; the New

Testament in the following additional languages: Ibanag, Cebuan; and certain portions of the Scriptures have been translated into the following additional dialects: Igorrote, Ifugao; and beginnings have been made in Moro, Moro Lanao, and Samareno.

With the extensive development of the American school system throughout the islands, in which there are now over 500,000 children, who are all of them becoming used to the English language, and with the percentage that still speak the Spanish, the use of these dialect Scriptures may sometime pass away. But the Word of Truth already introduced into these languages has been as a cup of cold water to millions of souls that would otherwise never have tasted of the Water of Life.

For five years from the 30th of November, 1899, Mr. Goodrich was in charge of the Agency of the Philippines. Progress was made in translation, in publication, and in the circulation of the Scriptures among the people. The printing was done largely in Japan where labour and material were better and cheaper. The lack of roads, the danger of highway robbers, the islands widely separated by great inland seas,— all made the work of circulation difficult. One of the colporteurs, Mr. Gugin, starting out on a colportage tour, was never seen again. His books were found, but no information could be gathered as to his death or what had become of his body. Mr. Bear, another of the colporteurs of those early days, was attacked by the cholera early one morning and died in the evening.

Encouragement, however, to press on the work comes from statements like those made by the missionaries who were now penetrating the islands.

The Rev. James B. Rodgers, missionary of the Presbyterian Board, of Manila, says: "We find in many places that the colporteurs are the real pioneers. Because, in a great measure, of their scattering of the printed Word we gain an entrance into towns which would otherwise be difficult to reach."

The Rev. Homer C. Stuntz, Superintendent, at that time, of the Methodist Episcopal Missions in the Philippines, now one of the Bishops of the Methodist Episcopal Church, said:

"If the Bible Society did not exist, one-half the time of our own missionary staff would need to be devoted to this pioneer work of translating and distributing the Word of God." He mentions an instance where an old lady, a devout Roman Catholic, visited a chapel, was interested in what she heard, bought a New Testament, carried it back with her to her home in Malolos; and this one copy of the Scripture led, by the blessing of God, to the establishment of three churches, in which in 1905 there were 400 members.

The development of the Independent or Aglipay Church movement led to a lively demand for Scriptures, both among the clergy and the common people. The towns and villages were curious to see the Scriptures in their own dialects. Sales at first were rapid. People leaped for the Scriptures as fish in an unfished trout pool would leap for a fly.

The circulation for the year	1899 was	888
For	1900	10,873
For	1901	52,793
For	1902	91,260
For	1903	116,586
For	1904	108,354
Making a total of		380,754

volumes circulated in the five years and one month of Mr. Goodrich's service in the islands. When one considers that this was in a country where the Scriptures were unknown for three hundred years, there is cause for great rejoicing.

While Mr. Goodrich was on furlough the Rev. George A. Miller was in charge, and on Mr. Goodrich's desire to enter the pastorate in America the Rev. J. L. McLaughlin, who had already spent five years in the islands in the Methodist Episcopal Mission, was appointed Agent. Under his care the translation work has gone on rapidly.

One of the special publications was a transliterated version of the Bible in Panayan, prepared for the Society in co-operation with the American Baptist Missionary Union, by the Rev. Dr. Eric Lund, the veteran translator, whose work in Spain was ready for use in the islands at the opening of mission work there. This version is being used by Presbyterian and Baptist missionaries in Iloilo and the regions round about.

After ten years' work in the islands nearly a million volumes were put into circulation by the American Bible Society and about 700,000 by the British and Foreign Bible Society. These were distributed among the six or seven millions of people in the islands, and the Agent writes: "Probably all sincerely desiring a portion of the Scriptures have already been supplied." Now a desire must be created where none exists. Ordinary means cannot carry and plant the seed of the Word in the places where it should be planted.

Fertile in expedients, in addition to the regular colportage and the sending of special colporteurs on long and arduous journeys into regions never before visited, and to co-operation with the missionaries and the growing native ministry, a novel scheme was invented to break down the indifference and bigotry of many communities.

The cockpit is an institution all over the Philippines. In the midst of the nippa houses that make the interesting barrios and larger communities the cockpit, itself a nippa structure, rises like a Town Hall in a New England village. Thatch-roofed, it covers two or three open areas where the people congregate, in one of which the excitement surpasses belief as the crowd watches the feathered creatures fight for victory. Into these towns, in an automobile prepared especially for the purpose, the Agent goes. All about through the village he gathers an interested crowd by an electric light that burns brilliantly from his moving car. He distributes handbills announcing that in the cockpit that evening there will be an exhibition of moving pictures and that any who purchase copies of the Scriptures which he has with him will receive a ticket to the exhibition. Two Filipino boys help to handle the "outfit," and on the screen are shown Bible pictures — the story of David, the story of Samson, and stereopticon scenes from the New Testament, all of which explain some portion of the Scriptures that have been circulated. Occasionally the one who is giving the lecture will say that the further particulars of these pictures can be found in the little books which he has with him, and it is also announced that a Philippine minister will be there the next Sunday to answer any questions which the people may want to ask concerning either the pictures or the books. In this way, in villages where a colporteur in ordinary visitation from house to house would only dispose of a few Gospels, thousands actually are taken in a day; and more than that, the people are interested in them.

This has led to opposition, and in one village the priest offered to admit to a rival picture exhibit all who would come bringing the Scriptures that they had bought as tickets of admission. In this way he gathered a few hundred out of the thousands and the next day ostentatiously burned them in the public plaza.

So the experiences of the days of Tyndall and St. Paul's Churchyard in London are reproduced in Vigan. Would that like results might follow and the Philippines become, as the British Isles, filled with Bible-loving people.

In the year 1912, while Mr. McLaughlin was on furlough, the Rev. Harry Farmer was in charge.

In spite of opposition the work has gone forward, the missionary societies have their important stations, a Protestant church membership has grown up of over 60,000 souls, and multitudes of others have an awakened conscience. In this youngest of its fields the Society has circulated a million and a half of Scriptures in eight languages and dialects, into all of which these holy writings have been translated for the first time.

CHAPTER LVI

THE BIBLE IN APOSTOLIC FIELDS

SOMETIMES suggested, sometimes stated in a bald and commonplace manner, an idea springs from reading the historical parts of the Old Testament that ancient Bible lands were soaked in blood. The year 1916, when this chapter is written on the Levant Agency, offers a parallel respecting parts of those lands familiar to the Apostles, and now included in diminishing degree within the Turkish Empire. During the twenty-five years between 1891 and 1915 there were three terrible massacres in Turkey besides the latest horror of the same class connected with Turkey's participation in the war now raging in Europe. There were also several wars, and one revolution that hurled a Sultan from his throne. The story of this period in the Levant Agency, then, is a story of work in circumstances which again and again have tested the fibre of all engaged in its labours.

During the first seventeen years (ending in 1908) of this period, the wishes of an arbitrary sovereign definitely hindered the work of Bible distribution in a large part of the agency field. Turkish officials happily did not give full effect to the wish of the Sultan, but their actions resembled those of the police in a city controlled by a rapacious ring. Year after year colporteurs were arrested, had their books seized on pretence of censorship examination, and were forbidden for weeks and perhaps months to travel according to the needs of their occupation. Such hindrances were mainly encountered in the northern provinces of Asiatic Turkey, but often the whim of an official interrupted Bible work in other provinces of the Empire.

The devices used by Turkish officials to hinder circulation of the Scriptures sprang partly from a hope of extracting blackmail from the colporteurs. But they had a real dread of the tendency and the power of Bible ideas. More than once the first verse of the 27th Psalm was copied out and sent to the Minister of the Interior as subversive: "The Lord is my light and my salvation; whom shall I fear?" To a Turkish official this implied overthrow of that terror of the Sultan's officers which seemed essential to a proper control of subjects.

Such opinions made it remarkable that Bible distribution work could be performed at all. Greater troubles awaited the Agency and its colporteurs, however. In 1893 the Turkish authorities at Mush in Eastern Turkey claimed to have discovered a plot for a general insurrection among the Armenian mountaineers of the neighbouring district of Sassun. To forestall any such movement a massacre of the Armenians in the district was carried out by Turkish troops aided by civilian volunteers who would get their pay in loot from the houses. Then began a general attitude of suspicion toward Armenians in all the country which greatly hindered Bible distribution. Much hardihood was required of Armenian colporteurs who travelled.

The European governments now urged the Sultan to adopt certain measures calculated to give protection to peaceable Armenians. The Sultan, after long delay, accepted the proposals of the Powers but before they were put into execution, massacres of the Armenian population began. One after another of the cities and towns where the richest Armenian communities were settled experienced some days of slaughter. These successive massacres continued from October, 1895, during almost a year, the last great outbreak taking place at Constantinople in 1896. There some 6,000 people were killed in the streets, their homes and shops were looted, and when it became clear that the police winked at such doings, the whole city was plunged into terror. Probably at least 100,000 Armenians, many of them the choice men of the community, were killed during this year of slaughter in Asiatic Turkey.

In 1909 a bloody massacre in the main limited to Cilicia, dear to St. Paul, took place in Adana and adjoining regions south of the Taurus Mountains. Several evangelical pastors and an American missionary were among the victims of this outbreak of fanaticism.

Syria and Egypt were not much affected by the massacres of 1895 and 1896 excepting as numbers of Armenian fugitives sought refuge in those sections of the Agency. A rather picturesque incident connected with the visit of the German Emperor to Jerusalem in 1898 was the presentation to him by Mr. Freyer of Beirut, the representative of the Bible Society, of a finely bound copy of the Bible in Arabic. This gift was courteously and pleasantly accepted, but every one felt that the visit of the Emperor to Turkey in that year would harden the heart of the Sultan.

Mohammedans as well as Christians in Turkey felt that the heart and hand of the Sultan were hard, and it was an occasion for great rejoicing among the people which was reflected in all letters from the Levant Agency when in 1909 the Sultan whose despotism had seared the helpless like a red hot iron during thirty years, was dethroned. A revolution occurred in Constantinople resulting in the acceptance by the Sultan of popular demands for a constitution and a parliament. This was in July, 1908, but the Sultan prepared a counter-revolution in 1909, whereupon a Turkish army from Macedonia marched on Constantinople, captured the Sultan, and placed his brother upon the throne. Free institutions were now established, among them freedom of the press. The new "freedom" might not pass muster in America, but the only restrictions upon any Christian workers under the new order of things in Turkey were the restrictions of common sense and of the rights of others.

In 1910 disturbances began in Egypt, where the Prime Minister was assassinated, and in Albania. In 1911 Italy declared war on Turkey on account of the Turkish action in Albania and wrested from Turkey the province of Tripoli in Africa, making peace late in 1912. Almost immediately Montenegro, Bulgaria, Servia, and Greece made an alliance and by a short and sharp war in 1912 drove the Turkish army and Turkish government into Constantinople. This was followed by war over the spoils between the Balkan States; Servia and Greece fighting with Bulgaria for possession of Macedonia. This continued through the year 1913, one incident of the turmoil being the assassination of the King of Greece at Salonica. Six months later Austria declared war upon Servia, in July, 1914, and by the first week in August the great European war had commenced, into which Turkey was drawn before many months.

The Turkish statesmen had not yet been converted from government by the sword as a principle of successful rule. Successive ministries have shown a fatal facility for taking advice as mischievous as the counsel of Hushai the Archite to Absalom upon whom the Lord willed to bring punishment. As the great war progressed Turkey more and more feared disloyalty on the part of the Armenians and Greeks scattered through the Empire. It chose the course of destroying the whole Armenian nation, and the full extent of the infamies which it perpetrated with this purpose will probably never be known.

At the time when this inhuman policy was adopted there were in Asiatic Turkey within the fields of the American Board 168 American missionaries, men and women; 1,204 native assistants; 137 church centres with 13,891 communicants and an average of a little over 50,000 attendants at the regular church services. This body of evangelicals in Asiatic Turkey, reported in 1914, was the fruit of almost a hundred years of evangelistic labour; it has been deported and scattered in great measure, if not entirely destroyed along with tens of thousands of Armenian members of the ancient church.

A land devastated by calamity and catastrophe forms the largest part of the field of the Levant Agency, concerning the state of which at the end of our century this chapter must convey some true impression. It was a wonder that any field work was accomplished by the Levant Agency and its band of colporteurs during years of such unrest and panic and overturning. During the massacres of 1895 Dr. Bowen wrote that in some parts of the country colporteur work was at a complete standstill. Of course it was not safe for a colporteur to travel when the country was overrun by roving bands of men with murder in their eyes. During the whole year 1895 a colporteur was kept at work at Mosul and another at Mardin in far off Mesopotamia; but neither one ventured outside of his own city. On the whole the colporteurs showed extraordinary pluck, however, through all that year of violence, venturing out whenever there seemed to be a lull in the storm. By the end of 1897 the Agency found it possible to employ thirty-eight colporteurs in Asiatic Turkey and to help correspondents in the same region to employ forty-nine men who gave part of their time to Bible distribution.

Hindrances to Bible work in the Levant now took on a new aspect. The terrible poverty of the survivors, stripped of all their goods during the massacres, was one hindrance; a feeling of political unrest another. But another difficulty encountered at this time was a strange growth of socialistic atheism among the younger Armenians and Greeks of the Turkish Empire. A strong socialistic propaganda among the Armenians was one of the immediate consequences of the massacres.

In 1911 the Levant Agency completed seventy-five years of its existence, and Dr. Bowen was particularly anxious to have attention called to the fact that it was still alive. The circulation during the year ending January 1st, 1911, was 145,000 volumes, which was an increase by 37,000 volumes over the circulation of the previous year. The demand for Arabic Scriptures was continually growing. During the last half of those seventy-five years, that is to say since 1872, the Society had paid the Presbyterian mission press in Beirut for printing and binding 1,342,266 volumes of Arabic Scriptures. These figures represent not only the vogue enjoyed by this book, but the close relations of the Bible Society to missions.

Bible translation had been fostered in the Levant by the Society from 1830 or thereabouts. In 1900 Dr. Bowen called attention to the fact that the work of Bible translation into the different languages of the Levant was substantially accomplished. As if this fact made it possible for the aged saint to go to rest, in January, 1901, the Rev. Dr. Elias Riggs, the veteran translator of the Armenian Bible, the Bulgarian Bible, and in association with others reviser of the Turkish Bible, finished his arduous labours upon earth. He was a noble Christian and a great man. Like many other men who are truly great, Dr. Riggs was simple in his habits and never claimed recognition of his talents.

The first Balkan war broke out while Dr. Bowen was in America recuperating from a very fatiguing journey of inspection and counsel to Persia.

During the Balkan wars the Agency employed every means to distribute Scriptures among the contending armies. Scriptures could be sent from Constantinople to Salonica, under various foreign flags without great delays, but when Bulgaria was fighting with Turkey it was extremely difficult to supply the colporteurs in Bulgaria from Constantinople. Nevertheless this was done to some extent, even while the two nations were at war, and it was reported by the colporteurs working among the troops on both sides that amid all the agonies of war yearnings for the love of God and for the sense of God in daily life were more potent than ever before.

Outweighing the difficulties which confronted Bible workers in Turkey during this period, pleasant evidences of interest in the Bible appeared where least expected. In Syria, Maronite Roman Catholics of the Lebanon, commonly classed among the most bigoted of men, began to come back from America with new ideas. They were apparently freed from domination of the priests, and willing or even anxious to read the Bible. Even more remarkable changes of attitude among Mohammedans appeared in all parts of the Agency field. Colporteurs were astonished to find kindly consideration among Mohammedans instead of opposition and violence. The number of Mohammedan readers of the Bible steadily increased in Bulgaria, in Asiatic Turkey, in Syria, and notably in Egypt. They often expressed hearty admiration for the book and it gradually became clear that during almost eighty years of Bible distribution in the Turkish Empire, the Scriptures have been acquiring a certain influence among the followers of Mohammed, notwithstanding their armour of hostility to Christians. In 1913 the circulation of Scriptures among Mohammedans in the Agency was more than double that of the previous year. Notwithstanding bitterness toward Christians in general on account of war, respect for the Scriptures seems to be increasing.

After the suppression of the censorship of the press, the circulation reports showed that the Mohammedan population had become a most important part of the field to be cultivated. Again and again Mohammedans have expressed the greatest indignation at the massacre of their Christian neighbours; and it seems clear that the wide dissemination of the Scriptures is producing a radical change of attitude toward Bible Christians. At one place in Turkey a colporteur was arrested by the police at the request of a priest on a charge of "trying to make Protestants," and was taken before the governor. "Yes, yes, I know," said the governor, "he wants to make men protest against wickedness." One colporteur fell into the hands of a band of brigands. They rushed at him furiously, but when he told them that he had nothing at all excepting the Bible, the book of God, they changed their tone, released him, and said, "We know you Protestants are good people; go on your way!"

In Cairo, Egypt, a Mohammedan barber found it worth while to buy a Bible for his shop, because his customers were always glad to have that book to read while waiting their turn. In 1913 a young student in a Mohammedan theological seminary decided that he needed more education than the seminary afforded, and entered a Christian college in Turkey. His first lesson in English was in the Psalms. When he came to the 23rd Psalm he said to his teacher, "Ah, I love that Psalm!" English and Turkish Bibles side by side, he went on with his studies, more and more interested. The Beatitudes were a revelation to his mind. As he read, "Blessed are the pure in heart for they shall see God," his face became radiant. The truth had entered into his heart and from that time on he was a different man.

In Egypt it was pleasant to see an unusual interest among timid native Christians in religious work for Mohammedans. A Copt had a brother liable to be drafted into the army. After the fashion of the Orientals, when he prayed that his brother might be spared he made a vow binding himself in case his wish was granted to buy one hundred Bibles for Mohammedans. The brother was not conscripted; the money for the Bibles was paid, and this Copt gave forty of them with his own hands to Mohammedans whom he considered worthy.

The great European war smote the Levant Agency more

heavily than any previous calamity. For seven months of 1914 everything was prosperous. Then came the outburst of August and the whole appearance of the field was changed. All financial transactions were arrested by the moratorium, and travel had to wait on the pleasure of army officers. At this time in Turkey, Bulgaria, and Albania the American Board had 203 missionaries, of whom 136 were women. The devotion with which these missionaries have endured the pain in order to encourage the fearful, help the sufferers, and save life is inspiring. The missionaries in Syria have not been forced out of their stations by the war, and in Egypt missionaries have felt few of the strains under which the missionaries in Turkey have laboured. While a considerable number of these, especially the British subjects from Canada, the feeble, and some of the unmarried women, have been advised to leave the field, some missionaries remain at almost every one of the fifteen American Board mission stations in Asiatic Turkey. Wherever there are missionaries, there Bible work is going on in greater or less extent.

At the end of 1914 Rev. Dr. Bowen was handling the affairs of the Agency at Constantinople with a subagent, the Rev. Mr. Popoff of Sofia, in Bulgaria; Mr. C. A. Dana was caring for the interests of the Society in Beirut, Syria, and Mr. M. Bakhit was superintending the colporteurs in Egypt advised by Rev. W. H. Reed of the United Presbyterian mission. Egypt being a possession of Great Britain, now at war with Turkey, communication with Constantinople is entirely cut off, but before the war broke out, Mr. Reed said that the colporteurs were reaching hundreds of towns and villages unreached by any other evangelistic agency. One of the colporteurs had visited some of the oases in the desert to the west of the Nile, penetrating as far as El Obeid, the capital of Kordofan. In the Soudan the colporteurs reported that the illiteracy of the Soudanese is rapidly passing. Not one in two hundred yet knows how to read, but the desire for education seems to possess all the young folks and the schools are crowded. This implies a tendency toward extension of the field for Bible distribution. In Syria any increase of colporteurs was prevented by the war, both because of the scarcity of money and of the risks of travelling. In Bulgaria the evangelical churches quite generally celebrated the 13th of December, 1913, as Bible day, when the pastors preached on the Bible and collections were made for the Bible Society. Bulgarians in the congregation who were not Protestants were interested in the subject and contributed with the others. It is quite clear that the number of Bible readers is increasing because of the calamities of the times. At the end of the 24th year of the fourth quarter of the century the Agency had put into circulation since 1891 2,308,800 volumes of Scripture.

The Society has expended for the great work in the lands of the Near East in ninety-one years (from 1825 to the end of 1915) the sum of $2,804,104.39.

The changes which have taken place and which are impending in the Turkish Empire and the Balkan states are quite beyond measure or estimate. Turkey is shrinking, losing territory and losing power. The Armenians are wasted but not destroyed. Bulgaria, which has always been in unrest since the first Balkan war, seems now to be in a peculiarly critical condition. All that any friends of the people of this great agency can do is to remember this situation in their prayers. Let the brave words of Dr. Bowen close this chapter, for they reveal our hope for the future. Speaking in the first months of the great European war on the many problems presented by the suddenness with which the armies clashed, Dr. Bowen said: "The American Ambassador was adapted to the peculiar demands of the time. Divine Providence brought Mr. Morgenthau to the Constantinople Embassy at this time." And for himself he adds, "Difficulties cleared away, we experienced the favour of Providence. We learned lessons in those days. The more trustfully we trudged along our way, the more confirmed our strength became."

CHAPTER LVII

THE PROBLEM OF MEANS

"THE poorest way to measure life, whether it be the life of an institution or the life of an individual, is simply to count the years that have been lived. As the poet says, we should 'count life by deeds, not years!' *The* life, the great life lived in Palestine nineteen centuries ago, was compassed in all its activities within less than four years, yet it has fashioned and moulded the life of the world with ever increasing power since that date."[1]

Not because of one hundred years of existence are we to celebrate the centennial anniversary of the American Bible Society, but because during each of those years it has sent forth many Bibles. The important point in the ceaseless labour outlined in this history is that thus the deeds wrought by the Bible have been in some degree manifested and so far God has been glorified. But the story of these labours is not complete until it has made clear the vital relation to the Society and the source, in the hearts of Christian people, of the gifts of money which have made and moved the 115,000,000 Bibles issued during the century.

There is a persistent but mistaken impression abroad that sales of books ought to support the Bible Society. Sales of books each year bring in a considerable sum, but this sum is not sufficient even to pay the cost of the books printed because a very considerable number of volumes are given away to the poor, to churches, and to missionary Societies. Moreover, though this sum were sufficient to pay for printing all the books used, it would not suffice for carrying on the work of the Society.

[1] Mr. Justice Brewer of the United States Supreme Court, on Bible Day, March 6th, 1904, at Washington.

The people for whom the Society exists form a large class composed of those who have no Scriptures, those who know not where to get Scriptures, and those who do not wish to get Scriptures. This large class has power to ruin the country if it is not enlightened and brought under the influence of the Bible. The situation of the Society is something like that of our Lord when He explained to the Pharisees that He came to call not the righteous, but sinners to repentance. Money to print books is not enough to sustain the work of the Society, because the Bibles when printed have to be carried to those who have none, in every country where the Society is working.

In any missionary or benevolent institution a natural impulse is often felt by its Managers to expend the money in the treasury, expecting more at once to be given. But wise Managers will earnestly invite contributions, and at the same time act cautiously, making no plans to give even for the best of causes unless there is a reasonable probability that gifts will come in. The churches and benevolent people of the different denominations make the final decision for the Society as to its issue and distribution of Scriptures. The Board takes note of the probability of donations. When these diminish anxiety takes the place of the usual confidence respecting appropriations for the work. In 1892 the Board was shocked to discover that the contributions from churches, whether direct or through Auxiliary Societies, and those from individuals were far less than twenty-five years before.[1] It was clear if the needed books were to be provided, the Board must make special appeals for money. Books in the languages of the immigrants were especially expensive, being imported from Europe, but it was absolutely impossible to leave the immigrants in such ignorance of the Bible as was the lot of most of them on arriving in the United States. It was certain that the people if they once understood the need, would increase their subscriptions.

Such appeals caused increase in the contributions during the next year, but the plans for necessary labours could not have been carried out had not legacies in unusual amounts

[1] From Churches and individuals in 1867, $60,545 — in 1892 $37,207; and from Auxiliaries in 1867, $113,309 — in 1892, $44,093.

A FISHER OF MEN

come into the Treasury during the last months of 1893. Legacies during ten years had averaged a little more than $126,000 each year. In 1893, the year of financial panic, $247,000 came into the Treasury from this source as if to meet a foreseen need. In the year ending March, 1896, the gifts from churches, Auxiliaries and individuals were less than gifts from the same sources in 1876. The Board of Managers found in 1896, too, that while the gifts from these three sources amounted to $67,102.17, $162,240.13 had been appropriated that very year for foreign missions alone.

In this case the deficiency was supplied by legacies received during the year and by a draft upon the surplus of legacies formerly received and held over for emergencies of this class. This experience brought to the minds of the Managers the fact that the churches are continually expanding their missionary work. As missions expand, either at home or abroad, demands upon the Society for Scriptures greatly increase. The Bible Society is the servant of the churches of all denominations; but it can supply Bibles for expanded missionary enterprises only so far as the churches and their members furnish the means. It was clear that steps must be taken to inform all the churches in the country of this situation.

Whether a famine of Bibles should smite every American mission field or money be provided to print the needed Bibles was for the churches to decide. If the churches preferred to do so they could supply their missions by printing their own Bibles. The only alternative was to supply money to the Bible Society. This would be far more economical. This dilemma the Board placed before the churches. The proof of this thesis was the fact that in the year ending March, 1896, the Society issued for the home field alone 175,484 volumes of Scripture more than it did twenty years before. The following year, 1897, however, the sum of the gifts from churches, Auxiliaries, and individuals was $8,000 less than the previous year; a situation which caused great solicitude. No alternative remained but to reduce expenditures. A commencement was made by reducing grants for Bible distribution in mission fields outside of the regular agencies of the Society. For Russia, France, and Italy grants were suspended, and for Germany, the Scandinavian countries, and Austria grants were considerably reduced because of the insufficiency of contributions.

It now began to be perceived that unless the Christian public thoroughly understands what the Society is doing, the Treasury will always be so nearly empty that a very small coin makes a noise when dropped into it. This fact is illustrated by the provision made for printing Scriptures for the blind by gifts to the Society that were specially designated. People see and sympathetically feel the need of those who cannot see. Effort to help them is of a kind which no one would wish to see curtailed. One of the evidences mentioned by our Lord to convince John the Baptist in his prison cell that He was indeed the Christ, we have not failed to note, was the fact that the blind received their sight.

We have already mentioned that the whole Bible in raised letters on the system of Dr. Howe was prepared at the expense of the Society in the years from 1836 to 1843. After more than 19,000 volumes had been distributed, Mr. W. B. Waite, of the New York Institution for the Blind, in 1874 invented a new system of printing for the blind known as the New York Point system. In the Point system a single Gospel was printed in that year and the whole Bible completed in 1894. Afterwards plates for the whole Bible in another point system known as American Braille were made at the St. Louis Institute for the Blind, and placed at the disposal of the Society. The whole Bible in this system also has been issued from the Bible House.

As to the expense of providing Scriptures for the blind it has been largely met by the interest of one man in their needs. Mr. Jonathan Burr, of Chicago, happened in a Sunday School to see three persons from one family, a sister and two brothers who had been born blind and were taking part in the exercises of the school by means of a copy of the New Testament in raised letters. When Mr. Burr found that this book had come from the American Bible Society, he included in his will a legacy to the Society to form a fund of which the interest is forever to be used for the issue by the Society of books for the blind. In 1915 Mr. W. B. Waite presented to the Society a printing press of his own invention for the

New York Point system. Personal understanding of the need by Christians of sympathetic hearts led to these generous gifts.

Operations of the Society less well known are often forgotten. Of this class are the grants sent to mission fields in Europe, in Arabia, and in Persia. Some such grants have been sent to Russia where, as has been already mentioned, through a Bible Committee many thousands of Scriptures have been sent to Esthonians and where the Society co-operated with the Imperial Russian Bible Society during more than thirty years in sending colporteurs on tours of six or seven thousand miles to the Far East of Siberia, in some cases when the thermometer registered fifty-eight degrees below zero, Fahrenheit. The total number of Scriptures circulated by means of such grants of the Society in Russia during this period is 214,841 volumes, of which 4,148 volumes went to Finland.

During sixty-four years the Methodist Episcopal Mission Conference in the German Empire has been enabled to publish and circulate large numbers of Bibles and Testaments in that Christian country, where, as in the United States, many families grow up without the Bible. The total number of Scriptures printed and circulated in Germany through grants of the Society during this period was 328,927. Germany's neighbour, Austria, is the field of a mission of the American Board which during some thirty-five years has received grants for the purchase of Scriptures and their distribution by colporteurs, particularly in the land of Huss. The police in one town in Bohemia called up a young woman who was an attendant at the Protestant Chapel. "How much money did you get," was demanded, "for becoming a Protestant?" "Not a cent," the woman answered, "but we have wasted less. Father used to be a drunkard and gambled everything away. Now he is kind; the Bible has entirely changed our family." Some of the converts through this Bible work are now labouring for the Bohemians in the United States. The whole number of Scriptures circulated in Austria from 1891 to 1915 by means of these grants is 93,257.

Italy is another country to which money for Bible distribution has been sent for many years. The Waldensian churches in the region of Florence, and the Methodist Episcopal missionaries at Rome have received considerable grants from the Bible Society. The whole number of Scriptures distributed in Italy by means of these grants during the period was 34,057.

Methodist Missions in Norway, Sweden, and Denmark have been aided in the same manner and report 16,551 volumes distributed. The Bible Society of France was able to print and circulate during this period through grants from the American Society 260,270 volumes. Some of these have gone to French troops in Cochin China, and some to the camps in Madagascar. The Evangelical Society of Geneva is another organisation labouring among the country districts in France, which during this period distributed a considerable number of volumes by means of American Bible Society grants.

Other grants have gone to Persia, where the American Bible Society has been the ally of missions of the American Board during many years. For some years the work in Persia was under the supervision of the Levant Agency; then for seventeen years the Rev. Mr. Whipple carried on this Bible work as a separate Agency; and after his resignation in 1896 the American Presbyterian missionaries in Persia received grants and distributed Scriptures each year. The number of Bibles, Testaments and Portions which the Society has enabled the missionaries to send out is 44,049. During seventy-seven years the Scriptures furnished by the Society have been a main reliance of the missionary work; but in 1913 an arrangement was concluded with the British and Foreign Bible Society by which the American Society's work in Persia was transferred to it; the British Society withdrawing its Agents from Central America at the same time.

Since 1895 the Society has made grants to the Reformed Church Mission in Arabia. The grants have been used to circulate Bibles, Testaments, and Gospel Portions, for the most part in Arabic, in Oman and Muscat and other parts of Arabia lying near the head of the Persian Gulf. With the money given by the Society during this period these devoted missionaries have put in circulation 55,616 volumes of Scripture chiefly among Mohammedans and very largely by sale. The main part of the work of the mission is Bible distribution. Next to the Koran the Bible is the most talked about book among the people of that region.

The American Board's Mission in Spain has been granted sums of money to maintain two or three colporteurs and to supply them with Scriptures. It is a most difficult country in which to work. Every book sold represents a victory over superstition and avarice. The number of Scriptures circulated during the twenty-five years for the Society is 21,902.

Grants have been made by the Society to four missions in India, besides those whose printing operations have been already described. The missions of the American Board in Ceylon and in the Madura region, and of the Reformed Church in America in the Arcot district, and of the Methodist Episcopal Church in the region of Pakur in Bengal, each have had small grants to foster Bible distribution. One of the missionaries in the Madura region said that the boys and girls in the school when offered their choice would more readily take a present of a Bible than of a jack-knife or a doll. The number of Scriptures circulated in India by the grants sent to these four missions during the period was 95,702.

All these grants, though sometimes small in amount, are important in results, and should be better known among American churches who sustain the Society. The effect of failure to renew a grant which has been made annually for several years may be disastrous. In 1905 when a warning of retrenchment was sent to the missions, Rev. Dr. H. H. Jessup, of Beirut, Syria, wrote an impressive entreaty for the Board to show mercy. He pointed out that in Bible work the Presbyterian Mission Press at Beirut is the agent and servant of the American Bible Society; that to make retrenchment in the appropriations for printing would cripple the press since it derives at least three-fourths of its support from the Bible Society. Moreover, it would mean a stoppage of Bible circulation, an essential work of any Bible Society.

In 1904 the failure of contributions for Bible work was so striking that an appeal was signed by President Roosevelt, Ex-President Cleveland, Chief-Justice Fuller and Justices Harlan and Brewer of the United States Supreme Court, and nearly a score of other distinguished men, for special contributions to supply money necessary for Bible distribution at home and abroad. The central principle of this appeal was, "No thoughtful man can doubt that to decrease the circulation and use of the Bible among the people would seriously menace the highest interests of civilized humanity."

This appeal brought an increase of donations, and in 1908 Mrs. Russell Sage made a most generous offer looking toward permanent relief. She proposed to give the Society $500,000 provided it could raise within one year $500,000 more, the two sums to form an endowment fund of $1,000,000 of which the interest only may be used each year. This offer was made known widely, but as it was not received until the year was partly gone, Mrs. Sage kindly extended her offer for another year. Tens of thousands of persons contributed to the fund. Donations ranged all the way from ten cents, the lowest, to $25,000, the highest gift from any single individual. Before March 31, 1910, the whole sum of $500,000 was subscribed, and Mrs. Sage sent the Treasurer of the Society her check for $500,000.

An endowment fund of one million dollars seemed to the public enough to meet every need. Further contributions to the Bible Society seemed unnecessary. But the interest on such an endowment would at best be about four and one-half per cent., or $45,000 each year, while the estimated appropriations for 1911 called for a little more than $790,000. In three years, 1910, 1911, 1912, by the wills of Christians who had studied and appreciated the work of the Society, like Mr. Bloodgood H. Cutter, who left his entire estate to the Society, and Mr. John S. Kennedy, whose gift was the largest ever received from one individual, legacies were received amounting to $1,749,000. These were drawn upon to maintain Bible work without reduction, although the contributions from the living were far below the amount necessary for the purpose.

In 1913 it was no longer possible to avoid the conclusion that the Bible work planned would far exceed in cost the amount which the people had planned to give for it, and appropriations for the year 1914, on recommendation of the Finance Committee, were reduced twenty per cent., thus defeating at the outset plans for using new opportunities for Bible distribution made by eager Agents in different parts of the world and of the many American missionaries elsewhere with whom the Society was in correspondence. In 1914 contributions from the living increased somewhat, but they were still so much less than was needed that the Board made a further reduction of ten per cent. on appropriations for 1915. In the meantime it has been forced to draw again upon the reserve fund, formed out of the unused portion of past legacies, to pay the current bills of the year. It has been pointed out by the Finance Committee that this reserve is nearly exhausted and that the Society will be obliged to curtail its work both at home and abroad unless measures are discovered for increasing contributions.

The financial experiences of the Society have thrown into the foreground a very important principle. The relation of this Bible work to the churches of the supporting denominations needs to be close and vital. General Synods, General Conferences, General Assemblies, General Conventions and National Councils by kindly official recommendations make such a relation possible. But it is when the facts are made clear to the Church members that this vital relation becomes most precious. Then their hearts are moved to intercessory prayer, and to setting apart as the Lord has prospered them regular donations while they live, and bequests to continue their support after they have passed from earth. Then by their inner impulse they form the habit of sharing in this unique enterprise as blessed as it is great. This inner impulse can shortly be described in the words of another: "We call the Bible the Book. It is the duty of the churches to add the word 'universal' to this name; 'The Book' must become 'The Universal Book!'"

CHAPTER LVIII

THY ORDINANCES ARE MY DELIGHT

On looking back over the Society's century with the Bible, the satisfaction felt and exhibited by those who have shared in the work will furnish pitying amusement to some; the enterprise of the Society will be qualified as sheer foolishness by the united judgment of many; for it offers to those engaged in it nothing of personal gain, it holds out no allurements of aggrandisement, it permits no slackening in eager service of an unseen Master. This history admits all this. It has not concealed the self-denials, strains, anxieties, dangers, sufferings which have marked its every period. Nevertheless the enterprise has brought to those engaged in it satisfaction and unstinted happiness. This profound truth cannot fail to arrest attention on any thoughtful reading of the record.

As has been seen, the idea which led to the formation of the Society was that of obedience to the last command of our Saviour, "Go ye into all the world, and make disciples of all nations, teaching them to observe all things, whatsoever I commanded you." All recognised that this command was associated with the mission of Jesus Christ to save the world, and sprang from the eternal purpose of God. The failings, the ignorance, and the sin to be overcome by knowledge of the Most High were really characteristics of the whole race, not of any one nation or tribe. It was the interest of the people which was at stake, and since the command to teach the people made their interest supremely important, it overshadowed any interest of self. Ignorance concerning God is like the germ of a physical disease; it has a slow incubation but final effects of great virulence. That the study of the Bible can avert some dangers of this ignorance has been illustrated repeatedly in this volume. In Cuba during the Spanish War, after the fighting before Santiago, a torn, muddy New Testament was picked up on the battlefield. On the fly-leaf was written a soldier's name and regiment, and a sentence which tells the whole story of enlightenment: "July 3rd, 1898. Trenches before San Juan after night attack: This book has been a great comfort to me."

It was before the eyes of the members of the Society at the very beginning that concentrated action is powerful and that a national object unites national feeling and wins its concurrence. As Dr. Mason said in his address to the people: "The members of the Society claim their place in this new age of Bibles." The one purpose before their minds enabled them to belittle the party lines of denominations.

The purpose with which the Society began in 1816 was the increase of circulation of the Bible without note or comment. It was a beautiful, poetic thought which led the Ancient Armenian Church to call the Bible by a name which has not been lost to this day. On the back of Armenian Bibles is stamped in gold the name, "The Breath of God." The Society was to send forth the text of God's word unchanged, as pure as it came to their hands. Its work was marked out in the home land as the furnishing of books for preachers and missionaries at the frontier and the carrying of them where home missions had not yet gone. Whether the people to whom they were taken were well-bred enough to appreciate benevolent service and yet like many in our day careless enough to substitute kindly acts to others for personal conviction of sin and repentance toward God; or whether they were in total ignorance and carelessness as to their need of cleansing by the Lord Jesus Christ, the purpose of the Society was simply the carrying out of the Saviour's intent that all should know whatever he had commanded. So the Society at the very beginning stood between the ignorance of people without the gospel and their opportunity to receive what they most needed. The man with the Bible was like a friendly stranger coming to a traveller lying parched with thirst and hopeless on the ground in one of the salt deserts of Asia, and giving him fresh hope by the news that by passing over one more ridge he can find abundant water.

The method of this work was that of Jesus Christ when He used to "go on to the next towns" to carry the gospel to the people. It was a method that exhibited the simplicity and entire practicability of the effort demanded by the command to teach the nations.

The Society hoped to find and unite the best influences in the community, in the family, or in the single individual, and so to urge on the circulation of Scriptures throughout the United States. Its aim was simply to make clear and unmistakable its sympathy for all the people; and the effect of it can hardly fail to be that shadowed in the Oriental proverb which says, "Go into a crowd and beg some one to carry your burden and the crowd will melt away; but ask to bear the burden of any one, and you will always find a multitude about you." Some of these were always found to be instantly moved, some after delay. Joy was brought into desolate homes; worthless men were changed to helpers. And the result of the work throughout has been to glorify God by convincing the labourers that it was His hand which enabled the Society to place in the United States up to the first of January, 1916, about 70,000,000 copies of Scripture, besides those circulated in foreign lands.

The benefits of Bible distribution have by no means been limited to the descendants of the Americans who founded the Society. These benefits have touched the millions of immigrants flocking to our country from almost all the nations of the earth, the coloured people whose needs constituted them a class for special interest and assistance after the Civil War, and the American Indians who have shown so remarkable readiness to receive the Bible in their own tongues that one of the experienced missionaries remarked, "God turned a leaf in the history of the Indian race when the whole Bible was translated into Dakota." Still another special class which the Bible distribution has blessed is the multitude of blind who are deprived of so much that makes for joy in life. Especially does work for the blind glorify God. Was not the fact that the blind received their sight one of the evidences mentioned by our Lord to convince John the Baptist in his prison cell that Jesus was the Christ?

The orders under which the founders of the Society acted had reference to the race, and not to any one group of persons. Naturally, then, the Constitution of the Society expressed a purpose, according to ability, to extend its influence to all other countries, whether Christian, Mohammedan, or pagan. The desire was expressed by the Board in one of its reports "to embrace every opportunity to ray out by means of the Bible the light of life and immortality to such parts of the world as are destitute and within reach of the Society." It was proper that the eagerness of the Managers to do this should at least equal the eagerness of merchants who in those days shipped New England rum to many ports in Asia, Africa, and the Pacific Islands.

The duty of the Society was clear to aid American missions, furnishing them books or money for making books where translations were to be made or the printing press brought into action; and wherever the missionaries had their hands already full of work to furnish them with men who would carry the books far afield. This was no little help to a work which might have seemed hopeless were it not that all gospel workers have to remember the forces which are working in their favour as certainly as the forces with which the Creator has endowed nature. In Tennyson's "Princess" the ground of such hope is well suggested in the lines, "No rock so hard but that a little wave may beat admission in a thousand years." So the Society's aid in Bible translation and Bible printing and distribution has had a direct influence upon the progress of the missions.

It is impossible to lay too much emphasis upon the providence which since 1832 has led the Society to help missions in their translations and publications of the Scriptures. By supporting translators, by printing the finished versions, by purchasing books from other societies to furnish to American missions, theSociety has co-operated with American missionary societies, giving them Bibles speaking in 164 different languages, and carrying books in the right language to those who had no books. The development of this great feature of the Society's work in one hundred years is illustrated at home by the growth of its printing department from the twelve hand presses of 1820 to the sixteen power presses now working in the Bible House, at times day and night, in order to keep up with the demand, and abroad by other presses engaged by the Society for the same service in Constantinople, Beirut, Bangkok, Shanghai and other centres in China, Yokohama in Japan, and Seoul in Korea.

In these foreign lands the Society's Agents through their colporteurs study new fields, exploring, considering the lives of the people, gauging their religious beliefs, their worship, and their aims in life, their hopes and their prospects — all with a view to betterment of their condition. Here the Society's undertaking is like the Red Cross work in war where men are sent out to carry bandages and instruments and remedies, in a labour of compassion for helpless sufferers to be sought out on the very battlefield. In olden times God spoke by the prophets; now He speaks by the Bible. The word delivered through the prophets pulled down and destroyed social systems. Now the written word in the Bible published to the ends of the earth builds up a new social organisation upon a solid and enduring foundation. It was well said by Rev. P. F. Leavens that "The sudden and rapid ingrafting of the Sacred Scriptures upon the living languages of the world is a main feature in the providential plan to fill the earth with the knowledge of the Lord."

What makes the work abroad reasonable and obligatory is the fact that the people of the lands where the Bible is not known are exactly like ourselves in nature and aspiration, excepting that they have no light on the path wherein they would go. A nation which does not know the Bible knows neither peace nor content. "The Bible is not an aid to the people's liberty; it is the very substance of the structure from foundation up." The effect of taking the Bible into these foreign lands is that peace and security are now found in many places where they were never before known, and the help of the God of love is now enjoyed where men used vainly to seek help from a block of carved wood or stone. By the divine leading the Society has become a foreign missionary society indispensable to the success of other American foreign missionary societies, although it was organised primarily with a view to home missions.

We have mentioned the millions of Scriptures which have been placed in the home field of the Society during these hundred years. In its foreign field, according to a conservative estimate, it has distributed some 45,000,000 volumes over many lands in four continents. This great mass of Scriptures has a direct relation to the success of missionaries in the field. Expressions are continually coming to the Bible House like this from the great missions of the American Board in Turkey, which say, "The history and the work of missionary Society and Bible Society are so interwoven that we feel that our annual meeting is in a good degree a report of your work also." A Secretary of the American Board spoke of the Bible Society as "The twin propeller of missions." The Methodist Episcopal Board of Foreign Missions has told its constituency concerning the Society, "It is the indispensable and efficient ally in missionary work throughout the world." The Presbyterian General Assembly has said of the Bible Society, "It is more than ever needed now," and the organ of the Protestant Episcopal Domestic and Foreign Missionary Society mentioned not so long ago that "Missions of the Church are dependent on the Bible Society for help." The United Presbyterian missionaries on the Sobat River in the Soudan, speaking of the Gospel in Shulla printed by the Society, remark that it makes evangelism more simple and more forceful since the message becomes both audible and visible. Similar friendly words might be quoted from Baptist missions, from missions of the Friends, of the Reformed Church in America, and of other denominations.

In reading the history of what the Bible has been doing at home and in many foreign lands during a century of labour, it were well if the reader, like Moses, might be impelled to turn aside and see this wonderful thing. The use which the Holy Spirit makes of Scripture is truly wonderful. A Hottentot girl in a missionary school, rebelling against the restraints of the quiet life, one night prepared to escape to her heathen home and its freedom. Collecting her few possessions, she tossed her Bible on the floor. It fell open and she instinctively turned to lay it on a table. As she took it up Pilate's appeal to the Jews, "Shall I crucify your King?" smote her heart. She was doing just that thing, crucifying Jesus Christ afresh. That verse tamed the girl's wild spirit and made her an humble servant of Christ. The revelation of God's love has come to more than one Siamese through the last verse of the book of Jonah, where His compassion is emphasised even in the last clause of the verse. A Fiji Islander told his missionary guide that the word which won his allegiance to Jesus Christ was the word which we know has won many an American, "Come unto me all ye that labour and are heavy laden and I will give you rest." The decisive moment in the life of Joseph Neesima, the Christian educator in Japan, was reached when his eyes fell upon the first verse of Genesis, "In the beginning God . . ." For years of patient hope Dr. Morrison, the translator of the Bible, was rewarded when his Chinese scribe, Leang Afa, confessed faith in Christ. The verse which led to this Chinaman's decision was that great verse in the Gospel of St. John, "For God so loved the world that He gave His only begotten Son that whosoever believeth on Him should not perish but have everlasting life." A proud Brahman in India, after seeking in vain rest to his soul in the holy writings of his own people, chanced upon a New Testament and found what he sought when Jesus Christ there said to him, "I am the door; by me if any one enter in he shall be saved and shall go in and out and find pasture." By a thousand proofs brought from the ends of the earth the original simple purpose of increasing the circulation of the Bible has thus redounded to the glory of God by drawing attention to its power.

The Bible has now become the most popular book in the world. "The sun never sets on its gleaming page. In all countries it is the awakener of spiritual life, the creator of lofty ideals, and the messenger which brings the soul into fellowship with Jesus Christ." In all missions to-day anxiety is banished about possessing Scriptures adequate to need, about purity of the text, or about means of preserving that purity — these great interests are safe in the hands of the Bible Societies. To share in the great enterprise which accomplishes such results is a privilege, and an act of worshipful service of God who has made the Bible Society His instrument.

Happiness and perennial joy go with those who strive to increase the circulation of the Bible in obedience to our Lord's command. The nature of the command ensures this, for its source is love and its fruit is peace. The nature of the human heart implies the same result, for all workers in the Bible cause will say that no satisfaction can equal that of conscience in the doing of the right thing. The Society to-day has a great background — a past that is rich in experience. As we turn over the pages of this history and seek its teachings our conviction is fixed that the Lord is the helper of this enterprise that glorifies Him. The political world has undergone changes since the Society's infancy which would have seemed incredible to the members of the organising convention, if a prophet had foretold them. Practically all nations are open to Bible distribution. The stupendous changes yet to come are vaguely foreseen as men watch the terrible devastations of universal war convulsing the eastern hemisphere. But past experience proves that when God overturns and overturns He brings out of catastrophe new things better than men ask or think. There are greater works before us.

And so at the end of a hundred years all members and supporters of the American Bible Society, still watchful, alert as Jacob when he wrestled for the blessing, untired in obedience to the great Command, can say with the Psalmist, "Lord, thy ordinances are my delight."

APPENDIX I

MEMBERS OF THE CONVENTION IN 1816 WHICH FORMED THE SOCIETY

Bassett, Rev. John, D.D., Bushwick, N. Y.
Bayard, Samuel, Princeton, N. J.
Beecher, Rev. Lyman, *Secretary of the Convention,* Litchfield, Conn.
Biggs. Thomas J., Nassau Hall, Princeton, N. J.
Blatchford, Rev. Samuel, D.D., Lansingburg, N. Y.
Blythe, Rev. James, D.D., Lexington, Ky.
Bogart, Rev. David S., Long Island, N. J.
Bradford, Rev. John M., D.D., Albany, N. Y.
Burd, William, Lynchburg, Va.
Caldwell, John E., New York.
Callender, Levi, Catskill, N. Y.
Chester, Rev. John, Albany, N. Y.
Clarke, Matthew St. Clair, Chambersburg, Pa.
Cooley, Rev. Eli F., Cooperstown, N. Y.
Cooper, James Fenimore, Cooperstown, N. Y.
Day, Orrin, Catskill, N. Y.
Eddy, Thomas, New York.
Ford, Henry, Cayuga County, N. Y.
Forrest, Rev. Robert, Delaware County, N. Y.
Griscom, John, New York.
Hall, Rev. James, D.D., Statesville, N. C.
Henshaw, Rev. J. P. K., Baltimore, Md.
Hornblower, Joseph C., Newark, N. J.
Humphrey, Rev. Heman, Fairfield, Conn.
Jay, William, Bedford, N. Y.
Jones, Rev. David, Newark, N. J.
Lewis, Rev. Isaac, D.D., Greenwich, Conn.
Linklaen, Gen. John, Cazenovia, N. Y.
McDowell, Rev. John, Elizabethtown, N. J.
Mason, Rev. John M., D.D., New York.
Milledoler, Rev. Philip, D.D., New York.
Morse, Rev. Jedediah, D.D., Charlestown, Mass.
Mott, Valentine, M. D., New York.
Mulligan, William C., New York.

Murray, John, Jr., New York.
Neil, Rev. John, D.D., Albany, N. Y.
Nott, Rev. Eliphalet, D.D., Schenectady, N. Y.
Oliver, Rev. Andrew, Springfield, N. Y.
Platt, Isaac W., Nassau Hall, Princeton, N. J.
Proudfit, Rev. Alexander, D.D., Salem, N. Y.
Rice, Rev. John H., Richmond, Va.
Richards, Rev. James, D.D., Newark, N. J.
Romeyn, Rev. John B., D. D., *Secretary of the Convention,* New York.
Sands, Joshua, Brooklyn, N. Y.
Sayres, Rev. Gilbert H., Jamaica, N. Y.
Sedgwick, Robert, New York.
Skinner, Ichabod, Conn.
Spring, Rev. Samuel, D.D., Newburyport, Mass.
Spring, Rev. Gardiner, New York.
Swift, Gen. Joseph G., Brooklyn, N. Y.
Taylor, Rev. Nathaniel W., New Haven, Conn.
Van Sinderen, Adrian, Newton, N. Y.
Vroom, Guysbert, B., New York.
Wallace, Joshua M., *President of the Convention,* Burlington, N. J.
Warner, Henry W., New York.
Williams, Rev. John, New York.
Williams, William, Vernon, N. Y.
Wilmur, Rev. Simon, Swedesboro, N. J.
Woodhull, Rev. George S., Cranberry, N. J.
Wright, Charles, Flushing, N. Y.

APPENDIX II

TABLE OF EARLY GRANTS MADE BY THE AMERICAN BIBLE SOCIETY FOR FOREIGN LANDS [1]

Bibles in different languages	7,824	volumes	
New Testaments and portions	31,032	volumes	
Total	38,856	"	valued at $17,905.44

GRANTS OF MONEY [2]

In the 2nd year:	
Mr. F. Leo, Paris	$ 500.
Rev. Mr. Dencke for translating the Epistle of John	100.
In the 7th year:	
American Missionaries in Ceylon	500.
Missionaries in Serampore	1,033.75
In the 10th year:	
American Missionaries at Malta for Arabic Scriptures	800.
In the 13 year:	
Rev. Jonas King, Athens, for Greek Scriptures	494.44
In the 14th year:	
Baptist General Convention for Burmese Scriptures	1,200.
In the 15th year:	
American Board for missions in Ceylon	600.
Total money grants	5,228.19
Aggregate of both together	$23,133.63

[1] Including grants for American Indians, then considered foreigners.

[2] Statement of Mr. John Nitchie, Gen. Agent, Nov. 10, 1831. Managers Minutes, Vol. 4, p. 371.

APPENDIX III

PRESIDENTS OF THE SOCIETY

William H. Allen, LL.D., 1872–1880
Hon. Elias Boudinot, LL.D., 1816–1821
Hon. Luther Bradish, LL.D., 1862–1863
Theophilus A. Brouwer, 1909–1911
Hon. Enoch L. Fancher, LL.D., 1885–1900
Hon. Frederick T. Frelinghuysen, 1884–1885
Hon. Theodore Frelinghuysen, LL.D., 1846–1862
Daniel Coit Gilman, LL.D., 1903–1908
Hon. John Jay, LL.D., 1821–1827
James Lenox, Esq., 1864–1871
Hon. John Cotton Smith, LL.D., 1831–1845
Hon. Richard Varick, 1828–1831
Hon. S. Wells Williams, LL.D., 1881–1884
James Wood, Esq., 1911–

APPENDIX IV

VICE-PRESIDENTS OF THE SOCIETY

Hon. John Quincy Adams, 1818–1848
William H. Allen, LL.D., 1881–1883
Joshua L. Baily, Esq., 1913–
Hon. Charles J. Baker, 1892–1894
Hon. Simeon E. Baldwin, LL.D., 1915–
Samuel Bayard, Esq., 1831–1840
Hon. E. E. Beard, 1892–
Hon. James A. Beaver, 1896–1914
Hon. John M. Berrien, 1844–1855
Marshall S. Bidwell, Esq., 1871–1872
George I. Bodine, Esq., 1910–1913
John Bolton, Esq., 1816–1839
Hon. Luther Bradish, 1848—Pres. 1862
Hon. David Josiah Brewer, 1893–1909
Elbert A. Brinckerhoff, Esq., 1894–1913
Theophilus A. Brouwer, Esq., 1886—Pres. 1909
George Brown, Esq., 1851–1860
James M. Brown, Esq., 1882–1890
Richard P. Buck, Esq., 1871–1884
Hon. William A. Buckingham, 1865–1875
Hon. Duncan Cameron, 1821–1853
Hon. Samuel B. Capen, LL.D., 1903–1914
Hon. James H. Carlisle, LL.D., 1888–1909
Isaac Carow, Esq., 1842–1850
Robert Carter, Esq., 1878–1889
Thomas B. Carter, Esq., 1889–1898
Hon. J. L. Chamberlain, 1871–1914
Aristarchus Champion, Esq., 1844–1871
Hon. Salmon P. Chase, 1865–1873
Charles Chauncey, Esq., 1848–1859
B. Preston Clark, Esq., 1915–
Gen. Matthew Clarkson, 1816–1825
Hon. DeWitt Clinton, 1818–1828
Hon. David Clopton, 1887–1892
Thomas Cock, M.D., 1839–1869

Gen. John H. Cocke, 1844–1866
Hon. Francis M. Cockrell, 1879–
William B. Crosby, Esq., 1853–1865
William H. Crosby, Esq., 1882–1892
Hon. Paul Dillingham, 1871–1891
Hon. William P. Dillingham, 1892–
Capt. Robert Dollar, 1915–
D. B. Douglass, Esq., 1844–1845
George Douglass, Esq., 1859–1862
Hon. Francis B. Drake, 1896–1904
Hon. Robert P. Dunlap, 1837–1860
Hon. Edward H. East, 1894–1905
Hon. W. W. Ellsworth, 1849–1868
Hon. Enoch L. Fancher, LL.D., 1867—Pres. 1885
Hon. Charles W. Fairbanks, 1915–
John Forrest, M.D., 1915–
Hiram Forrester, Esq., 1882–1888
Hon. John W. Foster, 1880–
Hon. Lafayette S. Foster, 1878–1880
Hon. Frederick T. Frelinghuysen, 1864—Pres. 1884
Hon. Theodore Frelinghuysen, 1831—Pres. 1846
James N. Gamble, Esq., 1915–
William Gammell, Esq., LL.D., 1885–1889
Freeborn Garretson, Esq., 1848–1866
Hon. Merrill E. Gates, 1894–
Hon. Daniel Coit Gilman, 1896—Pres. 1903
Hon. Charles Goldsborough, 1819–1835
Hon. Grant Goodrich, 1866–1889
Hon. Simon Greenleaf, 1849–1853
John Griscom, Esq., LL.D., 1851–1852
Felix Grundy, Esq., 1816–1841
Francis Hall, Esq., 1853–1866
W. T. Hardie, Esq., 1908–
Hon. Benjamin Harrison, 1896–1901
Hon. A. B. Hasbrouck, 1851–1879
Hon. Henry P. Haven, 1875–1876
Hon. Rutherford B. Hayes, 1880–1893
Alexander Henry, Esq., 1837–1847
Horace Hitchcock, Esq., 1896–1904
Hon. Jesse L. Holman, 1837–1842
Hon. Joseph C. Hornblower, 1840–1864
Maj. Gen. O. O. Howard, 1871–1909
James M. Hoyt, Esq., 1866–1895
Hon. Charles E. Hughes, LL.D., 1915–
Hon. James Jackson, 1879–1887

Hon. John Jay, 1816—Pres. 1821
Hon. John Jay, 1885–1894
Peter A. Jay, Esq., 1828–1843
Hon. William Jay, 1843–1858
Francis S. Key, Esq., 1818–1843
Francis T. King, Esq., 1868–1891
Hon. Andrew Kirkpatrick, 1818–1831
Judge J. F. Lamb, 1908–
John Langdon, Esq., 1816–1820
Hon. Abbott Lawrence, 1849–1855
J. Edgar Leaycraft, Esq., 1914–
James Lenox, Esq., 1853—Pres. 1864
Joshua Levering, Esq., 1915–
Zechariah Lewis, Esq., 1839–1841
Hon. Heman Lincoln, 1831–1869
Hon. Joseph Lumpkin, 1853–1867
Hon. James McDowell, 1849–1852
William M'Elroy, Esq., 1880–1887
Hon. Edward McGehee, 1849–1881
Hon. James B. M'Kean, 1867–1879
Hon. John M'Lean, 1837–1861
Hon. R. B. Magruder, 1839–1844
Hon. Charles Marsh, 1824–1849
Hon. John Marshall, 1830–1836
Christopher Matthewson, Esq., 1915–
James A. Maybin, Esq., 1853–1876
Hon. Horace Maynard, 1873–1882
Hon. C. G. Memminger, 1873–1885
Annis Merrill, Esq., LL.D., 1890–1905
Hon. W. H. Millsaps, 1908–
Hon. David Lawrence Morrill, 1821–1849
Hon. Joacquin Mosquera, 1833–1844
John R. Mott, LL.D., 1915–
Hon. Daniel Murray, 1818–1820
Hon. E. A. Newton, 1851–1862
Hon. Wm. J. Northen, 1894–1913
Cyrus Northrop, LL.D., 1886–
Joseph Nourse, Esq., 1816–1842
John Belton O'Neall, Esq., 1857–1865
Cortlandt Parker, Esq., 1871–1907
Pelatiah Perit, Esq., 1859–1863
Myron Phelps, Esq., 1852–1878
Hon. William Phillips, 1820–1828
Hon. Charles Cotesworth Pinckney, 1816–1826; 1837–1864.
Hon. John Pintard, 1832–1844

Robert Ralston, Esq., 1828–1837
Judge Robert F. Raymond, 1915–
Judge George G. Reynolds, 1908–1913
Samuel Rhea, Esq., 1842–1865
William A. Robinson, Esq., 1894–
Gen. Francisco De Paula Santander, 1832–1840
Matthew T. Scott, Esq., 1853–1858
Hon. H. H. Seldomridge, 1915–
E. H. Sholl, Esq., 1908–
Hon. Jacob Sleeper, 1864–1889
Hon. John B. Smith, 1895–1914
Hon. John Cotton Smith, 1816—Pres. 1832
Hon. Edward Spalding, LL.D., 1887–1895
Hon. Alden Speare, 1901–1902
Frank E. Spooner, Esq., 1907–
John Noble Stearns, Esq., 1894–1907
Caleb Strong, Esq., 1816–1820
Hon. Wm. Strong, LL.D., 1871–1895
George H. Stuart, Esq., 1866–1889
Peter G. Stuyvesant, Esq., 1839–1847
George Suckley, Esq., 1839–1846
James Suydam, Esq., 1866–1872
Benjamin L. Swan, Esq., 1853–1866
Hon. David L. Swain, 1853–1869
Augustus Taber, Esq., 1890–1898
James H. Taft, Esq., 1890–1906
John Tappan, Esq., 1842–1871
Hon. Smith Thompson, 1816–1843
Hon. William Tilghman, 1816–1827
Hon. Daniel D. Tompkins, 1816–1825
Charles Tracy, Esq., 1873–1885
Charles E. Tracy, Esq., 1895–1896
Hon. Allen Trimble, 1844–1869
Robert Troup, Esq., 1825–1832
C. C. Trowbridge, Esq., 1871–1883
Ezra B. Tuttle, Esq., 1913–1914
Hon. Howard Van Epps, 1889–1909
Stephen Van Rensselaer, Esq., 1828–1839
Hubert Van Wagenen, Esq., 1843–1852
Col. Richard Varick, 1820—Pres. 1828
Hon. Peter D. Vroom, 1839–1873
A. R. Walsh, Esq., 1867–1884
Hon. R. H. Walworth, 1851–1867
Hon. Bushrod Washington, 1816–1830

George W. Watts, Esq., 1908–
Hon. James Whitcomb, 1851–1852
Norman White, Esq., 1865–1883
William Whitlock, Jr., Esq., 1864–1875
Hon. Elisha Whittlesey, 1857–1863
John L. Williams, Esq., 1907–1915
Gen. William Williams, 1864–1870
F. S. Winston, Esq., 1865–1884
Hon. Robert C. Winthrop, LL.D., 1864–1894
F. H. Wolcott, Esq., 1873–1883
James Wood, Esq., 1903—Pres. 1911
William W. Woolsey, Esq., 1828–1840
Hon. Thomas Worthington, 1816–1828
Hon. George G. Wright, 1871–1896
Hon. Joseph A. Wright, 1854–1867

APPENDIX V

MEMBERS OF THE BOARD OF MANAGERS

John Adams, 1819—Treasurer 1828
John Agnew, 1826–1828
George Arcularius, 1819–1820
Henry M. Alexander, 1873–1878
C. Edgar Anderson, 1911–
Andrew C. Armstrong, 1875–1900
John Aspinwall, 1816–1847
William H. Aspinwall, 1842–1875
Daniel Ayres, 1839–1840
Joshua L. Baily, 1905—V. P. 1913
Henry J. Baker, 1860–1875
James S. Baker, 1894–1905
James L. Banks, M.D., 1868–1883
Albert S. Barnes, 1872–1873
William Bayard, 1816—Declined
George D. Beatys, 1903–
Gerard Beekman, 1892–
Stephen D. Beekman, 1823–1827
Robert L. Belknap, 1879–1896
Waldron P. Belknap, 1911–
Divie Bethune, 1816–1825
Marshall S. Bidwell, 1857—V. P. 1871
Edward Kirk Billings, 1899–1908
John Bingham, 1816–1834
Jacob Binninger, 1821–1828
Nathan Bishop, 1865–1881
Garrat N. Bleecker, 1830–1834
Leonard Bleecker, 1816–1837
Cornelius N. Bliss, 1883–1884
Henry W. Bookstaver, 1886–1891
James Boorman, 1834–1854
William T. Booth, 1874–1911
Samuel W. Bowne, 1897–1898
Samuel Boyd, 1816–1839
Elbert A. Brinckerhoff, 1877—V. P. 1894
Theophilus A. Brouwer, 1864—V. P. 1886
James M. Brown, 1867—V. P. 1882
John Crosby Brown, 1877–1882; 1884–1903

Silas B. Brownell, 1912–
Richard P. Buck, 1862—V. P. 1871
Ebenezer Burrill, 1816—Declined
Duncan P. Campbell, 1816–1821
James G. Cannon, 1911–1912
Isaac Carow, 1816—V. P. 1842
Thomas Carpenter, 1816–1825
Robert Carter, 1855—V. P. 1878
John Cauldwell, 1816–1822
William A. Cauldwell, 1880–1882
William N. Chadwick, 1834–1842
Charles Chauncey, 1821–1843
Benjamin Clark, 1818–1834
Matthew Clarkson, 1898–1899
De Witt Clinton, 1816—V. P. 1818
Thomas Cock, M.D., 1834—V. P. 1839
Bowles Colgate, 1876–1886
George Colgate, 1834–1837
William Colgate, 1822–1837
Isaac Collins, 1820–1827
Thomas Collins, 1816–1818
John B. Cornell, 1885–1888
Jasper Corning, 1834–1835.
J. D. Kurtz Crook, 1889–1897
William B. Crosby, 1830—V. P. 1853
William H. Crosby, 1864–V. P. 1882.
Stephen Crowell, 1869–1876
S. Van Rensselaer Cruger, 1875–1898
A. P. Cummings, 1849–1871
Churchill H. Cutting, 1882–.
Thomas Darling, 1827–1840
John B. Dash, 1819–1821
George W. Davidson, 1915–
Henry G. De Forest, 1875–1888
Robert W. DeForest, 1888–1893
Edward Delafield, M. D., 1825–1831
Frederick Depeyster, 1816–1819
Henry Dickinson, 1866–1895
Gabriel P. Disosway, 1838–1869
William E. Dodge, 1858–1883
William E. Dodge, 1883–1887
James W. Dominick, 1830–1852
James W. Dominick, 1853–1880
James Donaldson, 1841–1872

George Douglass, 1829–1841
Cornelius Dubois, Jr., 1842–1869
Frederick S. Duncan, 1903–
Theodore Dwight, 1819–1837
John H. Earle, 1869–1891
Thomas Eddy, 1816–1828
Franklin S. Edmonds, 1914–
Alfred Edwards, 1843–1868
John Elliott, 1887–1888
Jeremiah Evarts, 1816–1831
William M. Evarts, 1858–1862
Enoch L. Fancher, 1859—V. P. 1867
Thomas Farmer, 1816—Declined
George J. Ferry, 1883–1887
Richard Fletcher, 1838–1848
Samuel A. Foot, 1843–1847
William Forrest, 1832–1865
Hiram M. Forrester, 1866—V. P. 1882
Anderson Fowler, 1903–1904
Frederick Frelinghuysen, 1886–1888
Theodore Frelinghuysen, 1906–1907
James M. Fuller, 1869–1884
Andrew Gifford, 1816–1826
A. H. Gilbert, 1900–1905
Theodore Gilman, 1883–1891
George Gosman, 1816–1819
Timothy R. Green, 1832–1840
George Griffin, 1816–1825
John Griscom, LL.D., 1828–1834
Francis Hall, 1824—V. P. 1853
William Phillips Hall, 1906–
Schureman Halsted, 1855–1869
John A. Hardenbergh, 1894–1898
William H. Harris, 1898–
Oliver Harriman, 1885–1889
John C. Havemayer, 1876–1884
William Havemeyer, 1820–1830
Richard T. Haines, 1839–1870
Timothy Hedges, 1825–1860
Cornelius Heyer, 1816–1843
Richard M. Hoe, 1911–
Daniel J. Holden, 1892–1903
Horace Holden, 1835–1862
Dyer B. Holmes, 1911–1913

Silas Holmes, 1841–1849
William W. Hoppin, Jr., 1874–1879
S. S. Howland, 1848–1853
Ezra P. Hoyt, M.D., 1898–1903
Oliver Hoyt, 1877–1887
William Hoyt, 1888–1903
Charles A. Hull, 1905–1913
E. Francis Hyde, 1894–
Henry A. Ingraham, 1915–
Henry C. Ingraham, 1898–1911
Frederick Wolcott Jackson, 1879–1904
Philip Nye Jackson, 1905–1911
Schuyler B. Jackson, 1911–1914
John Jay, 1880—V. P. 1885
Henry W. Jessup, 1901–1905
William Johnson, 1816—Declined
John Keese, 1820–1831
William Kelly, 1840–1844
Robert Lenox Kennedy, 1871–1873
A. B. Ketchum, 1905–1906
Rufus King, 1816—Declined
Leonard Kirby, 1853–1854
Caleb Knevals, 1870–1900
William G. Lambert, 1864–1883
George W. Lane, 1871–1883
Thomas M. Latimer, 1909–
James T. Leavitt, 1884–1894
J. Edgar Leaycraft, 1902—V. P. 1914
James Lenox, 1838—V. P. 1853
Charles D. Leverich, 1897–
Robert Lewis, 1888–1891
Zechariah Lewis, 1816—V. P. 1839
Eleazar Lord, 1827–1843
Edgar MacDonald, 1911–
Peter McCartee, 1816–1819
Gates W. McGarrah, 1909–1911
John S. McLean, 1892–1911
G. S. Mackenzie, 1907–
Alexander Maitland, 1897—declined; 1899–1907
Arlando Marine, 1911–
Lewis D. Mason, M.D., 1909–
Ralph Mead, 1840–1867
Elbert B. Monroe, 1890–1894
H. D. Nicoll, M.D., 1894–1908

Henry A. Oakley, 1871–1896
George P. Ockershausen, 1896–1897
Isaac Odell, 1868–1886
Robert C. Ogden, 1897–1898
Eben E. Olcott, 1914–
D. W. C. Olyphant, 1833–1841
Alexander E. Orr, 1884–1914
John E. Parsons, 1873–1903
Robert B. Parsons, 1892–1898
Samuel Parsons, 1841–1842
George Foster Peabody, 1892–1905
James W. Pearsall, 1908–
Frederick T. Peet, 1840–1867
Pelatiah Perit, 1825—V. P. 1859
Anson G. Phelps, 1848–1854
Anson G. Phelps, 1854–1858
George D. Phelps, 1848–1872
James L. Phelps, M.D., 1826–1869.
Elijah Pierson, 1828–1832
John S. Pierson, 1887–1908
James A. Punderford, 1888–1914
Peter W. Radcliff, 1819–1827
Robert Ralston, 1816—V. P. 1828
Anson D. F. Randolph, 1882–1897
James F. Randolph, 1911–
George G. Reynolds, 1887—V. P. 1908
Nathaniel Richards, 1839–1856
Edward Richardson, 1838–1858
John R. B. Rodgers, 1816–1823
Benjamin W. Rogers, 1821–1829
Henry Rogers, 1816–1834
Henry Roosevelt, 1847–1849
Daniel L. Ross, 1867–1868
Sheppard Rowland, 1906–1908
Archibald Russell, 1840–1871
Henry Rutgers, 1816–1830
Joshua Sands, 1816–1819
William J. Schieffelin, 1896–
T. G. Sellew, 1889–1913
George I. Seney, 1865–1875
John Sergeant, 1830–1848
Thomas L. Servoss, 1838–1849
Smith Sheldon, 1872–1884
Thomas Shields, 1816–1821

Lemuel Skidmore, 1884–1892
William L. Skidmore, 1877–1897
John Slosson, 1843–1848
William Alexander Smith, 1882–1883
William A. Spencer, 1849–1854
William H. Spencer, 1912–
John P. Stagg, 1834–1836
Edmund D. Stanton, 1873–1874
Chandler Starr, 1853–1857; 1861–1876
Henry S. Stearns, M.D., 1899–
John Noble Stearns, 1874—V. P. 1894
William F. Stearns, 1873–1874
George E. Sterry, 1891–1908
John A. Stewart, 1878–1891
Thomas Stokes, 1816–1833
J. Marshall Stuart, 1913–
Frederick Sturges, 1875–1911
Jonathan Sturges, 1853–1874
Peter G. Stuyvesant, 1831—V. P. 1839
George Suckley, 1816—V. P. 1839
James Suydam, 1848—V. P. 1866
Benjamin L. Swan, 1828—V. P. 1853
J. G. Swift, 1816–1828
Augustus Taber, 1868—V. P. 1890
John R. Taber, 1905–
James H. Taft, 1871—V. P. 1890
Charles N. Talbot, 1848–1872
Arthur Tappan, 1828–1834
Jeremiah H. Taylor, 1838–1840
Najah Taylor, 1828–1860
Edward P. Tenney, 1898–1912
Charles Tracy, 1850—V. P. 1873
Charles E. Tracy, 1885—V. P. 1895
Charles H. Trask, 1884–1897
John Truslow, 1890–1903
Frederic M. Turner, 1905–1912
Ezra B. Tuttle, 1893—V. P. 1913
Winthrop M. Tuttle, 1915–
Charles Unangst, 1915–
Joshua M. Van Cott, 1873–1876
Cornelius Vanderbilt, 1883–1884
Abraham Van Nest, 1831–1832
Alexander Van Rensselaer, 1853–1878
Stephen Van Rensselaer, 1816—V. P. 1828

Adrian Van Sinderen, 1830–1838
Hubert Van Wagenen, 1823–1836
Washington R. Vermilye, 1853–1876
A. R. Walsh, 1843—V. P. 1867
Samuel Ward, 1835–1838
John Warder, 1816–1828
George Warner, 1816–1825
John H. Washburn, 1895–1899
John Watts, M.D., 1816–1831
Norman White, 1840—V. P. 1865
Thomas Whitaker, 1897–1914
James Wiggins, 1909–1913
S. V. S. Wilder, 1831–1843
Marinus Willet, M.D., 1831–1841
Mornay Williams, 1915–
Peter Wilson, 1816–1819
F. S. Winston, 1839—V. P. 1865
William Winterton, 1833–1837
Francis B. Winthrop, 1819–1823
F. H. Wolcott, 1852—V. P. 1873
John David Wolfe, 1854–1869
Howard O. Wood, 1913–
Isaac Wood, M.D., 1842–1868
James Wood, 1896—V. P. 1903
William H. S. Wood, 1878–1894
B. L. Woolley, 1836–1850
Edward J. Woolsey, 1844–1872
William W. Woolsey, 1816—Treasurer 1820
Charles Wright, 1816–1820
O. F. Zollikoffer, 1896–1897

APPENDIX VI

CORRESPONDING SECRETARIES OF THE SOCIETY

Rev. Nathan Bangs, D.D., 1827–1829
Rev. John C. Brigham, D.D., 1827–1862
Rev. Spencer H. Cone, D.D., 1833–1836
Rev. John Fox, D.D., 1898–
Rev. Edward W. Gilman, D.D., 1871–1900
Rev. William I. Haven, D.D., 1898–
Rev. Joseph Holdich, D.D., 1849–1878
Rev. Albert S. Hunt, D.D., 1878–1898
Rev. Edward P. Ingersoll, D.D., 1901–1906
Rev. Thomas McAuley, D.D., LL.D., 1825–1839
Rev. Alexander McLean, D.D., 1874–1898
Rev. James H. McNeill, 1853–1861
Rev. John M. Mason, D.D., 1816–1820
Rev. James Milnor, D.D., 1819–1840
Rev. Samuel Irenaeus Prime, D.D., 1849–1850
Rev. John B. Romeyn, D.D., 1816–1819
Rev. T. Ralston Smith, D.D., 1866–1871
Rev. Charles G. Sommers, D.D., 1825–1833
Rev. Joseph C. Stiles, 1850–1852
Rev. Wm. J. R. Taylor, D.D., 1874–1892
Rev. Selah Strong Woodhull, D.D., 1820–1825

FINANCIAL SECRETARY

Rev. Edmund S. Janes, D.D., 1840–1844
Rev. Noah Levings, 1844–1849

TREASURERS

John Adams, Esq., 1828–1832
Garrett N. Bleecker, Esq., 1832
William Foulke, Esq., 1886–
Abraham Keyser, Esq., 1838–1840
John Nitchie, Esq., 1836–1838
Hubert Van Wagenen, Esq., 1832–1836
Hon. Richard Varick, 1816–1820

William Whitlock, Jr., Esq., 1840–1875
William W. Woolsey, Esq., 1820–1827

RECORDING SECRETARY AND ACCOUNTANT

J. Pintard, LL.D., 1816–1832
Robert F. Winslow, Esq., 1832–1836

RECORDING SECRETARY

Rev. Henry Otis Dwight, LL.D., 1907–

AGENT

John E. Caldwell, Esq., 1818–1819

AGENT AND ACCOUNTANT

John Nitchie, Esq., 1819–1832

GENERAL AGENT

Caleb T. Rowe, Esq., 1854–1898

GENERAL AGENT AND ASSISTANT TREASURER

Joseph Hyde, Esq., 1836–1854
John Nitchie, Esq., 1832–1836

ASSISTANT TREASURER

Henry Fisher, Esq., 1853–1869
Andrew L. Taylor, Esq., 1869–1886

ASSISTANT CORRESPONDING SECRETARY

Rev. L. B. Chamberlain, M.A., 1915–

ACTING RECORDING SECRETARY

Rev. Henry J. Scudder, B.D., 1914–

EDITOR AND LIBRARIAN

Rev. George Bush, 1835–1839

APPENDIX VII

MINISTERS WHO HAVE SERVED OR ARE SERVING ON COMMITTEES OF THE BOARD

Rev. William Adams, D.D., 1846–1881
Rev. J. W. Alexander, D.D., 1846–1849; 1854–1858
Rev. Rees F. Alsop, D.D., 1914–
Rt. Rev. E. G. Andrews, D.D., 1888–1907
Rev. W. W. Atterbury, D.D., 1899–1912
Rev. L. W. Bancroft, D.D., 1883–1890
Rev. G. T. Bedell, 1846–1860
Rev. D. Bigler, 1850–1856
Rev. Nehemiah Boynton, D.D., 1905–1906
Rev. Cornelius Brett, D.D., 1892–1906
Rev. W. I. Budington, D.D., 1861–1874
Rev. Henry A. Buttz, D.D., 1897–
Rev. S. Parkes Cadman, D.D., 1907–
Rev. Wm. H. Campbell, D.D., 1858–1873
Rev. T. W. Chambers, D.D., 1873–1896
Rev. G. B. Cheever, D.D., 1846–1861
Rev. A. Huntington Clapp, D.D., 1871–1886
Rev. Rufus W. Clark, D.D., 1859–1861
Rev. Henry Evertson Cobb, D.D., 1914–
Rev. Edward B. Coe, D.D., LL.D., 1900–1914
Rev. D. B. Coe, D.D., 1874–1888
Rev. George R. Crooks, D.D., 1881–1897
Rev. George R. Crooks, D.D., 1860–1862
Rev. Howard Crosby, D.D., LL.D., 1880–1891
Rev. John R. Davies, 1896–1899
Rev. John DeWitt, D.D., LL.D., 1897–1913
Rev. Thomas De Witt, D.D., 1846–1873
Rev. Richard B. Duane, 1871–1875
Rev. Howard Duffield, 1892–1906
Rev. Isaac Ferris, D.D., 1846–1873
Rev. James Floy, D.D., 1853–1857
Rev. Archibald C. Foss, 1865–1869
Rev. Cyrus D. Foss, 1869–1876
Rev. R. S. Foster, 1851–1852
Rev. Wm. H. Foulkes, D.D., 1912–1913

Rev. C. A. Goodrich, 1858–1860
Rt. Rev. D. A. Goodsell, D.D., 1908–1909
Rev. Wm. Green, D.D., LL.D., 1892–1897
Rev. W. L. Harris, D.D., 1877–1887
Rev. Thomas S. Hastings, 1864–1868; 1871–1874
Rev. Albert S. Hunt, D.D., 1866–1878
Rev. J. F. Hurst, D.D., 1876–1881
Rev. Mancius S. Hutton, D.D., 1848–1880
Rev. E. P. Ingersoll, D.D., 1890–1892; 1898–1902
Rev. R. E. Inglis, D.D., 1915–
Rt. Rev. E. S. Janes, D.D., 1846–1876
Rev. E. H. Jewett, D.D., 1890–1899
Rev. Lot Jones, 1858–1866
Rev. Wm. V. Kelley, D.D., 1898–
Rev. James M. King, 1878–1899
Rev. C. P. Krauth, D.D., 1875–1883
Rev. John M. Krebs, D.D., 1854–1868
Rev. G. T. Krotel, D.D., 1868–1907
Rev. Joseph H. Kummer, 1865–1866
Rev. W. J. Lindsay, 1862–1865
Rev. James MacDonald, 1850–1854
Rev. J. McGoffin M'Auley, 1847–1848
Rev. Thomas McAuley, D.D., 1846–1847
Rev. E. McChesney, D.D., 1888–1898
Rev. J. McClintock, D.D., 1848–1853; 1858–1860
Rev. J. W. McLane, 1848–1864
Rev. John McLeod, D.D., 1857–1873
Rev. T. B. McLeod, D.D., 1900–1905
Rev. Stephen Martindale, 1846–1849
Rev. Henry E. Montgomery, D.D., 1866–1869
Rev. J. O. Murray, 1867–1871
Rev. William H. Norris, 1857–1866
Rev. F. M. North, D.D., 1902–
Rev. Howard Osgood, D.D., 1878–1882
Rev. Ray Palmer, D.D., 1867–1871
Rev. George Peck, D.D., 1846–1849
Rev. Henry C. Potter, D.D., 1882–1883
Rev. George Potts, D.D., 1853–1855; 1858–1865
Rev. Howell Powell, D.D., 1871–1875
Rev. J. E. Rankin, 1886–1890
Rev. C. H. Read, 1846–1848
Rev. John M. Reid, 1855–1857
Rev. A. A. Reinke, 1886–1890
Rev. J. B. Remensnyder, D.D., LL.D., 1907–
Rev. N. L. Rice, D.D., 1865–1867

Rev. James F. Riggs, D.D., 1897–
Rev. William Roberts, D.D., 1865–1869
Rev. Edward Robinson, D.D., 1846–1858
Rev. E. P. Rogers, D.D., 1880–1882
Rev. Philip Schaff, D.D., 1866–1874
Rev. Henry J. Schmidt, D.D., 1858–1874
Rev. M. L. Scudder, 1852–1855
Rev. J. Preston Searle, D.D., 1914–
Rev. E. T. Senseman, 1856–1861
Rev. Wm. G. R. Shedd, D.D., 1864–1872
Rev. George Shelton, 1858–1863
Rev. Daniel Smith, 1849–1851
Rev. Henry B. Smith, D.D., 1858–1874
Rev. John Cotton Smith, D.D., 1860–1882
Rev. T. Ralston Smith, D.D., 1871–1879
Rev. W. Snodgrass, D.D., 1849–1850
Rev. Gardiner Spring, D.D., 1846–1864
Rev. Joseph C. Stiles, 1851–1853
Rev. Ross Stevenson, 1915–
Rev. H. A. Stimson, D.D., 1907–
Rev. Charles F. E. Stohlmann, D.D., 1861–1869
Rev. R. S. Storrs, Jr., D.D., 1848–1858
Rev. Wm. J. R. Taylor, D.D., 1874–1892
Rev. Wm. M. Taylor, D.D., 1884–1895
Rev. J. P. Thompson, D.D., 1847–1850; 1864–1865
Rev. Charles C. Tiffany, D.D., 1899–1905
Rev. Wm. R. Tompkins, 1861–1867
Rev. Samuel H. Turner, D.D., 1846–1858
Rev. B. B. Tyler, D.D., 1890–1897
Rev. Stephen H. Tyng, D.D., 1846–1858
Rev. H. J. Van Dyke, Jr., D.D., 1887–1892
Rev. T. E. Vermilye, D.D., 1846–1858
Rev. Alexander H. Vinton, D.D., 1864–1870
Rev. S. H. Virgin, D.D., 1888–1901
Rev. William Hayes Ward, D.D., LL.D., 1895–
Rev. J. B. Weston, D.D., 1897–1908
Rev. Erskine N. White, D.D., 1876–1887
Rev. Wm. R. Williams, D.D., 1846–1847; 1858–1874
Rt. Rev. Luther B. Wilson, D.D., 1912–
Rev. Theodore Woolsey, D.D., LL.D., 1861–1884.

APPENDIX VIII

REGULATIONS RESPECTING APPROPRIATIONS FOR EXPENSE INCURRED IN TRANSLATING THE SCRIPTURES

1. Upon the application of Missionary Societies, annual appropriations will be made to them toward defraying the current expenses of translation.

2. If the time and services of a missionary, approved by this Board, are wholly given to the work of translating the Bible, the Board will provide for his support during the time necessary for accomplishing the work; but if only part of his time is given to it, a proportionate allowance will be made.

3. Such charges for the services of native scribes and helpers as may be approved by a committee of missionaries in the same field, may fairly be added to those for the support of the principal translator.

4. The Board will expect annual reports of the work accomplished and the time devoted to it; and the version, while in progress and when completed, will be regarded as the property of the American Bible Society.

5. In appropriating money for the translation, printing, and distribution of the Sacred Scriptures in foreign languages, the Managers feel at liberty to encourage only such versions as conform, in the principles of their translation, to the common English version, at least so far that all the religious denominations represented in this Society can consistently use and circulate said versions in their several schools and communities.

6. No translation shall be printed and published with the funds of the American Bible Society until a committee of missionaries or others, skilled in the language, shall have given it their approbation, except in cases where no such committee of revision can be procured.

APPENDIX IX

REGULATIONS RESPECTING THE PUBLICATION AND DISTRIBUTION OF THE SCRIPTURES IN FOREIGN LANDS

1. Upon the recommendation of the Committee on Distribution, grants of books and appropriations of money will be made by the American Bible Society to Missionary Societies and others, to promote the circulation of the Holy Scriptures in foreign lands.

2. The principal objects to be had in view, in making appropriations of funds, are the following:

(a) To meet the expense of printing and binding the Scriptures in versions which have received the previous approval of the Board of Managers, it being deemed essential for such approval that the version be faithfully translated from the original, and that it be free from objection on denominational grounds. The publication must be in the form of complete portions of Scripture without note or comment.

(b) To purchase copies of the Scriptures which, though not published by the Society, have received its sanction.

(c) To pay the necessary expense of transportation of books to the places of distribution.

(d) To pay the expense of distributing the Scriptures by the agency of native believers, when their employment has been authorized by the Society.

3. As a rule, even among the heathen, the Scriptures should be sold at some price, although that may be much less than the cost.

The proceeds of sales of books granted by this Society, or printed with its funds and afterward sold, should be put again at its disposal. Unexpended funds, and books left on hand which are not needed, should be held subject to its orders. From each Mission annual statements will be expected, exhibiting in detail the amounts of money received and expended, and showing also the extent of distribution and the stock of books remaining on hand. Narratives of incidents connected with the work are also desired for publication in the "Bible Society Record."

4. Applications for funds should reach the Society early in

the month of February of each year, that the annual appropriations may be made by the Board on the first Thursday of March.

The American Bible Society expects that due credit will be given for its donations, by those to whom its grants are confided for distribution.

APPENDIX X

LIST OF 164 LANGUAGES IN WHICH THE TRANSLATION, PRINTING, OR DISTRIBUTION OF THE SCRIPTURES HAVE BEEN PROMOTED BY THE SOCIETY

Ainu
Albanian
Amharic, Abyssina
Arabic
Arapahoe, American Indian
Armenian (Ancient)
Armenian (Modern)
Armenian (Ararat)
Armeno-Turkish
Arrawack, Guiana
Azerbaijan Turkish
Benga, West Africa
Bengali
Bengali (Roman)
Bicol, Philippines
Bohemian
Bohemian-Slovak
Bulgarian
Bulu, West Africa
Burmese
Chinese, Mandarin, Peking
" Swatow Colloquial
" Swatow Colloquial (Roman)
" Mandarin, Bp. Schereschewski
" Mandarin, Union Version
" Mandarin (Roman)
" Classical (Wenli)
" Classical, Bridgman, Culbertson and Boone
Chinese, Classical, Union Version
" Easy Wenli, Union Version
" Easy Wenli, Blodgett and Burdon Version
" Easy Wenli, Schereschewski Version
" Canton Colloquial
" Canton Colloquial (Roman)
" Fuchow Colloquial
" Hinghua Colloquial (Roman)
" Ningpo Colloquial
" Peking Colloquial (Roman)
" Shanghai Colloquial
" Shanghai Colloquial (Roman)
" Shantung Colloquial (Roman)
" Suchow Colloquial
" Sam Kiong Colloquial
Cambodian
Cebuan (Visayan), Philippines
Chamorro, Guam
Cherokee, American Indian
Chimanyika, Africa
Choctaw, American Indian

Creolese, Curacao
Croatian
Dakota, American Indian
Danish
Delaware, American Indian
Dikele, West Africa
Dutch
English
" American revised version
Esperanto
Esthonian, Reval, Russia
Fijian
Finnish
Flemish, Belgium
French
Gaelic
Galla, Borders of Abyssinia
German
Gilbert Islands, Micronesia
Grebo, Liberia
Greco-Turkish
Greek, Ancient
Greek, Modern
Gujerati, India
Hawaiian
Hebrew
Hebrew-Arabic
Hebrew-Spanish
Hindi
Hungarian
Ibanag, Philippines
Icelandic
Ifugao, Philippines
Ilocano, Philippines
Irish
Italian
Japanese
" Kunten (Chinese Letters)
" (Roman)
Javanese
Karen (Sgau)
Kurdish (Armenian letters)
Kurdish (Arabic letters)
Korean (Eunmun)
" (Mixed Script)
Kusaien, Micronesia
Lanao Moro, Philippines
Laos, Siam
Latin
Lettish
Lithuanian
Luragoli, Kavirondo-West Africa
Malay
Marathi, India
Marshall Islands, Micronesia
Mohawk, American Indian
Mongolian, Lake Baikal
Mortlock Islands, Micronesia
Mpongwe, West Africa
Muskokee, American Indian
Nauru, Micronesia
Navaho, American Indian
Nez Perces, American Indian
Norwegian
Ojibwa, American Indian
Pahari, India
Pampangan, Philippines
Pangasinan, Philippines
Panayan (Visayan)
Panjabi, India
Persian
Polish
Ponape, Micronesia
Portuguese
Portuguese Revised
Quechua
Roumanian
Ruk, Micronesia
Russian
Ruthenian
Samareno (Visayan)
Sanskirt, India
Santali-Bengali, India
Scottish "Broad"
Sechuana, Africa

Seneca, American Indian
Servian
Sesuto, South Africa
Shan, Burma
Sheetswa, East Africa
Shulla or Shilluk, Africa
Siamese
Singhalese (Ceylon)
Slavic
Slovak
Slovenian
Spanish, Moderna
" Scio
" Valera
Swedish
Syriac (Ancient)
" (Modern)
Tagalog, Philippines
Talain or Pequin, India
Tamil, India
Telugu, India
Tonga, East Africa
Turkish
Urdu or Hindustani
Uriya, Orissa, India
Visayan or Bisayan, see Cebuan, Panayan, and Samareno
Welsh
Wolof, West Africa
Yiddish
Zambal
Zapotec
Zulu

EMBOSSED SCRIPTURES FOR THE BLIND, 14 LANGUAGES AND SYSTEMS

Arabic, Braille System
Arabic, Moon System
Armenian, Braille System
Armeno-Turkish, Braille System
Chinese, Mandarin, Braille
English, Boston Line Letter
English, New York Point
English, American Braille System
English, Moon System
Japanese, Braille System
Korean, New York Point
Portuguese, Braille System
Siamese, Braille System
Spanish, Braille System

APPENDIX XI

NAMES OF MISSIONARY TRANSLATORS OR REVISERS AIDED OR SUPPORTED BY THE SOCIETY

American Indians:

Ainslee, Rev. George,	Nez Perces
Allan, Rev. George,	Quechua, Peru
Brink, Rev. L. P.,	Navaho
Buckner, Dr. H. F.,	Muskokee
Hall, Rev. Sherman,	Ojibwa
James, Dr. Edwin,	Ojibwa
McDonald, Archdeacon Robert,	Ojibwa
Ramsay, Rev. J. R.,	Muskokee
Riggs, Rev. S. R.,	Dakota
Roberts, Rev. J.,	Arapahoe
Robertson, Mrs. A. E. W.,	Muskokee
Spalding, Rev. H. H.,	Nez Perces
Stucki, Rev. J.,	Winnebago
Torrey, Rev. C. C.,	Cherokee
Turner, Mrs. C. M.,	Quechua, Peru
Williamson, Rev. T. S.,	Dakota
Worcester, Rev. S. A.,	Cherokee
Wright, Rev. A.,	Choctaw, Seneca

Africa:

Bushnell, Rev. Albert,	Mpongwe, Dikele
Dorward, Rev. Mr.,	Zulu
Frazer, Rev. M. E.,	Bulu
Good, Rev. A. C.,	Bulu
Kilbon, Rev. C. W.,	Zulu
McCleary, Rev. C. W.,	Bulu
Nauer, Rev. F. G.,	Benga
Ousley, Rev. Benjamin,	Sheetswa
Payne, Rt. Rev. John,	Grebo
Preston, Rev. I. M.,	Dikele
Rees, Rev. E. J.,	Luragoli
Richards, Rev. E. H.,	Sheetswa, Tonga
Rood, Rev. I.,	Zulu
Taylor, Rev. J. D.,	Zulu
Wilcox, Rev. W. C.,	Zulu
Wilder, Rev. G. E.,	Zulu
Wilson, Rev. D. A.,	Mpongwe

China:

Aiken, Rev. E. E.,	Mandarin, Union
Allan, Rev. C. N.,	Mandarin, "
Baldwin, Rev. C. C.,	Fuchow Colloquial
Baldwin, Rev. S. L.,	" "
Baller, Rev. F. W.,	Mandarin, Union
Blodgett, Rev. H.,	Mandarin, Easy Wenli
Box, Rev. E.,	Shanghai Colloquial
Bramfitt, Rev. Thomas,	Mandarin, Union
Brewster, Dr.,	Hinghua Colloquial
Bridgman, Dr. E. C.,	Wenli (Classical)
Burdon, Rt. Rev. J. S.,	Mandarin, Easy Wenli
Chalmers, Rev. John,	Wenli (Classical, Union)
Chestnut, Miss Eleanor, M.D.,	Sam Kiong Colloquial
Clayton, Rev. G. A.,	Mandarin (in Braille)
Culbertson, Rev. M. S.,	Wenli (Classical)
Davis, Rev. D. H.,	Shanghai Colloquial
Davis, Rev. John W.,	Easy Wenli, Union
Edkins, Rev. Dr. Jos.,	Wenli (Classical), Union
Farnham, Rev. Dr.,	Shanghai Colloquial, Union
Fitch, Rev. G. F.,	Suchow dialect
Genahr, Rev. I.,	Easy Wenli, Union
Gibson, Rev. J. G.,	Swatow, Easy Wenli, Union
Graves, Rev. R. H.,	Canton dialect, Easy Wenli, Union
Goodrich, Rev. C.,	Mandarin, Union
Happer, Rev. Dr.,	Canton Colloquial
Henry, Rev. Dr.,	" "
Hykes, Rev. J. R.,	Mandarin
Judd, Rev. C. H.,	Shantung, Colloquial
Lewis, Rev. Spencer,	Mandarin, Union
Lloyd, Rev. Mr.,	Wenli (Classical), Union
Lowrie, Mrs. R.,	Peking Colloquial
Maclagan, Rev. P. J.,	Wenli (Classical)
Mateer, Rev. C. W.,	Mandarin, Union
Martin, Rev. W. A. P.,	Mandarin
Nagel, Rev. A.,	Wenli (Classical), Union
Nevius, Rev. J. L.,	Mandarin, Union
Noyes, Rev. Dr.,	Canton, Colloquial
Owen, Rev. George,	Mandarin, Union
Parker, Rev. A. P.,	Easy Wenli
Pearce, Rev. T. W.,	Wenli (Classical), Union
Schaub, Rev. M.,	" (Classical)

Schereschewski, Rt. Rev. S. I. J.,	Mandarin, Easy Wenli
Sheffield, Rev. D. Z.,	Wenli (Classical), Union
Silsby, Rev. J. A.,	Shanghai Colloquial
Thomson, Archdeacon,	Shanghai Colloquial
Wherry, Rev. J.,	Wenli (Classical), Union
Ware, Rev. James,	Shanghai Colloquial
Woodin, Rev. Dr.,	Foochow Colloquial

Hawaii:

Andrews, Rev. L.,	Hawaiian
Bingham, Rev. Hiram,	"
Bishop, Rev. A.,	"
Clark, Rev. E. W.,	"
Dibble, Rev. S.,	"
Green, Rev. J. S.,	"
Richards, Rev. W.,	"
Thurston, Rev. A.,	"

India:

Ballantine, Rev. H.,	Marathi
Bate, Rev. J.,	Hindi
Bateman, Rev. R.,	Urdu
Chamberlain, Rev. Jacob,	Telugu
Hall, Rev. Gordon,	Marathi
Hay, Rev. J.,	Telugu
Janvier, Rev. L.,	Panjabi
Newell, Rev. Samuel,	Marathi
Newton, Rev. E. P.,	Panjabi
Newton, Rev. John,	Panjabi
Sutton, Rev. A.,	Uriya (Orissa)
Tracy, Rev. W.,	Tamil
Winslow, Rev. M.,	Tamil

Japan:

Amerman, Rev. J. L.,	Japanese Colloquial
Batchelor, Rev. J.,	Ainu
Brown, Rev. S. R.,	Japanese
Davison, R. C. S.,	"
Fyson, Rt. Rev. P. K.,	"
Foss, Rt. Rev. H. F.,	"
Greene, Rev. D. C.,	"
Gutzlaff, Rev. Charles,	"
Harrington, Rev. C. K.,	"
Hepburn, Dr. J. C.,	"

Learned, Rev. D. W.,	Japanese
Piper, Rev. John,	"
Maclay, Rev. R. S.,	"
Verbeck, Rev. G. F.,	"
Williams, Rt. Rev. D. C.,	Chino-Japanese
Korea:	
Appenzeller, Rev. H. G.,	Korean
Gale, Rev. J. S.,	"
Jones, Rev. G. H.,	"
Moffet, Rev. S. A.,	"
Reynolds, Rev. W. B.,	"
Scranton, Dr. W. B.,	"
Trollope, Rev. M. N.,	"
Underwood, Rev. H. G.,	"
Micronesia:	
Bingham, Rev. Hiram, Jr.,	Gilbert Islands
Delaporte, Rev. P. A.,	Nauru
Doane, Rev. E. T.,	Ebon (Marshall Islands) Ponape
Gulick, Rev. L. H.,	Ponape
Logan, Rev. R. W.,	Mortlock, Ruk
Pease, Rev. E. M.,	Ebon (Marshall Islands)
Pierson, Rev. G.,	Ebon (Marshall Islands)
Price, Rev. F. M.,	Ruk, Chamorro
Rife, Rev. C. W., M.D.,	Marshall Islands
Snow, Rev. B. G.,	Ebon (Marshall Islands) Kusaien
Sturges, Rev. A. A.,	Ponape
Whitney, Rev. J. F.,	Ebon (Marshall Islands)
Philippines:	
Conant, Mr. E. C.,	Pampangan
Goodrich, Rev. J. C.,	Ilocano
Hanna, Rev. W. H.,	Ilocano
Lund, Rev. Eric,	Visayan of Panay
Mumma, Rev. M. W.,	Ilocano
Peterson, Rev. B. O.,	Ilocano
Williams, Rev. P. H.,	Ilocano
Siam:	
Bradley, Rev. D. B.,	Siamese
Carrington, Rev. John,	Siamese
Dunlap, Rev. E. P.,	Siamese
Irwin, Rev. Robert,	Laos
McClure, Rev. W. G.,	Siamese

McGilvary, Mrs. Daniel,	Laos
McGilvary, Rev. E. B.,	Laos
McKean, Dr. J. W.,	Laos
Mattoon, Rev. S.,	Siamese
Van Dyke, Rev. J. W.,	Siamese
Wilson, Rev. J.,	Laos

Turkey:

Adger, Rev. J. B.,	Armenian
Andrus, Rev. A. N.,	Kurdish
Christie, Rev. Dr. J.,	Hebrew-Spanish
Dwight, Rev. H. O.,	Turkish
Goodell, Rev. W.,	Armeno-Turkish
Herrick, Rev. G. F.,	Turkish
Hoskins, Rev. F. E.,	Arabic
Labarree, Rev. Benjamin,	Azerbaijan Turkish
Long, Rev. A. L.,	Bulgarian
Perkins, Rev. Justin,	Syriac, Modern
Pratt, Rev. A. T.,	Turkish
Riggs, Rev. Elias,	Armenian, Bulgarian, Turkish
Schauffler, Rev. W. G.,	Hebrew-Spanish, Turkish
Smith, Rev. Eli,	Arabic
Spence, Rev. D. B.,	Hebrew-Spanish
Van Dyck, Rev. C. V. A.,	Arabic
Weakley, Rev. R. H.,	Turkish
Wright, Rev. J. N.,	Azerbaijan Turkish

Miscellaneous:

Baez, Rev. D. B.,	Spanish
Brown, Rev. W. C.,	Portuguese
Diez, Rev. Francisco,	Spanish
Drees, Rev. Charles W.,	"
Howland, Rev. John,	"
Kyle, Rev. J. M.,	Portuguese
Pratt, Rev. H. B.,	Spanish
Smith, Rev. J. R.,	"
Stallybrass, Rev. E.,	Mongolian
Thompson, Rev. Henry C.,	Spanish

APPENDIX XII

CONSTITUTION OF THE AMERICAN BIBLE SOCIETY,[1] 1916

ARTICLE I

This Society shall be known by the name of the AMERICAN BIBLE SOCIETY, of which the sole object shall be to encourage a wider circulation of the Holy Scriptures without note or comment. The only copies in the English language, to be circulated by the Society, shall be of the version set forth in 1611, and commonly known as the King James Version, whether in its original form as published in the aforesaid year or as revised, the New Testament in 1881 and the Old Testament in 1885, and published in these years under the supervision of the Committee of Revision, or as further revised and edited by the American Committee of Revision and printed under its supervision in 1901.

ARTICLE II

This society shall add its endeavours to those employed by other Societies, for circulating the Scriptures throughout the United States and their Territories; and shall furnish them with plates, or such other assistance as circumstances may require. This Society shall also, according to its ability, extend its influence to other countries, whether Christian, Mohammedan, or pagan.

ARTICLE III

All Bible Societies shall be allowed to purchase, at cost, from this Society, Bibles for distribution within their own districts; and the officers of all such Bible Societies as shall hereafter agree to place their surplus revenue, after supplying their own districts with the Bible, at the disposal of this Society, shall be entitled to vote in all meetings of the Society.

ARTICLE IV

Each subscriber of three dollars annually shall be a Member.

[1] The modified constitution is inserted here for comparison with the original form of 1816.

ARTICLE V

Each subscriber of thirty dollars at one time shall be a Member for Life.

ARTICLE VI

Each subscriber of one hundred and fifty dollars at one time, or who shall by one additional payment, increase his original subscription to one hundred and fifty dollars, shall be a Director for Life; but he shall not be such Director when he is in receipt of any salary, emolument, or compensation for services, from the Society.

ARTICLE VII

Directors shall be entitled to attend and speak, and if constituted Directors before June 1, 1877, shall be entitled to vote at all meetings of the Board of Managers.

ARTICLE VIII

A Board of Managers shall be appointed to conduct the business of the Society, consisting of thirty-six laymen, of whom twenty-four shall reside in the city of New York or its vicinity. One-fourth part of the whole number shall go out of office at the expiration of each year, but shall be re-eligible.

Every Minister of the Gospel, who is a Member for Life of the Society, if he be not entitled to receive any salary, emolument or compensation for services from the Society, shall be entitled to meet and vote with the Board of Managers, and be possessed of the same powers as a Manager himself.

The Managers shall appoint all officers, and call special general meetings, and fill such vacancies as may occur, by death or otherwise, in their own Board.

ARTICLE IX

Each Member of the Society shall be entitled, under the direction of the Board of Managers, to purchase Bibles and Testaments at the Society's prices, which shall be as low as possible.

ARTICLE X

The annual meetings of the Society shall be held at New York or Philadelphia, at the option of the Society, on the second Thursday of May, in each year; when the Managers shall be chosen, the accounts presented, and the proceedings of the foregoing year reported.

ARTICLE XI

The President and Vice-Presidents, for the time being, shall be considered, *ex-officio,* members of the Board of Managers. The Treasurer and Secretaries shall, in addition to their other duties, attend meetings of the Board, and of the Committees thereof to render such aid in imparting information, recording and reading proceedings and minutes, and in preparing reports, as may be required of them.

ARTICLE XII

At the general meetings of the Society, and the meetings of the Managers, the President, or in his absence, the Vice-President first on the list then present, and in the absence of all the Vice-Presidents, such member as shall be appointed for that purpose, shall preside at the meeting.

ARTICLE XIII

The Managers shall meet on the first Thursday in each month, or oftener, if necessary, at such place in the city of New York as they shall from time to time adjourn to, but when the first Thursday falls on a legal holiday the meeting shall be on the second Thursday.

ARTICLE XIV

The Managers shall have the power of appointing such persons as have rendered essential services to the Society, either Members for Life, or Directors for Life.

ARTICLE XV

The whole minutes of every meeting shall be signed by the Chairman.

ARTICLE XVI

No alteration shall be made in this Constitution, except by the Society at an annual meeting, on the recommendation of the Board of Managers.

ARTICLE XVII

The President, or, in his absence, the Vice-President first on the list in the city of New York, *may,* and, on the written request of six members of the Board, *shall* call a special meeting of the Board of Managers, giving three days' notice of such meeting and of its object.

ARTICLE XVIII

The Board of Managers may admit to the privileges of an Auxiliary, any Society which was organised and had commenced the printing, publication, and issuing of the Sacred Scriptures before the establishment of this Society, with such relaxation of the terms of admission, heretofore prescribed, as the said Board, two-thirds of the members present consenting, may think proper.

APPENDIX XIII

THE AGENCIES OF THE SOCIETY

HOME AGENCIES

Coloured People of the South, Rev. J. P. Wragg, D.D., 35 Gammon Ave., Atlanta, Ga.

Northwestern Agency, Rev. S. H. Kirkbride, D.D., McCormick Building, 332 South Michigan Ave., Chicago, Ill.

South Atlantic Agency, Rev. M. B. Porter, 205 North Fifth Street, Richmond, Va.

Western Agency, Rev. Arthur F. Ragatz, D.D., Y. M. C. A. Building, Lincoln and 16th Streets, Denver, Colo.

Pacific Agency, Rev. A. Wesley Mell, Y. M. C. A. Building, 200 Golden Gate Ave., San Francisco, Cal.

Southwestern Agency, Rev. J. J. Morgan, 1304 Commerce Street, Dallas, Texas.

Eastern Agency, Rev. W. H. Hendrickson, 137 Montague Street, Brooklyn, N. Y.

Central Agency, Rev. George S. J. Browne, D.D., 424 Elm Street, Cincinnati, Ohio.

Atlantic Agency, Rev. Leighton W. Eckard, D.D., 701 Walnut Street, Philadelphia, Pa.

FOREIGN AGENCIES

Levant Agency, Rev. Marcellus Bowen, D.D., Bible House, Constantinople, Turkey.

La Plata Agency, Rev. Francis G. Penzotti, Box 304, Lavalle 1467, Buenos Ayres, Argentina.

Japan Agency, Herbert W. Schwartz, M.D., 53 Main Street, Yokohama, Japan.

China Agency, Rev. John R. Hykes, D.D., 14 Kiukiang Road, Shanghai, China.

Brazil Agency, Rev. H. C. Tucker, Caixa do Correio, 454, Rio de Janeiro, Brazil.

Mexico Agency, Rev. W. F. Jordan, 123 Uvalde St., San Antonio, Texas, U. S. A.

West Indies Agency, Rev. W. F. Jordan, 123 Uvalde St., San Antonio, Texas, U. S. A.

Korea Agency, Rev. S. A. Beck, Seoul, Korea.
Venezuela Agency, Rev. Gerard A. Bailly, Apartado de Correo 419, Caracas, Venezuela.
Siam Agency, Rev. Robert Irwin, 426 Pramuen Road, Bangkok, Siam.
Central America and Panama Agency, Rev. James Hayter, Apartado 119, Guatemala City, Guatemala.
Philippines Agency, Rev. J. L. McLaughlin, Box 755, Manila, P. I.

APPENDIX XIV

RECEIPTS

RECEIPTS OF THE AMERICAN BIBLE SOCIETY IN EACH YEAR SINCE ITS ORGANIZATION [1]

Year	Date	Receipts	Year	Date	Receipts
1st	1816–17	$37,779.35	51st	1866–67	$734,089.14
2d	1817–18	36,564.30	52d	1867–68	723,106.68
3d	1818–19	53,223,94	53d	1868–69	731,734.73
4th	1819–20	41,361.97	54th	1869–70	747,058.69
5th	1820–21	47,009.20	55th	1870–71	729,464.70
6th	1821–22	40,682,34	56th	1871–72	689,923.47
7th	1822–23	52,021.75	57th	1872–73	669,607.06
8th	1823–24	42,416.95	58th	1873–74	664,436.06
9th	1824–25	44,833.08	59th	1874–75	577,569.80
10th	1825–26	53,639.85	60th	1875–76	527,198.27
11th	1826–27	60,194.13	61st	1876–77	543,579.55
12th	1827–28	75,879.93	62d	1877–78	446,954.04
13th	1828–29	101,426.72	63d	1878–79	462,274.66
14th	1829–30	143,449.81	64th	1879–80	608,342.28
15th	1830–31	116,900.74	65th	1880–81	606,484.96
16th	1831–32	86,875.18	66th	1881–82	502,223.32
17th	1832–33	83,556.03	67th	1882–83	598,641.91
18th	1833–34	86,537.63	68th	1883–84	640,719.06
19th	1834–35	98,306.29	69th	1884–85	587,914.34
20th	1835–36	101,771.48	70th	1885–86	523,910.59
21st	1836–37	83,259.79	71st	1886–87	493,358.35
22d	1837–38	91,904.57	72d	1887–88	557,340.18
23d	1838–39	79,545.24	73d	1888–89	499,823.56
24th	1839–40	94,880.24	74th	1889–90	597,693.05
25th	1840–41	116,485.05	75th	1890–91	512,388.18
26th	1841–42	132,637.08	76th	1891–92	556,527.29
27th	1842–43	124,728.77	77th	1892–93	578,930.76
28th	1843–44	153,678.05	78th	1893–94	662,729.80
29th	1844–45	159,738.68	79th	1894–95	526,824.26
30th	1845–46	196,182.48	80th	1895–96	437,223.05
31st	1846–47	203,494.63	81st	1896–97	380,803.12
32d	1847–48	251,804.68	82d	1897–98	392,942.28
33d	1848–49	236,428.94	83d	1898–99	464,985.13
34th	1849–50	284,459.59	84th	1899–1900	350,173.82
35th	1850–51	276,882.53	85th	1900–01	378,972.10
36th	1851–52	308,744.81	86th	1901–02	450,558.76
37th	1852–53	346,542.42	87th	1902–03	377,742.41
38th	1853–54	394,340.50	88th	1903–04	448,037.21
39th	1854–55	346,767.09	89th	1904–05	396,885.50
40th	1855–56	393,167.25	90th	1905–06	438,677.02
41st	1856–57	441,805.67	91st	1906–07	548,343.88
42d	1857–58	390,759.49	92d	1907–08	534,020.24
43d	1858–59	415,011.37	93d	1908–09	502,345.56
44th	1859–60	435,956.92	94th	1909–10	533,470.80
45th	1860–61	389,541.52	95th	1910–11	747,766.64
46th	1861–62	378,132.08	96th	1911–12	929,906.58
47th	1862–63	422,588.00	97th	1912–13	728,246.32
48th	1863–64	560,578.60	98th	1913–14	696,609.26
49th	1864–65	677,851.39	99th	1914	840,291.52
50th	1865–66	642,625.64			
			Total	....	$38,016,919.18

[1] These figures do not include Trust Funds, the *income* of which can only be used, invested Funds received for Reinvestment, or amount borrowed temporarily from banks.

APPENDIX XV

ISSUES

BIBLES AND NEW TESTAMENTS ISSUED IN EACH YEAR SINCE ITS ORGANIZATION

Year	Bibles	Tests, etc.	Total	Year	Bibles	Tests, etc.	Total
1st	6,410	....	6,410	51st	324,215	933,745	1,257,960
2d	17,594	....	17,594	52d	315,525	871,669	1,187,194
3d	23,870	7,248	31,118	53d	339,595	1,047,016	1,386,611
4th	26,800	14,713	41,513	54th	329,774	1,000,866	1,330,640
5th	26,772	16,474	43,246	55th	316,857	790,870	1,107,727
6th	28,910	24,560	53,470	56th	298,352	802,519	1,100,871
7th	28,448	26,357	54,805	57th	313,714	887,531	1,201,245
8th	31,590	28,849	60,439	58th	317,365	673,207	990,572
9th	30,094	33,757	63,851	59th	281,703	645,197	926,900
10th	31,154	35,980	67,134	60th	269,303	581,167	850,470
11th	35,876	35,745	71,621	61st	239,546	641,510	881,056
12th	75,734	58,873	134,607	62d	297,452	560,041	857,493
13th	91,248	108,874	200,122	63d	343,902	843,952	1,187,854
14th	130,254	108,329	238,583	64th	394,545	961,494	1,356,039
15th	171,972	70,211	242,183	65th	422,208	1,052,395	1,474,603
16th	54,843	60,959	115,802	66th	371,728	1,153,045	1,524,773
17th	36,941	54,227	91,168	67th	438,063	1,238,169	1,676,232
18th	34,083	76,749	110,832	68th	499,379	1,308,836	1,808,215
19th	47,709	75,527	123,236	69th	429,716	1,118,459	1,548,175
20th	65,974	155,720	221,694	70th	369,714	1,067,726	1,437,440
21st	51,354	154,886	206,240	71st	391,865	1,055,405	1,447,270
22d	45,083	113,215	158,298	72d	420,242	1,084,405	1,504,647
23d	45,333	89,604	134,937	73d	410,282	1,030,173	1,440,455
24th	54,227	103,034	157,261	74th	412,862	1,083,195	1,496,057
25th	64,304	87,898	152,202	75th	450,180	1,047,457	1,497,637
26th	101,416	155,650	257,066	76th	411,618	886,578	1,298,196
27th	82,912	133,693	216,605	77th	410,093	984,770	1,394,863
28th	114,766	199,816	314,582	78th	400,176	1,047,483	1,447,659
29th	145,970	283,122	429,092	79th	403,434	1,177,694	1,581,128
30th	161,974	321,899	483,873	80th	391,437	1,358,846	1,750,283
31st	209,416	418,348	627,764	81st	317,472	1,196,027	1,513,499
32d	232,272	422,794	655,066	82d	252,530	1,109,743	1,362,273
33d	205,307	359,419	564,726	83d	194,564	1,186,328	1,380,892
34th	205,037	428,358	633,395	84th	215,426	1,191,375	1,406,801
35th	209,821	382,611	592,432	85th	238,081	1,316,047	1,554,128
36th	221,450	444,565	666,015	86th	283,288	1,440,503	1,723,791
37th	260,381	538,999	799,380	87th	302,121	1,691,437	1,993,558
38th	277,584	537,815	815,399	88th	304,952	1,465,939	1,770,891
39th	256,087	493,809	749,896	89th	290,847	1,540,249	1,831,096
40th	240,776	427,489	668,265	90th	274,185	1,962,574	2,236,759
41st	258,846	511,211	770,057	91st	272,077	1,638,776	1,910,853
42d	260,997	451,048	712,045	92d	262,518	1,633,423	1,895,941
43d	269,826	451,269	721,095	93d	312,922	1,840,106	2,153,028
44th	267,466	486,306	753,772	94th	327,636	2,499,195	2,826,831
45th	295,858	426,020	721,878	95th	393,230	2,838,492	3,231,722
46th	161,374	932,468	1,093,842	96th	430,098	3,261,103	3,691,201
47th	175,554	1,083,563	1,259,117	97th	399,734	3,649,876	4,049,610
48th	238,063	1,262,501	1,500,564	98th	412,229	4,838,947	5,251,176
49th	239,097	1,591,659	1,830,756	99th	352,469	6,053,854	6,406,323
50th	256,498	894,030	1,150,528	Total	23,456,549	86,469,665	109,926,214

INDEX

A

Abeel, David, 118, 240.
Academy of Music, Jubilee celebration in, 320.
Adams, John, Treasurer of Society, 90.
Adams, John Quincy, Vice-President of Society, 98; death of, 197; presides at Bible convention in Washington, 204.
Adams, Rev. Dr. William, address of, at funeral of Secretary Brigham, 266–267; Jubilee appeal sent out by, 319; Jubilee sermon by, 319.
Adger, J. B., Bible translator, 167.
Africa, plans to evangelise, in 1798, 7; first American colonists sail for, 59; Scriptures distributed in, 144, 242, 315–317; first American missions in, 241; translation of Scriptures into native languages of, 241–242; Scriptures printed for, 365–366.
African Scriptures, issued by Society, 447.
Agencies, list of, 400 n., 574–575.
Agents, number of, in service in 1842, 178; importance of work of, in distributing Bibles among the destitute, 293–294; spirit of fraternity among different denominations promoted by, 294; utter devotion to God's purposes an essential in character of, 294; withdrawal of, from Vermont, Virginia, and Rhode Island, 295; duties of, 460.
Aglipay Church in Philippines, development of, leads to demand for Scriptures, 509.
Aitken, Robert, first English Bible printed in America by, 3.
Alabama Bible Society, 176; resumes Auxiliary relationship, 280.
Albany County Auxiliary, 340.
Alexander, Rev. Mr., missionary in Egypt, 426.
Alf, Rev. Alfred, Sub-Agent in China, 501.
Allan, Rev. George, translation for Quechua Indians by, 477.
Allen, Dr. William H., quoted, 339; elected President, 348; death of, 348.
Allison, Dr., Congress petitioned by, to order Bibles printed, 3.
American Bible Society, first President, 3; gift from British and Foreign Bible Society to, 9, 34; organisation of, first proposed, 16–20; first act in formation of, 18; organised, 21–30; original form of constitution, 25–27; first officers, 29; ratification meeting held in City Hall, 30; first Board of Managers, 29; appreciation of, by other societies, 33–36; letter to, from British Society, 35; denounced, 36; auxiliary relationship to, 42–47; statement by Board of Managers in regard to Auxiliary Societies, 45; difficulties encountered in Auxiliary system, 46–47; first issue of Bibles by, 49; stereotype plates given to, by New York Bible Society, 49; meets need of Bibles in foreign languages, 51; model for form of administration, 52; quotation from Board of Managers' first report, 52; gift of German and Spanish Bibles from British Society to, 53; independence of, 53; gift of Bibles from, to United States Navy, 54; work among foreign countries begun, 58–60; confronted by illiteracy, 63; first salary paid by, 65; early depositories of, 67; Bible House on Nassau Street, 67; growth of, 83; adopts resolutions for first General Supply in United States, 86; foreign work of, broadened, 102–110, 119–120; adopts rule to supply Bibles to

American Foreign Missions, 103–104; foreign activities of, 112; discussion by, of plan for General Supply of world, 113–117; plans to increase circulation of the Bible, 117–118; difficulties attending plans for expansion, 122–123; desire to aid publication of foreign translations of Bible, 130–131; appeals to, from foreign missionaries, 131–132; attitude of, as a federation, toward slavery question, 136–139; need of agents to oversee foreign distribution, 144–146, 148; co-operation with missionaries undertaken, 148; twenty-fifth anniversary of, 162–163; pressing problems in home field, 164; problems of reaching frontier districts, 172; republishes statement of 1834 in 1845, 185; adopts resolutions for Second General Supply in United States, 198; distribution in Italy, 212; money grants of, to Germany up to 1861, 212; distribution through missionaries in Turkey, 227–228; grants to Jaffna Auxiliary, 238; grant to India for translation, 239; appropriation by, to assist revision of Chinese Bible, 244; encouragement from the South to, 256; Bibles sent to Virginia Bible Society by, 263; Army Agency of, 279; grant to Bible Society of France by, 299; re-statement in 1863 of policy toward nations, 299; expansion of field in fifty years, 326, 327, 328; presents plates of Arabic Bible to British Society, 331–332; charges of mismanagement brought against, 333; generous donations to, during war period, 334; from Boston, 337–338; influences which hamper work of, 337–343; table showing financial stress following war times, 338; financial condition of, after war, 338–340, 341, 342, 345; education of public to power of Bible necessary to support of, 343; bequests to, 345, 523; changes in charter and constitution, 364; unjust criticism of, 370–372; seventy-fifth anniversary of, 431–439; record of labours of seventy-five years, 432–437; library of the, 445–446; present number of Auxiliaries, 457; effect of increased immigration on Home Agencies of, 464; foreign language Bibles in depository of, 464–465; number published and circulation of Chinese Bibles by, 502; need of appeals for money to carry on work of, 521–523; appeal of 1904 for contributions, 528; reduction of appropriations necessary in 1914 and 1915, 529; purpose of formation of, 530, 531; aim of, 532; those benefited by, 532; development of work of translation, 533–534; estimate of total foreign distribution, 534; table of early grants made by, 540.

American Board of Commissioners for Foreign Missions, formed, 11; removal of, from Bible House, 449.

American Colonisation Society, 59, 73.

American and Foreign Bible Society, formation of, in 1836, 157.

American and Foreign Christian Union, grant to, 302, 306.

American Missions, grants to, in twenty-five years, 133.

American Mission Press, in Madras, 156; in Malta, 227.

American Presbyterian Mission, in Lodiana District, 239.

Americans, Bible destitution among, 466.

American Standard Revision, 446.

American Sunday School Union, receives New Testaments for children, 88; supplied with Bibles by Society, 157.

American Tract Society, arrangement with, for distribution of Scriptures in West, 202–203.

Anderson, Rev. Dr. Rufus, 79; quoted, 104, 166; address by, at Jubilee, 322.

Andover Theological Seminary, missionary spirit in, 81.

Andrus, Rev. Dr., translator of Bible into Kurdish, 363, 423–424.

Annual Report, issued by Society, 446.

Anti-Slavery Society, proposal made by, to Board, 137–139.

Appenzeller, Rev. H. G., missionary to Korea, 418; work of, on Korean Version, 486.

Apocrypha question, 100–101.

Arabia, grants by Society to Reformed Church Mission in, 526.

Arabic letters drawn by Dr. Smith, 330.
Arabic Version of Bible, 233–234, 330, 331.
Arawack, version of Book of Acts published in, 223.
Argentina, Mr. Milne's field, 390.
Armenian, Version of Bible in, 149, 227, 360; Bible printed in, at Bible House (1858), 199; Reference Bible in, 425.
Armenian Massacre, of 1893, 513; of 1909, 513.
Armenians, readiness of, to receive the Bible, 227; missionaries sent to, 227–228; Bible distribution among, 228 ff.; persecution of Evangelical Armenians by Armenian Church, 230; Socialistic propaganda among, 516.
Armenian women send money to supply Bible to Korea.
Armeno-Turkish Version of Bible, 227, 229, 231–232; revision of, 425–426.
Armies, Bibles supplied to, in Civil War, 269–276.
Asiatic Turkey, distribution in, 422, 423.
Aspinwall, John, on first Board of Managers, 29; death of, 196.
Aspinwall, William H., death of, 354.
Aston-Binns, Rev. T., of England, at seventy-fifth anniversary, 431.
Atlantic Agency, organised, 462; circulation in, 465.
Austria, difficulty of distribution in, 211, 383–384; circulation in (1891–1915), 525.
Auxiliary Bible Societies, founding of, 40; theory of, 40–42; line marked between, and other Bible societies, 44; change of system in connection with National Society, 84–87; growth in number, 92; donations to Society up to 1832, 94; perplexities created by inefficient, 123–127; system of, main financial reliance of Society, 125, 154; distribution by, 174, 175–177; number lost to main Society in seceded States in Civil War, 257; Bibles supplied to soldiers in Civil War by, 272–273; amount of donations received from, in 1866, 284; important activities of, in period following Civil War, 291–295; Jubilee meetings of, 318; assistance of, during financial stress, 340; inefficiency of many, 342; partial explanation of dissolution of some, 452; revision of roll of, 456.
Auxiliary New York Bible Society, becomes Auxiliary of National Society, 33, 44; takes name of New York Bible Society, 93.
Avederanian, Hohannes, Mohammedan convert, 430.
Ayachucho, colporteur attacked in, 475.
Azerbaijan Turkish Version, 363.

B

Bachellor, Rev. John, preparation of Ainu Version of Psalms by, 484.
Baez, Rev. Victoriano D., member of Committee on revision of Spanish Version, 480, 481.
Bailly, Mr., Agent in Venezuela, 478, 575.
Baird, Rev. W. F., Agent of Bible Society among Southern coloured people, 282.
Bakhit, M., Sub-Agent in Egypt, 519.
Ballagh, Rev. Dr., incident in Japan described by, 415.
Bangkok, Scriptures printed in, 366.
Banks, Dr. James L., death of, 354.
Baptist Board of Missions, resolutions adopted by, relative to foreign translations of Bible, 142.
Baptist Church, approval voted at General Convention of, 33.
Baptist missionaries, work of, in Germany, 211–212.
Baptist Missionary Society, established 1792, 7.
Bath and Wells, Bishop of, sermon by, on results of Society's labours, 373.
Baughman, Rev. J. A., Agent in Michigan, 179.
Baxter, Dr., letter from, on world supply, 113.
Bayard, Samuel, member of Committee on Constitution, 25; member of first Board of Managers, 29; at death bed of Dr. Boudinot, 69.
Bayard, William, on first Board of Managers, 29.
Bear, Mr., colporteur in Manila, 508.
Beck, Rev. S. A., Agent in Korea, 486.
Beecher, Rev. Dr. Lyman, one of secretaries of first Convention, 22; quoted, 24; member of Committee

on Constitution, 25; mentioned, 86; death of, 287.
Beirut, Scriptures printed at, 366.
Benga, Scriptures printed in, 366.
Bengali translation of Bible, controversy over, 139–142.
Benson, Rev. H. H., 370.
Bergne, Dr., Secretary of British and Foreign Bible Society, 225; quoted on receipt of Arabic plates from Society, 332.
Berlin, Scriptures printed in, 366.
Bethune, Divie, on first Board of Managers, 29; tracts circulated by, 32; death of, 99.
Bethune, Rev. G. W., quoted, 107.
Bettelheim, Rev. Dr., translator of Scriptures into Japanese, 313; offer of translation to Society, 314.
Bible, brought to America by early settlers, 1; sale of, stopped by Revolution, 3; English Versions of, 134; power of, to change men, 167–170, 475, 536; influence of, on nations, 168–170.
Bible Board, created by Methodist Episcopal Church South, 458.
Bible Day, observance of, 450; in Bulgaria (1913), 520.
Bible distribution, results produced by, 4, 89–91; reasons for undertaking, in Latin America, 55–56. *See* Distribution.
Bible House, Nassau Street, enlarged, 84; Astor Place, cornerstone of, laid, 193; expansion of work in, 194; Bibles in foreign languages printed at, 199; payment of mortgage on, in 1863, 283; improvements in book-making at, 365; repairs and improvements made in, 365; increase of printing at, 446.
Bibles, twenty thousand imported from Holland (1777), 3; cities where printed in eighteenth century, 3–4; constant renewal of general supply of, 89; distribution of, through Life Members, 173; by pastors, 173–174.
Bible Societies, obstacles encountered by local, 95.
Bible Society of France, organised, 1864, 299, 319.
Bible Society Record, illustrated monthly, issued by Society, quoted on Jubilee, 320; mentioned, 446.
Biblical Library, founded by British and Foreign Missionary Society, 53.
Bidwell, Marshall S., Vice-President of Society, 353.
Bidwell, Rev. Mr., suggests work in Siberia, 381.
Biggs, Rev. Dr. T. S., death of, 287.
Bingham, Rev. Hiram, missionary to Sandwich Islands, 162, 163; translator, 167.
Bingham, Rev. Hiram, Jr., Gilbert Islands translator, 362; mentioned, 436; death of, 448, 449.
Bingham, John, on first Board of Managers, 29.
Bishop, Dr. Nathan, death of, 354.
Bissell, Rev. Mr., work of, in Austria, 383.
Blackford, Rev. Mr., missionary at Rio Janeiro, 224, 304; Agent in Brazil, 396.
Blanco, Gen. Guzman, liberal views of, 398.
Bleecker, Garrat N., Treasurer, 100.
Bleecker, Leonard, on first Board of Managers, 29.
Blind, New Testament prepared for the, 156; printing of Bible for the, 200–201; embossed Scriptures for the, published, 365; Spanish Gospel of St. John printed for, 473; Bible printed in Point system and in Braille for, 524; list of systems, 564.
Bliss, Rev. E. M., appointed Assistant Agent, 426.
Bliss, Rev. Dr. I. G., Agent in Turkey, 234–235, 316, 421, 422, 424, 426, 427; plan of, for Bible House in Constantinople, 317; address by, at Jubilee, 323; mentioned, 328; report of, on cost of translations in Turkey, 360.
Blodgett, Rev. Dr., missionary in North China, 311; Chinese New Testament translation by, 361.
Blythe, Rev. Dr. James, member of Committee on Constitution, 25; mentioned, 49; extract from letter regarding Latin Americans, 75.
Board of Managers, list of members of, 547–553.
Board of Revisers in Korea, 486.
Bogota, Scriptures sent to, 223.
Boker, George H., United States Minister to Turkey, 422.

Bolivia, Mr. Milne's field, 390; restriction removed in, 476.
Bolles, Rev. C. A., retirement of, 370.
Bolton, John, Vice-President, 30.
Bombay, effect on Jews of distribution in, 167.
Bond, Rev. Richard, Agent, 179.
Boone, Bishop, member of Committee on Chinese Bible translation, 310; teaches Chinese to Mr. Schereschewski, 498.
Booth, W. T., death of, 445.
Boudinot, Dr. Elias, first President American Bible Society, 3; statement issued by, 16; quoted, 17, election of, as President, 29; mentioned, 35, 66, 73, 74, 122; extract from letter of acceptance of office, 38; extract from letter of, 61; residence of, in Burlington, N. J., 61; presides at annual meetings, 61; death of, 69; portrait of, by Sully, 70; age of, at death, 269.
Bowen, Rev. Dr. Marcellus, Agent for the Levant, 427, 515, 516, 517, 519, 520.
Boyd, Samuel, on first Board of Managers, 29.
Bradish, Luther, elected President of Bible Society, 268; sketch of career, and death, 268; age at death, 269.
Brahmins, sway of, 237.
Brazil, attempt to found Huguenot colony in, 223; work of American missionaries in, 224; organised work of Bible distribution in, 224–225; Agency in, 396–397, 470, 473–475.
Breckenridge, Rev. John, quoted, 152.
Bremen, Scriptures printed in, 366; Methodist Episcopal Mission in, 382.
Brewer, David J., death of, 443; quoted, 521; signed appeal for contributions, 528.
Brewer, Rev. Josiah, suggestion of work in foreign parts by, 105, 112; missionary to Smyrna, 132.
Bridel, Rev. Mr., sent from France in 1848, 209.
Bridgman, Rev. Dr. E. C., missionary at Canton, China, 106, 132, 167, 244; member of committee on Chinese Bible translation, 310.
Brigham, Rev. John C., Bibles sold by, in Peru, 77; quoted, 78; address quoted, 79–80; chosen Assistant Secretary, 80; elected Secretary for Domestic Correspondence, 80; mentioned, 125; report of, at twenty-fifth anniversary, 162; death of, 266; Dr. Adams' tribute to, 266–267; mentioned, 355, 395.
Brinckerhoff, Elbert A., death of, 444.
British and Foreign Bible Society, established, 8; money granted American Society by, 9; letter from, to Dr. Boudinot, 35–36; mentioned, 40, 41, 51, 52, 53, 56, 57, 62, 76, 77, 100, 103, 104, 116, 126, 148, 149, 211, 212, 213, 222, 224, 227, 232, 234, 240, 243, 263, 283, 302, 319, 360, 390, 449, 453, 464, 474, 477, 480, 483, 484, 485, 497, 504, 505, 506, 507, 526; one hundredth anniversary of, 450.
Brooklyn Bible Society, 454, 463.
Brooks, Phillips, seventy-fifth anniversary address by, 431; quoted, 437–439.
Brouwer, Theophilus Anthony, elected President of Society, 443; death of, 443.
Brown, James, Vice-President, 30.
Brown, James M., Vice-President, 352.
Brown, Rev. John C., Bibles distributed among Protestants of North Russia and Finland through plan of, 213–214.
Brown, Rev. Dr. S. R., translator in Japanese, 361.
Brown, Rev. William M., Agent in Brazil, 396.
Browne, Rev. Dr. G. S. J., Central Agency Secretary, 462.
Brunetière, quoted, 2.
Buck, Richard P., Vice-President, 353.
Buckingham, William A., Vice-President, 350.
Buel, Rev. F., San Francisco Society organised by, 177; Agent for California, 202.
Buenos Aires, grant of Testaments to public schools of, in 1819, 57; mentioned, 79, 81, 222, 223; salesroom in, 476.
Bulgarian New Testament, 329.
Bulgarian Version of Bible, 360, 425; circulation of, 428.
Bunker, Rev. D. A., Superintendent of Society's work in Korea in 1901, 484; in 1907, 485.
Burdon, Bishop, translation of Chinese New Testament by, 361.

Burma, Scriptures distributed in, 144.
Burr, Jonathan, legacy of, for the blind, 524.
Burrill, Ebenezer, on first Board of Managers, 29.
Burton, Rev. J., of Canada, at seventy-fifth anniversary, 431.

C

Caldwell, John E., first General Agent, 67, 192.
Calhoun, John C., quoted, 48.
Calhoun, Rev. Simeon H., Agent for foreign distribution, 148–152, 156, 158, 159, 227, 229–232; Bibles distributed outside of Turkey by, 230–231.
California, effect of discovery of gold in, on work of Bible Society, 201–202.
California Bible Society, co-operation of, in organisation of Pacific Agency, 462.
Cameron, Duncan, death of, 196.
Cameron, Rev. W. W., Agent pro tem, in Siam, 491; work of, in Shanghai, 501.
Campbell, Duncan P., on first Board of Managers, 29.
Canada, Scriptures distributed in, 144.
Canton, Sub-Agency in, 501.
Canton Colloquial Version, 493, 497.
Capen, S. B., death of, 444.
Cape Palmas Mission in Africa, 315.
Caracas Bible Society, 76, 222.
Carew, Rev. Dr. E. D., missionary at Buenos Aires, 223.
Carey, William, establishment of Baptist Missionary Society due to, 7; work in connection with Bible printing in India, 59, 60.
Carpenter, Thomas, on first Board of Managers, 29.
Carrington, Rev. John, Agent in Siam, 409, 490, 491; Princeton gives degree of Doctor of Divinity to, 492; death of, 492.
Carter, Robert, Vice-President, 353.
Carthagena, Spanish Bibles sent to, 76, 222, 225.
Casey, Gen., quoted, 394.
Castells, F. deP., colporteur in Manila, 505.
Cauldwell, Dr., on world supply, 113.
Cauldwell, John, on first Board of Managers, 29.
Centennial Bible, issuing of, 365.
Central Agency, organised, 462; Bible destitution in, among Americans, 466.
Central America, distribution in, 220–221, 303–304; Agencies in, 397; Society established in, 470; British and Foreign Society transfers work in, to American Society, 480.
Ceylon, American Board mission in, 59; missionaries in, receive aid from Board, 102, 144, 236, 238, 308.
Chamberlain, Rev. Dr. Jacob, explores territories of Nizam of Hyderabad, 308; revision of Telugus version by, 363; shells accepted as coin by, 403.
Chamberlain, J. L., presides at assembly in Bible House on seventy-fifth anniversary, 431; death of, 444.
Chamberlain, Rev. L. B., elected Assistant Corresponding Secretary, 445.
Chamorro Version, 448.
Champlain Bible Society, distribution by, among French Canadians, 203.
Changsha, Sub-Agency in, 501.
Charles, Thomas, mentioned, 453.
Charleston, S. C., Auxiliary, 175; supplies troops passing through city (1846–47), 183; mentioned, 340.
Charnock, Stephen, quoted, 2.
Chase, Salmon P., Vice-President of Bible Society, 291, 350.
Chengtu, Sub-Agency in, 501.
Chestnut, Eleanor, M.D., translation of Sam Kiong Version by, 497.
Chicago Bible Society, grant of money to, after fire (1871), 337; nucleus of Northwestern Agency, 460.
Chickering Hall, seventy-fifth anniversary celebration held in, 431.
Chile, distribution in, 76, 77, 79, 147, 222, 223, 476; Dr. Trumbull's mission in, 390.
China, distribution in, 144, 310–312, 404–408; advance in missionary work in, after 1842, 242; controversy in, over translation of "God," 310; Agencies in, 401–408, 409; printing presses owned by American missions in, 401, 402; obstacles to distribution in, 403; price paid for Bibles in, 403; increase of circulation in, from 1893 to 1915, 493; Emperor buys a Bible,

495; internal disorders in (1897–1916), 493–495; distribution among students of Nanking in 1894, 499; distribution in, at present time, 502.
Chinese Bible, arrival of, at Bible House, 102; fund for, 124; translation of, 242–243; controversy attending translation, 243–245; American Committee on, 310.
Chinese Bridgman-Culbertson Version, 411 n.
Chinese in California, efforts to reach, at time of gold discovery, 201–202.
Chinese Colloquial Versions, 496–497.
Chinese Exclusion Bill, effect of, on Agents, 408.
Chippeway version of New Testament, 200.
Choate, Joseph, representative of Society at Centenary Meeting in London, 450.
Choctaw, Scriptures in, 200.
Cholera epidemic of 1849, effect on work of Bible Society, 201.
Christian Advocate, 178.
Christian Commission, distribution of Bibles by, during Civil War, 272, 274, 275; account of aims and work of, 275; co-operation of, in distribution, 333.
Christian Watchman and Reflector, review of controversy of 1836 published in, 142.
Christie, Rev. Dr., work of, as translator, 425.
Chungking, Sub-Agency in, 501.
Church Missionary Society, formed (1798), 7.
Cincinnati Young Men's Bible Society, supplies troops passing through city (1846–47), 183
City Hotel, annual meetings held in, 67.
Civil War, events of period preceding, 246–257; breaking out of, 256–257; course of Bible Society during, 258 ff.; Bibles supplied to soldiers, 269–275; work carried on by Christian Commission, 275–276; damages wrought in South by, 277–278.
Clark, Rev. Dr. N. G., urges circulation of Chinese Scriptures, 401.
Clark, Rev. William, Missionary in Milan, 305.
Clarkson, Gen., presiding officer at Board meetings in absence of Dr. Boudinot, 62; death of, 99.
Clatsop County, Oregon, Auxiliary Society, 188.
Cleveland, Ex-President, signs appeal for contributions, 528.
Clinton, De Witt, on first Board of Managers, 29; mentioned, 32; death of, 98.
Cock, Dr. Thomas, member of Versions Committee, 253; death of, 288.
Cocke, John H., death of, 288.
Collins, Rev. V. D., agent of American Bible Society in South America, 222–223.
Colombia Bible Society, organised at Bogota, 76; mentioned, 79, 144; Society established in, 470.
Coloured people, problem presented by, after close of Civil War, 281–282; admitted to some Southern Bible Societies, 282; Agency for, 460.
Colporteurs, employed to assist Agents, 180; money granted for maintaining, 311; some types of, in Constantinople, 328; martyrdom of, in China (1899), 496; number of, in China at present, 501.
Colton, Rev. A. E., Field Agent, 458.
Committee on Agencies, appointed, 123.
Committee which drafted constitution of American Bible Society, 25.
Committee on Versions, members of, 249; trials of, 250–253.
Cone, S. H., mentioned, 117; elected a Corresponding Secretary, 120; dissent of, on Bengali Testament controversy, 140; resignation of, as Secretary, 142.
Confederate States' Bible Society, organised in 1862, 260.
Conference of Auxiliaries, held in 1900, 454; resolutions adopted at, 454–456.
Congress, called upon to remedy Bible famine in 1777, 3.
Connecticut Bible Society, organised, 9; support by, of plan for General Bible Society, 17; donation from, to American Society, 88; Bibles given to soldiers by, 272; Auxiliary relationship terminated, 457; Centennial of, 457.
Connecticut Congregational Association, charges of mismanagement of Society refuted by, 332; quoted, 345.
Connecticut Missionary Society, exploration in West by, 11.

Connecticut Religious Tract Society, established, 7.
Conservator of Sects, American Bible Society denounced by, 36.
Constantinople, Bible House in, 317, 420; Scriptures printed in, 366.
Constitution of American Bible Society, modified and revised (1904), 446; given in full, 570–573.
Convention of 1816, list of members of, 538–539.
Convention at Washington in 1844, 204.
Cooper, James Fenimore, delegate to first Convention American Bible Society, 22.
Copp, A. A., colporteur in China, 404, 409.
Coquimbo, opposition to distribution in, 147.
Corbeau, Father Telmonde at, 203.
Cote, Dr., Missionary in Rome, 387.
County Bible Society Annual Meeting, 451–452.
Crane, Mr., chosen Assistant Secretary, 80.
Creolese, translation of Bible into, 329.
Crimean War, Bible distribution in Turkey during, 232–233.
Crisis of 1857, effects of, felt by Bible Society, 246–248.
Cristobal, Bible House at, 480.
Crosby, William B., death of, 288.
Crouse, Rev. F. C., Sub-Agent in China, 500.
Crowe, Rev. F., Missionary in Guatemala, 223.
Cuba, Bibles sold in by Roman Catholic clergy, 77; Scriptures sent to, 218; distribution in, 389.
Culbertson, Rev. Dr., member of Committee on Chinese Bible translation, 310.
Cumberland County Society (N. J.), mentioned, 340, 457.
Cumings, A. P., member of Finance Committee, 352.
Cummings, J. W., Jubilee sermon by, 319.
Cutter, B. H., entire estate given to Society, 528.

D

Dakota, large field for work in, in 1906, 461.
Dakota Indians, version of Scriptures in language of, 200.
Dalzell, James, Agent ad interim at Shanghai (1889–1890), 409.
Dana, C. A., Sub-Agent in Syria, 519.
Danish Scriptures, 126.
Dardier, Mr., Agent of Geneva Society, 386.
Davis, Rev. Dr., 411.
De Castello, Rev. R. M., investigates European publishing houses for Society, 464.
Deems, Professor, quoted on sale of Bibles by recipients, 203; quoted concerning effect of Bible in benighted districts, 206.
Delaporte, P. A., translation of New Testament into Nauru, 447.
Delegates to first Convention American Bible Society, 22–23.
De Luca, Italian colporteur, establishes night school in Ladd, Ill., 461; further work of, 461.
Dencke, Rev. Mr., translation of Bible into Delaware language undertaken by, 51, 167.
Denmark, distribution in, 297–298.
De Palma, Joaquin, sent to Venezuela by Society, 398.
Der Kevork, Armenian priest, 228–229.
De Sacy, version of Bible by, brought out in Paris, 58.
Destitution, reports of, to Society, 83–84; plans to relieve in United States, 86, 198, 293, 345; in the world, 113.
Dickinson, Rev. Dr., Field Agent, 458.
Diez, Rev. Francisco, member of Committee on Revision of Spanish Version, 480.
Distribution, developed under pressure of claim of home field, 171–181; by auxiliaries, 174–177; through Agents, 177–181; good results following ease of, through army lines, 334; on railroads, 374; to children (1890), 375; by voluntary workers, 501; regulations respecting, in foreign lands, 560–561.
District Superintendents, work of, and discontinuation of, 453.
Doane, Rev. Mr., Scripture translated into Ponape language by, 362.
Doering, Rev. Dr., in charge of Methodist mission at Bremen, 382.
Dodge, William E., death of, 354.

Donaldson, James, member of Finance Committee, 352.
Donations, total in fifty years, 326.
Douay Version of Bible, printing of, not constitutional, 130.
Douglass, George, death of, 287.
Douglass, James, donation to Society by, 159.
Dred Scott decision, indirect effects of, on Bible Society, 253.
Drees, Rev. Charles W., church organised by, at Callao, Peru, 393; member of Committee on Revision of Spanish Version, 480, 481.
Du Bose, Rev. Mr., of Suchow, 406, 408.
Duffield, Mr., Agent of British and Foreign Bible Society, in South America, 222.
Durbin, Rev. H. J., Agent, 179.
Dutch Scriptures, 126.
Dwight, Rev. H. O., elected Recording Secretary, 445.
Dwight, H. G. O., translator of Scriptures, 167; at Nicomedia, 228.

E

Earle, John, death of, 354.
Eastburn, Bishop, quoted, 23; charge to clergy on Society's Jubilee, 324.
Eastern Agency, organised, 462.
Easy Wenli Version, work on revision of, 361, 497.
Eckard, Rev. Dr. L. W., Atlantic Agency Secretary, 462.
Ecuador, mentioned, 79; liberty of worship granted in, 475.
Ecumerical Missionary Conference of 1900, 449.
Eddy, Thomas, on first Board of Managers, 29.
Egypt, distribution in, 316.
Elliott, Rev. W. S., Eastern Agency Secretary, 462; returns to China, 463; Sub-Agent in China, 501.
Ellsworth, W. W., death of, 288.
English Version of Bible, Society responsible for excellence of, 133.
Esthonians, distribution among, 213, 299, 380.
Europe, results of turbulent conditions in, from 1848 to 1850, 208–216.
Evarts, Jeremiah, on first Board of Managers, 29, 32, 58.
"Extracts from Correspondence," issued by British and Foreign Bible Society, 52.

F

Fancher, Enoch L., elected President, 349; presides at seventy-fifth anniversary celebration, 431; death of, 441.
Fanshaw, Mr., room in building occupied by, used as depository, 192.
Farmer, Rev. Harry, work of, in Philippines, 511.
Farmer, Thomas, on first Board of Managers, 29.
Farnam, Rev. George E., Western Agency Secretary, 463; death of, 463.
Ferris, Rev. Dr. Isaac, chairman of Distribution Committee, 190; Jubilee sermon by, 320.
Ferris, Rev. Dr. J. M., delegate to seventy-fifth anniversary, 431.
Field Agents replace District Superintendents, 457; office abolished, 459.
Fielstedt, Rev. Mr., missionary at Bucharest, 231.
Financial stress of 1836, 157–158.
Finland, aid given Bible work in, by American Society, 213, 214.
Fisher, Henry, Assistant Treasurer of Society, 356; death of, and tribute to, 289.
Fisk, Rev. Pliny, 227.
Fitch, Dr., of Suchow, mentioned, 406.
Fletcher, Rev. J. G., Agent in Brazil, 224, 304.
Flinn, Rev. Glenn, Southwestern Agency Secretary, 462; resigns, 463.
Foochow Colloquial Version, 493.
Foreign Agent, advantages gained by appointing, 149–152.
Foreign countries to which Bibles were sent in 1834, 144.
Foreign distribution, Agency for, established, 148.
Foreign languages, number of, Society printed Bibles in (1816–32), 97; Scriptures in, circulated (1816–1841), 162; Scriptures printed in, or aided in printing by Society by end of 1841, 166; books sent out in, by Mr. Calhoun's Agency, 232; Bible distribution in, during Civil War period, 327; Bible read in twenty-seven different, 373; Bibles in, kept in Society's depository, 464–465; list of, in which Scriptures are translated, 562–564.

Foreign languages and dialects, Scriptures in, mentioned: Albanian, 232; Arabic, 149, 233, 235, 316, 329; Arapahoe, 447; Arawack, 223; Armeno-Turkish, 135, 149, 227, 231, 235, 360, 425; Azerbaijan Turkish, 363; Benga, 366, 447; Bicol, 507; Bulgarian, 327, 329, 360, 425, 428; Bulu, 447; Burmese, 109; Cambodian, 490; Canton, 493, 497; Cebuan, 507; Chamorro, 448; Cherokee, 135, 200, 329, 366; Chickasaw, 366; Chihuahua, 301; Chinese, 102, 132, 135, 166, 242–244, 310; Choctaw, 135, 200; Creolese, 329; Dakota, 200, 329, 359, 366; Danish, 126; Delaware, 51, 135, 167, 366; Dutch, 126, 314; Esthonian, 213, 299, 380; Foochow, 310, 493; French, 51, 59, 232; Gaelic, 51; German, 51, 126, 230, 231, 232; Gilbert Islands, 362, 447; Grebo, 135, 166, 241; Hawaiian, 102, 106, 135, 166, 238, 329; Hebrew-Spanish, 135, 151, 235, 360, 425; Hindi, 239, 308; Hindustani, 135; Hinghua, 497; Ibanag, 508; Ifugao, 508; Igorrote, 508; Ilocano, 507; Italian, 126, 232; Japanese, 314, 359–360, 361, 482–489; Korean, 360, 418; Kurdish, 363, 424; Laos, 360, 490; Mandarin, 311, 360, 497; Marathi, 106, 167, 308; Marshall Islands, 362; Modern Greek, 104, 149, 235; Mohawk, 106, 135, 200; Mongolian, 144; Moro, 508; Moro Lanao, 508; Mortlock Islands, 362; Mpongwe, 242, 366, 447; Muskokee, 366, 447; Nauru, 447; Navaho, 447; Nez Percés, 366; Ojibwa, 106, 135, 200, 366; Pampangan, 507; Panayan, 507, 509; Pangasinan, 507; Persian, 232; Ponape, 362; Portuguese, 76, 126, 155, 360; Punjabi, 239, 308; Quechua, 58, 76, 476, 477; Samareno, 508; Sam Kiong, 497; Seneca, 135; Shanghai, 497; Shantung, 497; Sheetswa, 362, 447; Siamese, 135, 240, 490, 492; Soochow, 497; Spanish, 51, 56, 57, 59, 76, 126, 379; Swedish, 126; Syriac, 156, 232, 235; Tagalog, 507; Tamil, 102, 106, 135, 238, 239, 308; Telugu, 135, 308, 363; Tonga, 362, 447; Turkish, 135, 360, 425–426; Urdu, 239, 308; Uriya, 135, 308; Welsh, 126; Zambal, 507; Zapotec, 473; Zulu, 129, 242, 316, 362, 366, 447.

Foreign Missions Conference of the United States and Canada, formation of, 450.

Foreign Versions fostered by Society, 562–564.

Formosa, colporteurs sent to, 493.

Forrester, Hiram M., Vice-President, 352.

Foster, Lafayette S., Vice-President, 351.

Foulke, William, Treasurer of Society, 356; assumes Mr. Rowe's duties, 441.

Fox, Rev. Dr. John, elected Corresponding Secretary, 442; mentioned, 449; sent as Society's delegate to Shanghai Conference of 1907, 497.

France, distribution in, 144, 209–211, 299, 526; difficulty of distribution in, 384–385.

Freedmen's Bureau, effort to care for negroes through, 282.

Frelinghuysen, Frederick T., mentioned, 291; election of, as President, and death of, 349.

Frelinghuysen, Theodore, copy of address of, placed in cornerstone of Bible House, 193; elected President in 1846, 196; quoted, 215; attitude toward South during Civil War, 259; death of, 265–266; honours paid to memory of, 266; age at death, 269.

French, Rev. Dr. George, Field Agent, 458.

French Bible printed by American Bible Society, 51.

French and Foreign Bible Society, formed, 58; money sent to, by Society for immigrants sailing from Havre, 126; aided by Society (1848–1850), 209–211; mentioned, 214, 299.

French Protestant Bible Society, mentioned, 299.

Fuchow, Scriptures printed in, 366.

"Fukien or Gospel Printing Company" of Yokohama, 489.

Fuller, Chief-Justice, signs appeal for contributions, 528.

Fulton County Auxiliary Society, work of one member of, 206–207.

Fyson, Rev. P. K., work of, on translation of Japanese version, 361.

G

Gaboon Mission in Africa, 315.
Gaelic Bible, imported by American Bible Society, 51.
Galitzin, Prince, quoted, 34.
Galusha, Jonas, Vice-President, 29.
Gammell, Dr. W., Vice-President, 351.
Gammon, Charles F., Sub-Agent in China and guide of allied troops, 496; assists Agent in China, 501.
Garden Street Dutch Reformed Church, 21.
Garretson, Freeborn, death of, 288.
Gaston, William, Vice-President, 30.
Gatrell, Dr. T. J. N., mentioned, 495.
General Agents of Society, 555.
General Assembly of the Presbyterian Church, note of appreciation and good will of, 33.
General Supply of Bibles to destitute, in United States, first (1829), 86; second (1856), 198; third (1866), 293, 368, 369; fourth (1882), 344–345, 372–377; in the world, 113; special gifts for, 88.
Geneva Evangelical Society, grants of money to, 385, 526.
Geneva Italian Committee, money granted to, 305.
Germans, Bibles distributed among, resident in southern Russia, Wallachia, and Moldavia, 230.
German Scriptures, printed by Society, 51, 126, 199; money granted for printing of, 298.
Germany, expressions of good-will from, 34; circulation of Bible in, through aid of American Society, 211–212, 525.
Gifford, Andrew, on first Board of Managers, 29.
Gilbert Islands, translation of Bible into language of, 362; converts from, 436; story of translation of Bible for, 448–449.
Gilman, Dr. Daniel Coit, elected President of Society, 442; death of, 443.
Gilman, Rev. Edward W., Secretary of Society, 355, 381; death of, 441; address of, at Missionary Conference, 449.
Goble, Rev. J., translator of Scriptures into Japanese, 361, 412.
Golubeff, Russian colporteur, 381.
Goodell, Rev. William, translator of Bible into Armeno-Turkish, 65, 167; missionary at Constantinople, 158, 159, 227, 228, 229, 231–232; on relation of Bible to work of missionaries in the Levant, 229; mentioned, 425.
Goodrich, Grant, Vice-President, 351.
Goodrich, Rev. J. C., appointed Agent in Manila, 506, 508.
Gordon, Mr., colporteur in China, 404.
Gore, Dr. Arthur, Agent in Mexico, 395.
Gosman, George, on first Board of Managers, 29.
Grant, Dr., appeal of, for Syriac Scriptures, 156.
Grant, President U. S., presentation of Bible to, 291; quoted, 375.
Grants, table of early, made by Society, 540.
Gray, William, Vice-President, 29.
Grebo language, Gospel of John translated into, 241.
Greece, Scriptures distributed in, 144, 227; withdrawal of Society from, 345.
Greeks in Turkey, opposition to distribution among, 427.
Greek Testament, printed 1833, 132.
Green, Dr., missionary to Sandwich Islands, 131.
Greene, Rev. Dr. D. C., quoted, 358; translator of Scriptures, 361.
Greene, Rev. Frederick D., Financial Agent, 458.
Griffin, George, quoted, 10; address by, 30.
Griscom, John, member of first Convention, 22; death of, 196.
Grundy, Felix, Vice-President, 30.
Guarapuava, distribution in, 435.
Guatemala, mentioned, 223.
Gugin, Mr., colporteur in Manila, 508.
Guicciardini, Count, mentioned, 212.
Gulick, Rev. Luther H., Agent for China and Japan, 312, 401, 403, 405, 408–409, 411, 412.
Gulick, Rev. Thomas L., investigations of, in Cuba, 389.
Gulick, Rev. W. H., distribution by, in Central America, 304; quoted, 387.
Gundert, Dr., quoted, 358.

Gutzlaff, Rev. Dr. Charles, quoted on need of Bibles in China, 112, 124; translation into Japanese attempted by, 313.

H

Hall, Rev. H. C., missionary in Seville, 306.
Hall, Rev. Sherman, New Testament translated into Ojibwa by, 200.
Hallock, Rev. Dr., mentioned, 79.
Hallock, Mr., matrices of Arabic letters made by, 330.
Halsey, Rev. L. H., contribution from, 96.
Hamburg and Altona Bible Society, extract from letter from, 34; results of postage due on letter from, 64.
Hamilton, Alexander, statue of, 98.
Hamilton, Rev. Hiram P., Agent in Mexico, 395; death of, 472.
Hamilton, Mrs. Hiram P., appointed Agent in Mexico, 472; death of, 473.
Hankow, Sub-Agency in, 500.
Harlan, Justice, signs appeal for contributions, 528.
Harrison, Benjamin, death of, 443; honorary chairman of Missionary Conference, 449.
Hasbrouck, Abraham B., Vice-President, 351.
Hatcher, Mr., Agent in Tennessee, 179.
Havana, Cuba, gift of Archdiocese of, 77; Scriptures sent to, 144.
Haven, H. P., Vice-President, 350.
Haven, Rev. Dr. William I., elected Corresponding Secretary, 442; mentioned, 449, 472; visit of, to Missionary Conference in Edinburgh, 480.
Hawaiian Bible, printed, 103, 106; presented to Society, 162.
Hawaiian Missionary Society, printing press given to Mr. Delaporte by, 447–448.
Hawaiian Testament printed at Bible House, 199.
Hay, Rev. Dr., revision of Telugus version by, 363.
Hayes, Rutherford B., death of, 443.
Hayter, Rev. James, appointed Agent for Central America, 479.
Hayti, work of American Bible Society in, 218–219; checked by Roman Catholics, 219.
Hebrew-Spanish Bible, 360, 425.
Henderson, Rev. Dr., Field Agent, 458.
Hendrickson, Rev. W. H., Eastern Agency Secretary, 463.
Henry, Alexander, death of, 196.
Henshaw, Mr., delegate to first Convention American Bible Society, 22.
Hepburn, Dr. J. C., one of first missionaries to Japan, 313; at Yokohama, 314; translator of Scripture, 361; "Jewelled Order of the Rising Sun" presented to, by Emperor of Japan, 488.
Herr, Rev. W., retirement of, as District Superintendent, 370.
Herrick, Rev. Dr. George F., member of Committee on Revision of Turkish version, 426.
Heyer, Cornelius, on first Board of Managers, 29.
Heye, Miss, grants to, from Society, 383.
Hickey, Rev. James, Agent in Mexico, 299; mentioned, 393.
Hicks, Mr. F., missionary in Panama, 304.
High Wenli Version, work on revision of, 361, 497.
Hinghua Colloquial Version, 497.
Hirst, Rev. Godfrey, Sub-Agent in China, 500.
Hobart, Bishop, controversy of, with Dr. Mason, 36.
Hodge, Rev. Dr. Charles, Jubilee sermon by, 319.
Hogg, Rev. Dr., missionary in Egypt, 422.
Holden, Rev. R., missionary in Para, 224, 304.
Holdich, Rev. Dr. Joseph, Secretary of Society, 197, 290, 332, 355.
Holland Bibles sent to Japanese, 314.
Holmes, Rev. Sylvester, mentioned, 126.
Home Agencies, establishment of, 450; secretaries of, 460–463; distribution in foreign languages by, 465; number of volumes distributed by, in 1916, 469.
Home Mission work first undertaken by American Bible Society, 55–58.
Honolulu, Scriptures printed in, 309.

Hooker, Rev. W. C., Sub-Agent in China, 501.
Hopkins, Mark, quoted, 165; benediction pronounced by, at Jubilee, 323.
Hornblower, Joseph C., delegate to first Convention American Bible Society, 22; death of, 287.
Horton, Rev. J. F., Northwestern Agency Secretary, 461; resigns, 463.
Hotels, supplying of Bibles to (1846), 201.
Howard, Maj. Gen. O. O., address by, at Jubilee, 322; death of, 443.
Howe, Dr. Samuel G., prepares New Testament for the blind, 156; mentioned, 524.
Howland, Rev. John, member of Committee on Revision of Spanish Version, 480.
Hughes, Rev. Joseph, establishment of Bible Societies due to, 8; mentioned, 453.
Huguenots, attempt to found colony of, at Rio Janeiro, 223.
Hunan, distribution in, 404.
Hungary, distribution in, 231.
Hunt, Rev. Dr. Albert S., Secretary of Society, 356; death of, 440.
Hunterdon County (N. J.) Auxiliary, mentioned, 457.
Hyde, Joseph, elected General Agent, 121.
Hykes, Rev. Dr. John R., appointed Agent for China, 493; mentioned, 494, 500, 501, 502; quoted on Philippines, 503–505.

I

Illinois Bible Societies, distribution by, 176.
Illinois Bible Society, formed, 12.
Immigrants, Auxiliary Societies at points of landing of, 126; Bibles supplied to, 188–190; Bibles printed for, with English translation, 189.
Imperial Bible Society of Russia, mentioned, 381, 525.
Incas, Bible translated into language of, 58.
Independent Church in Philippines, 509.
India, first missionaries to, 11; Society assists missionaries to print Bible in, 60, 308; distribution in, 144, 236, 399–400, 527; difficulties encountered by missionaries in, 236–237; sway of Brahmins in, 237; progress of missionaries, 237–238; amount of grants of money for Bibles by Bible Society, 238; Sepoy mutiny in, 239–240; Scriptures published in languages of, 308.
Indiana Bible Society, formed, 12.
Indian languages, Bible printed in, 51–52, 135, 199–200, 329, 366, 447.
Indians, Bibles sent to Canadian, 97; benefited by dissemination of Bible, 200; local Bible Societies among, 200; distribution among, 377.
Information, literature of, prepared and distributed by Secretaries of Society, 446.
Ingersoll, Rev. Dr. E. P., elected Corresponding Secretary, 442; death of, 442; representative of Society at Centenary meeting in London, 450.
Innsbruck, American mission at, 383.
Irwin, Rev. Robert, Assistant Agent, and Agent in Siam, 492.
Italian Bible Society in Rome, New Testaments printed by, 387.
Italians, work among, in Illinois, 461.
Italian version of Bible, ordered for immigrants, 126.
Italy, distribution among Sicilians in, 212; in Northern, 213; grants of money for distribution in, 305, 526; difficulty of distribution in, 387, 388.
Ito, Baron, recommends Bible to Mikado, 414.

J

Jackson, General Andrew, 11, 175.
Jackson, General "Stonewall," a collector for the Society, 250.
Jackson, F. Wolcott, death of, 444.
Jacobi, Rev. Dr., missionary, quoted, 298; retirement of, 382.
Jaffna Bible Society, 238.
Jalapa, distribution in 220.
James, Capt., work of, in Japan, 414.
Janes, Rev. Dr. E. S., appointed Financial Secretary, 121; finances improved through encouragement of, 155; elected Bishop of M. E. Church, 195.
Japan, first American Missionaries sent to, 313; work of distribution in, 313–315, 412–417; opposition to

distribution in, 412; printing Scriptures and distribution in, by General Committee, 417, 483; division of field in, 484; distribution at time of war with Russia, 487; circulation among students in, 488.
Japanese, Holland Bibles sent to, 314.
Japanese ambassadors' visit to Bible House, 313-314.
Japanese Version of Scriptures, 313, 314-315, 360, 411; revision of, by Committee, 489.
Japan Evangelical Alliance, proposal of, for revision of Japanese Version, 489.
Java, Bibles sent to, 112, 144.
Jay, John, Vice-President, 29, 66; elected President, 71; resignation of, as President, 72; quoted on divine origin of Bible Society movement, 72; influence of, 74; statue of, 98; age of, at death, 269.
Jay, William, delegate to first Convention, American Bible Society, 23; member of Committee on Constitution, 25; address by, 30; quoted on controversy concerning American Bible Society, 37.
Jenkins, Rev. Dr., member of Committee on Chinese Bible translation, 310.
Jessup, Rev. Dr. H. H., missionary in Syria, 527.
Jesuits, destruction of Bibles by member of, in Clinton County, N. Y., 203.
Johnson, William, on first Board of Managers, 29.
Jones, Rev. David, member of Committee on Constitution, 25.
Jones, William, Vice-President, 29.
Jordan, Rev. W. F., undertakes Mexican Agency, 473.
Jubilee celebration of 1866, 318-323; foreign representatives to, 320; sermons preached at, 319, 320.

K

Kemper, Bishop, missionary to Indians, 200.
Kenmure, Rev. Alexander, Agent in Korea, 485.
Kennedy, John S., large gift from, 528.
Kentucky Bible Society at Lexington, reorganised, 12; request of, leads to statement of relation of Auxiliaries to National Society, 43; mentioned, 49.
Key, Francis S., connection with American Colonisation Society, 73.
Kidder, Rev. D. P., Methodist missionary to Brazil, 224.
Kimber, Rev. J., delegate to seventy-fifth anniversary, 431.
King, Rev. Jonas, Scriptures distributed by, 104, 132; address by, at Jubilee, 323.
King, Rufus, on first Board of Managers, 29.
King James Version of the Bible, three hundredth anniversary of the publication of, 450.
Kirk, Rev. Mr., 210.
Kirkbride, Rev. Dr. S. H., Western Agency Secretary, 461; transferred to Northwestern Agency, 463.
Kirkpatrick, Andrew, death of, 99.
Kiukiang, Sub-Agency in, 500.
Koran, printing of, in India, 240.
Korea, missionaries sent to, 418; breadless, 447; religious restrictions removed in, 482; Scriptures translated for, 482.
Korean Version, of Gospels, 360, 418; of New Testament, 485; of Old Testament, 486.
Kurdish Version of New Testament, 363.

L

Labaree, Rev. Benjamin, Azerbaijan Turkish translation by, 363.
Labrador, Bibles sent to, 112.
Lallave, M. Alonzo, colporteur in Manila, 504, 505; translation by, 507.
Lambdin, Mr., Bibles distributed by, 376.
Lambert, William G., member of Finance Committee, 353.
Landes, Rev. G. A., work of, in Guarapuava, 435.
Lane, George W., member of Finance Committee, 353.
Langdon, John, Vice-President, 29.
Laos language, translation of Matthew in, 360.

La Plata Agency of Bible Society, beginning of, 296; territory of, 470.
Latin America, Bibles sold in (1826), 78; cosmopolitan character of work in, 81; progress of work of Society in, 217–225, 299–305; expenditures in, 299, 302–305.
Law, Rev. Dr. Thomas H., Field Agent, 457.
Lawrence, Mr., Agent of the Trinitarian Bible Society, 387.
Leamington, Rev. Robert, work of, in Guarapuava, 435.
Leavens, Rev. P. F., quoted, 534.
Lenox, James, elected President of Bible Society, 269; presides at Jubilee celebration, 320; resignation and death of, 348.
Leo, Rev. Ferdinand, edition of De Sacy version by, 58.
Levant, opposition to distribution in the, 316; colporteurs in, 425; hindrances to work in, in recent years, 512–516, 518–519; completion of seventy-five years of work in, 516; circulation in, 516, 520.
Levings, Rev. Dr. Noah, elected Financial Secretary, 195.
Lexington, S. C., Auxiliary, set of resolutions received from, 285.
Libby Prison, Bibles at, 264.
Life Directors, distribution by, 173.
Life members, distribution by, 173.
Liggins, Rev. Mr., one of first missionaries to Japan, 313.
Lincoln, Abraham, Bible, 3; resolution of grief passed upon death of, 290–291.
Lincoln, Heman, death of, 288.
Lodiana, Scriptures printed in, 366.
Logan, Rev. Mr., Mortlock Island translation by, 362.
London Missionary Society, formed (1795), 7.
London Religious Tract Society, formed (1799), 7.
Long, Rev. Dr. A. L., work of, on Bulgarian Version, 360.
Long, Rev. W. R., retirement of, as District Superintendent, 370.
Long Island Bible Society, mentioned, 340.
Loomis, Rev. Henry, Agent in Japan, 408, 416, 417, 419, 482, 483, 487; retires, 488.
Louisiana Auxiliary Bible Society, work of distribution by, in Spanish provinces (1817), 56.
Louisville Bible Society, quoted on distribution of Bibles to both armies in Civil War, 292.
Lucknow, Scriptures printed in, 366.
Lumpkin, J. H., death of, 288.
Lund, Rev. Eric, translation for Philippines by, 507, 509.
Lyman, Mr., missionary to Java, 112.
Lynch, Mr., Bibles sold by, in Peru, 76.

M

Macao, mission station in China, 242.
McAuley, Rev. Thomas, elected a secretary for Domestic Correspondence, 99; mentioned, 113.
McCarty, Peter, on first Board of Managers, 29.
McClay, Rev. Dr., member of committee on Chinese Bible translation, 310.
Maclay, Rev. R. S., translator of Scriptures, 361.
MacDowell, Rev. Dr. John, delegate to first Convention American Bible Society, 23; death of, 287.
McGehee, Edward, Vice-President, 351.
McKean, James B., Vice-President, 351.
McKim, Rev. A. J., Society's Agent in Cuba, 389.
McLaughlin, Rev. J. L., appointed Agent in Manila, 509.
McLean, Rev. Dr. Alexander, Secretary of Society, 355, 431; death of, 440.
McLean, John, Vice-President, 196; death of, 287.
McNeill, Rev. James H., elected Secretary, 197; resigned to go with South in Civil War, 256; death of, 256 n.
Madison, George, Vice-President, 29.
Maine Bible Society, Centennial of, 457.
Malta, American Mission Press at, 227.
Mandarin Version, 311; work on revision of, 361, 497.
Maracaibo, Spanish Bibles sent to, 76.
Marathi Bible, new edition aided, 106; effect of translation upon

Jews, 167; work of American missionaries upon, 240.
Marine Bible Societies, 93.
Marshall, John, elected Vice-President, 99.
Marshall Islands, translation of Bible into language of, 362.
Marshman, Rev. Mr., work at Serampore, 59.
Marsovan, result of tract sent to, 228.
Martin, Rev. Dr., missionary in China, 312.
Maryland, destitution in, 63.
Mason, Rev. Dr. John M., at first Convention, 24; member of Committee on Constitution, 25; address of, to people of United States, quoted, 27–29, 531; elected secretary for Foreign Correspondence, 30; mentioned, 32; controversy of, with Bishop Hobart, 36; resignation of, as Secretary for Foreign Correspondence, 66.
Massachusetts Bible Society, organised, 9; mentioned, 108, 340; contribution of, toward New Testament for blind, 156; distribution by, 175; Bibles given to soldiers and sailors in Civil War by, 272; Centennial of, 457.
Massachusetts Missionary Society, established, 7; appoints missionary to explore West and Southwest, 11; undertakes second tour, 12–13.
Massachusetts Society for Promotion of Christian Knowledge among Indians, established, 7.
Matamoras, Spanish Bibles sold in, 77.
Matsuyama, Mr., assistant in translating Japanese version, 361.
Matthews, Rev. Dr., pastor Garden Street Dutch Reformed Church (1816), 21.
Maxwell, William, quoted, 76.
Maybin, Joseph A., Vice-President, 350.
Mayhew, Mr., Agent in Indiana, 179.
Maynard, Horace, Vice-President, 351.
Mayor of New York City, host of Board of Managers, 34.
Mell, Rev. A. Wesley, Pacific Agency Secretary, 463.
Melville, Mr., Agent of British and Foreign Bible Society at Odessa, 231.
Memminger, C. C., Vice-President, 351.
Memphis and Shelby County (Tenn.) Auxiliary, distribution to soldiers by, 264.
Mesopotamia, distribution in, 232–233, 423.
Methodist Bible and Tract Society, dissolution of, recommended, 121.
Methodist Episcopal Missions, grants of money to, in Norway, 297; in Germany, 211, 212, 298; in Brazil, 224.
Mexican War, Bibles distributed during, 176, 183; creates new responsibilities, 182.
Mexico, Scriptures distributed in, 79, 144, 184, 220, 299, 301, 472, 473; Mr. Hickey's work in, 299–300; Agencies in, 394, 395; Society established in, 470.
Mexico City, Spanish Bibles sold in, 77.
Micronesia, work in, 309, 328, 329; work of translation in, 362; mentioned, 447.
Miller, Rev. G. A., Pacific Agency Secretary, 462.
Miller, Rev. George A., work of, in Philippines, 509.
Miller, Hugh, appointed Agent in Korea, 485.
Mills, Rev. Mr., Missionary in Tungchow, 311.
Mills, Samuel, constitution of British and Foreign Bible Society drafted by, 11.
Mills, Samuel J., student at Williams College, 10; missionary exploration of West by, 11; second western tour of, 13; quoted, 14–15; at first Convention, 24; mentioned, 59; last labours and death of, 73.
Milne, Andrew, Agent in South America, 302, 390, 391, 396, 398, 475; effects of forty years of service of, 476; death of, 477.
Milne, Rev. Dr., one of translators of Bible into Chinese, 102.
Milnor, Rev. Dr. James, elected Secretary for Domestic Correspondence, 65–66; presents resolutions to relieve destitute, 86; mentioned, 120, 162, 355; resolutions written by, 141; death of, 195.
M'Ilvaine, Bishop C. P., tribute of, to Dr. Spring, 321.
Ministers, list of, who have served on Society's Committees, 556–558.

Mobile Auxiliary, grant made to, 264.
Mohammedan, gift from a, to be used in giving the Bible to freedmen, 284.
Mohammedanism, characteristics of religion of, 226.
Mohammedans, interest in Bible awakened among, 234, 235; Koran printed for, in India, to offset Bible translations, 240; interest in Christianity of, 429; important work to be done among, 518, 527.
Mongolian, Old Testament printed in, 144.
Monod, Rev. Dr. F., Secretary of French and Foreign Bible Society, 211, 214.
Monroe County Bible Society, statistics of local needs made, 85.
Montevideo, Mr. Milne's field in, 390.
Montsalvatge, Ramon, Agent of the Society for Spanish South America, 221–222.
Moore, Bishop, letter from, on world supply, 113.
Morgan, Rev. J. J., Southwestern Agency Secretary, 463.
Mormons, Bible distribution among, 177; encouragement by, 375.
Morris, Rev. M. N., report of investigation of Society made by, 333.
Morrison, Rev. Dr., translation of Bible into Chinese by, 102, 242, 243, 536.
Morse, Rev. Dr. Jedidiah, delegate to first Convention American Bible Society, 22; member of Committee on Constitution, 25.
Mortlock Islanders, translation of Bible into language of, 362.
Mosquera, Don Joaquin, elected Vice-President of Society, 81.
Mosser, Rev. J., 370; retirement of, as District Superintendent, 370.
Mott, Dr. Valentine, delegate to first Convention American Bible Society, 22; death of, 287.
Moyes, Rev. James, Sub-Agent in China, 500.
Mpongwe language, printing of Gospel of John in, 242; New Testament printed in, 315; Scriptures printed in, 366, 403.
Munson, Rev. Mr., missionary to Java, 112.
Murray, John, Jr., on first Board of Managers, 29.
Muruoka, Mr., founder of "Fukien or Gospel Printing Company" of Yokohama, 489.
Myers, Rev. H. V. S., Agent in charge in China during Dr. Hykes' absence, 501.

N

Nanking, Sub-Agency in, 500.
Nashville, Tenn., Bible Society, formed, 12; mentioned, 175.
Natal, translations of Bible made by missionaries in, 316.
Natchez Bible Society formed, 12; Bibles supplied to immigrants, 126.
Nauru version, 448.
Neesima, Joseph, Japanese educator, 415, 536.
Negroes. *See* Coloured people.
Nesbit, R., Agent at Para, 224.
New Granada, opportunities for distribution watched for in, by Society, 304.
New Hampshire Bible Society, donation from, to American Society, 88, 175; supplies the soldiers, 272; mentioned, 340; Centennial of, 457.
New Hampshire Missionary Society, established, 7.
New Jersey Bible societies, 178.
New Jersey Bible Society, organised, 9; resolution adopted by (1814), in favour of a General Bible Society, 16; new proposal of, 18; mentioned, 108.
New Orleans Bible Society, formed, 12, 176; supplies immigrants, 126; supplies troops passing through city (1845–47), 183.
New York Auxiliary Bible Society, supplies troops passing through city (1845–47), 183; mentioned, 174, 189, 454; Bibles distributed by, during Civil War, 273; Scriptures supplied to army and navy by, 292; aid given to, by Society, 341; auxiliary relationship terminated, 457.
New York Bible Society, organised, 9; explorers furnished by, 12; objects to plan of General Bible Society, 17; becomes an Auxiliary, 33; gift of stereotype plates to American Bible Society by, 49; donation sent by, to missionaries

in Serampore, 60; coalescence with Auxiliary New York Bible Society, 93. *See* also Young Men's N. Y. Bible Society.
New York Female Bible Society, 92, 93, 94, 95; contribution of, toward New Testament for the blind, 156; Bible given by, to chapel in Tyrol, 383.
New York Historical Society, host to Board of Managers, 34.
New York Hospital, governors of, host to Board of Managers, 34.
New York Marine Bible Society, 93; absorbed by Young Men's Society, 94.
New York Public Library, books and manuscripts of Society transferred to custody of, 445.
Nicaragua, Agent of American Bible Society shot in, 220–221.
Nicoll, Dr. H. D., death of, 444.
Nicomedia, Bible distribution in, 228.
Nitchie, John, chosen General Agent, 67; elected Treasurer, 120.
Nizam of Hyderabad, territories of, explored, 308.
Nolan, Rev. Thomas, representative of British Society to Jubilee, 320; Jubilee address by, 321.
Norris, Rev. W. H., Agent for Central America, 304; appointed special Agent to Santo Domingo, 388.
Norris, Rev. W. H., Agent to Mexico, 184, 220.
North Carolina, Bibles granted to, 87.
Northwestern Agency, mentioned, 460; circulation in, 465.
Norwood, Rev. Joseph, Agent in Venezuela, 399, 477–478, 479.
Nott, Rev. Dr. Eliphalet, delegate to first Convention American Bible Society, 23; member of Committee on Constitution, 25; address by, 30; death of, 287.
Nourse, Joseph, Vice-President, 30.

O

Ohio State Bible Society, formed, 12.
Ojibwa version of New Testament, 200.
Okuma, Count, quoted on Bible, 488.
Oliver, Robert, Vice-President, 30.
Oncken, Rev. Dr. J. G., German Scriptures distributed by, 212, 383.
O'Neall, J. B., death of, 288.
Oneida County Bible Society (N. Y.), use of canal boats by, 124.
Orange County (N. Y.) Auxiliary, mentioned, 109, 340, 457.
Oregon, new field for work in, 184.
Oregon Auxiliary Bible Society, organised, 188.
Oregon Indians, missions to, established, 188.
Orient, work of Bible Society in the, 226–235.
Ormiston, Rev. Dr. William, representative to Jubilee, 320.
Orr, Alexander E., death of, 445.
Ousley, B. F., translator of Tonga Version, 362.
Owen, John, Secretary British and Foreign Bible Society (1816), 35, 36.
Owhyee (Hawaii), Bibles presented to Kings of, 59.
Ozark Mountains, Bible destitution in, 466.

P

Pacific Agency, organised, 462; circulation in, 465.
Pacific Railroad, effect of completion of, on work of Bible Society, 289–290.
Palmquist, Rev. Per, work in Sweden of, 382.
Panama, distribution on Isthmus of, 220; work in Canal Zone begun, 480.
Panayan, version in, 509.
Panoplist, The, quotation from, 5.
Paraguay, mentioned, 222; Mr. Milne's field in, 390.
Paris, Scriptures printed in, 366.
Parks, Rev. W. A., retirement of, as District Superintendent, 370.
Parrot, Mr., sells Spanish Bibles in Mexico City, 77.
Parsons, Rev. Levi, early missionary to Turkey, 227.
Parvin, Mr., explorations in South America by, 79.
Pascal, Rev. Cæsar, representative of French Society to Jubilee, 320; Jubilee address by, 322.
Patterson, Rev. Dr. W. M., Agent in Venezuela, 398, 399.

Patton, Rev. Mr., quoted, 122.
Pearce, Mr. E. H., retirement of, 370.
Pearse, Mr., sells Spanish Bibles in Matamoras, 77.
Pearse, Rev. Mr., Missionary to Calcutta, 139.
Pearson, Rev. Dr. John, Field Agent, 458.
Pease, Rev. E. M., translator of Scriptures into language of Marshall Islands, 362.
Peck, Rev. J. O., delegate to seventy-fifth Anniversary, 431.
Peking, Sub-Agency in, 500.
Pennsylvania Bible Society, becomes an Auxiliary, 121; distribution by, 175; notable donations by, as Jubilee offering, 283; contribution from, to send Testaments and Psalms to New Orleans, 291–292; Centennial of, 457; co-operation of, in organisation of Atlantic Agency, 462.
Penzotti, Rev. Francisco, good results from unjust imprisonment of, 391; mentioned, 398, 479; appointed Agent in Brazil, 477.
Perit, Peletiah, death of, 288.
Perkins, Rev. Justin, missionary to Persia, 151.
Permanent Committee on the Bible Cause, appointed by General Assembly of Presbyterian Church (in U. S.), 458.
Persia, distribution in, 227, 316; work of Society in, transferred to British and Foreign Society, 480, 526; grants to, 526.
Peru, work among Quechua Indians in, 76; mentioned, 77, 79; distribution in, 303, 390; restrictions removed in, 475.
Peshtimaljian's Armenian school, 228.
Petersburg Auxiliary Society, mentioned, 113.
Phelps, George D., death of, 354.
Phelps, Myron P., Vice-President, 350.
Philadelphia Bible Society, organised, 8; explorers furnished by, 12; French Testaments sent to New Orleans by, 13; objects to plan of General Society, 17; extract from letter to, 34; terms of recognition of, as Auxiliary, stated by Society, 45; attitude of, toward becoming Auxiliary to American Bible Society, 46; Bibles supplied Pennsylvania by, 85; donation from, to American Society, 88; mentioned, 108, 121; sends Bibles to Spain, 174.
Philippine Islands, Spanish Bibles sent to, 97; distribution in, 379, 506, 509, 510; Dr. Hykes' report of, 503–505; problems of translation for, 507; Scriptures translated into dialects of, 507–508; unique method of distribution, 510.
Phillips, Rev. Mr., Agent to Oregon, 188.
Phillips, Rev. Thomas, representative of British Society to Jubilee, 320; address by, at Jubilee, 321.
Phillips, William, death of, 98.
Pierson, John S., distribution of Bibles by, to sailors, 379; death of, 444.
Pierson, Rev. Mr., Agent of Society in Hayti, 219.
Pinckney, Charles C., Vice-President, 30; death of, 288.
Pinkerton, Mr., arrangement by, to publish modern translations for use in Jerusalem, 149–150.
Pintard, John, appointed Recording Secretary and Accountant, 65; elected Vice-President, 99.
Piper, Rev. John, work of, on translation of Japanese Version, 361.
Pittsburg Auxiliary, supplies immigrants passing through, 126; and troops passing through city (1845–47), 183.
Pixley, Rev. Dr., of Zulu Mission, 362.
Plummer, Rev. Dr. William S., quoted, 96; on World Supply, 113, 115, 117.
Poinsett, J. H., mentioned, 78.
Ponape language, Bible translated into, 362.
Popoff, Rev. Mr., Sub-Agent in Bulgaria, 519.
Porter, Mr., mentioned, 406; distribution by, in Syria, 426.
Porter, Rev. M. B., South Atlantic Agency Secretary, 461.
Porto Rico, Scriptures sent to (1820), 57; distribution in, 218.
Portuguese Scriptures, 126, 360; printed in New York, 155, 199; revision of, 474.
Posey, Thomas, Vice-President, 30.
Pratt, Rev. A. T., revision of Turkish version begun by, 426.

Pratt, Rev. Dr. H. B., preparation of Version Moderna by, 130, 479; missionary at Bogota, 223; work of on translation of Spanish version, 360; death of, 479.
Prayer, question of having, at Board meetings, 62.
Presbyterian Board of Home Missions, assistance to, in preparation of Navaho version, 447.
Presbyterian Mission in Shanghai introduced sale of Scriptures, 311.
Presbyterian Mission Press in Beirut, Arabic Bible printed at, 331.
Presidents of Society, election of, 29, 71, 72, 97, 196, 268, 348, 349, 442, 443; list of, 541.
Price, Rev. Mr., translation of Scriptures into Chamorro language by, 448.
Prime, Rev. S. I., elected Secretary, (1849), 197.
Prince, George H., Agent in St. Petersburg, 380, 381.
Printing for Society abroad, 366.
Protestant Bible Society of Paris, formed (1818), 58.
Protestant Episcopal Mission, grant to, in Mexico, 302.
Protestant Evangelical Community, established in Turkey, 230.
Prothero, Mr., colporteur in China, 404.
Proudfit, Dr., quoted on question of supplying Bibles to destitute, 86.
Prussian War, distribution to soldiers in, 298.
Pueblo, distribution in, 220.
Punderford, James A., death of, 445.
Punta Arenas, result of distribution in, 475.
Purdie, S. A., Friends' missionary in Mexico, 394.

Q

Quakers "Holy Experiment" established in Pennsylvania by, 1.
"Quarterly Extracts," issued by American Bible Society, 53.
Quechua Indians, translation for, 76, 477.

R

Ragatz, Rev. Dr. A. F., Western Agency Secretary, 463.
Ralston, Robert, on first Board of Managers, 29, 32.
Randolph, A. D. F., death of, 444.
Rankin, Melinda, Scriptures distributed among Mexicans by, 220, 301.
Rankin, Rev. W. B., 370.
Reed, Rev. W. H., of United Presbyterian mission in Egypt, 5, 19.
Reid, Rev. H. A., army chaplain, quoted, 274.
Religious Tract Society in London, 7.
Renville, Mr., assistance of, in Dakota translation, 359.
Revision Committees in China, 496, 497.
Reynolds, Rev. S., retirement of, as District Superintendent, 370.
Rhea, Vice-President Samuel, death of, 288.
Rhea, Rev. S. H., translation of Azerbaijan Turkish version undertaken by, 363.
Rhode Island Bible Society, Centennial of, 457.
Rice, John H., delegate to first convention, 23; member of Committee on Constitution, 25.
Riggs, Rev. Dr. Elias, Bible translation by, 167; printing of Bible in Armenian supervised by, 199; translator of Bulgarian version, 360; work of, as translator, 425, 426; death of, 516.
Riggs, Dr. S. R., grant of money to, by Society for printing Dakota translation, 200; translations of, 329, 359.
Righter, Rev. Chester N., Agent of Bible Society in Turkey, 232-233.
Rijutei, Mr., Korean official, conversion of, 418.
Riley, Rev. H. C., missionary in Mexico City, 302, 394.
Rio Janeiro, attempt of Huguenots to found colony at, 223.
Roberts, Rev, Mr., translation of St. Luke into Arapahoe by, 447.
Robertson, Mr. and Mrs. A. E. W., New Testament translated into Muskokee by, 366, 447.
Robertson, Dr., missionary to Greece, 132.
Robinson, Rev. Charles, missionary in Siam, 240.
Robinson, Rev. Dr. Edward, member of Committee on Versions, 249.

Rochester, meeting called in, to relieve local destitution, 85.
Rockland County Auxiliary, mentioned, 340, 457.
Rodgers, Rev. James B., missionary in Manila, quoted, 508.
Rodgers, John R. B., on first Board of Managers, 29.
Rodriguez, Col., influence of Bible on, quoted, 301.
Roman Catholic Church, attitude of American Bible Society toward, 217–218; opposition of, in Latin American countries, 219, 221–222, 223, 224; control of men's mind and conduct in Mohammedan system compared to that of, 226.
Roman Catholic Congress at Bahia, Brazil, New Testament Portions issued by, 474.
Roman Catholic Mission in Japan, edition of Gospels published by, 484.
Roman Catholic priests, distribution opposed by, 203–204, 298, 303, 305, 306, 332, 396–397, 457, 471, 473–474, 475, 478, 511; encouragement by, 375.
Roman Catholics, Testaments received by soldiers among, in Civil War, 274.
Roman Catholic version of Bible printed, 82.
Romeyn, Rev. Dr. John B., one of Secretaries of first Convention, 22; elected Secretary for Domestic Correspondence, 30; mentioned, 32; resignation of, 65.
Roosevelt, President, signs appeal for contributions, 528.
Root, Elihu, visit of, to South America, 475, 477.
Ropes, William, 213.
Rosario, Mr. Milne's field in, 390.
Ross, Rev. John, translation of Korean version of New Testament made by, 418.
Rowe, Caleb T., General Agent, death of, 441.
Russia, expressions of good-will from, 34; Scriptures distributed in, 144, 299, 380, 525; aid given Bible work in, by American Society, 213; Bibles distributed among Germans of Southern, 230; Imperial Bible Society of, 381.
Russian Bible Society, publication of Scriptures by, 149; Bible published in Ancient Armenian by, 227.
Rutgers, Henry, on first Board of Managers, 29; mentioned, 32.

S

Sage, Mrs. Russell, gift of, to Society, 528.
St. Croix, Island of, Scriptures sent to (1820), 57.
St. Louis Bible Society, 176.
St. Thomas, Scriptures sent to, 218.
Salonica, Scriptures introduced into Greek schools in, 428.
Sam Kiong Colloquial Version, 497.
Samoa, Gilbert Islands Bible sent to, 362.
Sampson, Rev. Mr., introduces Scriptures into Greek schools in Salonica, 428.
San Domingo, Scriptures sent to, 218; difficulty of distribution in, 388.
Sands, Joshua, on first Board of Managers, 29.
Sandwich Islands, Missionaries leave for (1819), 59; Scriptures distributed in, 144. *See* Hawaii.
San Francisco Bible Society, organised, 177; work of, at period of gold discovery, 201–202.
Santander, F. B., elected Vice-President of Society, 81.
Saratoga County Auxiliary, mentioned, 340.
Sarkis, Arabic version by, 330.
Sauer, Christopher, first Bible printed in America by, 2.
Sayre, Rev. Dr. G. H., death of, 287.
Scandinavia, money granted to missionaries in, for distribution, 297, 526.
Schauffler, Rev. Dr., Hebrew-Spanish version of Psalms prepared by, 151; money granted to, for translation, 159; work of, as translator of Turkish, 167, 425, 426.
Schereschewski, Bishop, translation of Scriptures into Mandarin by, 310, 311, 361; tribute to, 497–499.
Schermerhorn, J. M., first Missionary to explore West, 11.
Schmidt, George, colporteur in South America, 303; death of, and tribute to, 391.

Schwartz, Dr. Herbert W., appointed Agent in Japan, 488.
Scio version of Bible, printed, 82; plates of, destroyed, 130.
Scotland, National Bible Society of, mentioned, 100, 483, 485, 497.
Scranton, Dr., missionary to Korea, 418.
Scudder, Dr. John, missionary to India, 131, 159; appeal of, from Madras, 156.
Scudder, Rev. Henry J., elected Acting Recording Secretary, 445.
Scudder, Rev. Moses L., appointed General Delegate to Conferences and Synods, 197.
Secretaries of American Bible Society, importance of position of, 289–290; division of work of, 290; list of, 554, 555.
Sellew, T. G., death of, 445.
Serampore, Bible printing in, 59.
Servia, distribution not permitted in, 428.
Seward, William H., mentioned, 126; quoted, 127.
Shanghai, Scriptures printed in, 366; Missionary Conferences in, 406–407.
Shanghai Colloquial Version, 497.
Shantung Colloquial Version, 497.
Shelby, Isaac, Vice-President, 29.
Shields, Thomas, on first Board of Managers, 29.
Siam, work of translation in, 240; Scriptures printed in, 309; Agency in, 409.
Siamese Version, preparation of, 240–241; completion of, 492.
Siberia, distribution in, 381, 382.
Sickles, Gen. Daniel E., Bibles released in Spain through influence of, 306.
Sierra Leone, Bibles sent to coloured colonists in, 59.
Simonton, Rev. Mr., missionary at Rio Janeiro, 224, 304, 396.
Simpson, Rev. J. J., Agent in Kentucky, 172, 179.
Singapore, mission station at, 242.
Sioux version of Scriptures, 200.
Slaves, action of Board toward supplying with Bibles, 137, 185–187.
Sleeper, Jacob, Vice-President, 351.
Smith, Rev. Daniel, Western tour of, 13.
Smith, Rev. Dr. Eli, translator of New Testament into Arabic, 233–234; pattern of Arabic letters drawn by, 330; translation of Bible into Arabic begun by, 331.
Smith, Captain John, Jamestown provided with a church by, 2.
Smith, John Cotton, Vice-President, 29; elected President, 97–98; quoted, 133, 168; address delivered by, at twenty-fifth Anniversary, 162; death of, 196; age of, at death, 269.
Smith, Rev. Dr. T. Ralston, Secretary of Bible Society, 289, 290, 355.
Smyrna, Mission Press in, 149.
Snow, Rev. Mr., missionary in Kusaie, 309.
Society for the Promotion of Christian Knowledge, 7.
Society for Propagation of Gospel in Foreign Parts, 7.
Somerset County (N. J.) Auxiliary, mentioned, 457.
Sommers, Rev. Charles, elected a Secretary for Domestic Correspondence, 99; becomes Corresponding Secretary of American and Foreign Bible Society, 142.
Soochow Colloquial Version, 497.
Soudan, decrease of illiteracy in, 519.
South America, early work of American Bible Society in, 144, 221–225; labours of British and Foreign Bible Society in, 224–225; permanent Agent appointed to Argentina, 295–296; distribution in, 303; Agencies in, 390–393.
South Atlantic Agency, organised, 461; circulation in, 465.
South Carolina Bible Convention, cordial resolution passed at, 254.
Southern States, Auxiliary Societies in, sever relations after opening of Civil War, 259–260; conditions in, at close of Civil War, 277–278; renewal of relations by Auxiliaries in, 279–281.
South Sea Islands, plan to evangelise, 7.
Southwestern Agency, organised, 462; circulation in, 465.
Southwestern Bible Society, Bible House built by, 176; distribution by, 189; co-operation of, with American Bible Society, 280; activ-

ities of, in period following Civil War, 291–292.
Spain, Bibles distributed in, 174, 386; opposition to distribution in, 306, 527; grants to American Mission in, 387, 527.
Spalding, Rev. Mr., Methodist missionary to Brazil, 244; appeal of, 155.
Spanish Version, printed by American Bible Society, 51, 126, 199, 476; revision of, 473, 480, 481.
Spaulding, Rev. H. H., translator of Bible into Nez Perce dialect, 366.
Spring, Rev. Gardiner, delegate to first Convention American Bible Society, 22; mentioned, 194; chairman of Committee on Versions, 249, 253; address by, at Jubilee, 321; death of, 347.
Stalker, Rev. James, of Scotland at seventy-fifth anniversary, 431.
Stallybrass, Rev. E., aided to print Mongolian Testament, 144.
Stamboul, Bible House in, 420–422.
Standard Bible, preparation and issuance of, 249; storm of criticism directed against, 250; action taken by Bible Society concerning, 250–253.
"Standing Committee" of Board formed, 64.
Starr, Chandler, death of, 354.
Sterry, G. E., death of, 444.
Stevens, Bishop, quoted, 361.
Stevenson, Rev. Dr. J. M., delegate to seventy-fifth anniversary. 431.
Stiles, Rev. Joseph C., election and resignation of, as Secretary, 197.
Stockholm, Scriptures printed in, 366.
Stokes, Thomas, on first Board of Managers, 29.
Stone, Dr. Mary, Hospital of, at Kiukiang, 493.
Storrs, Rev. R. S., Jr., member of Committee on Versions, 249, 250–253; Jubilee sermon by, 320; President of American Board of Missions, 431.
"Story of the American Bible Society," publication issued by Society, 446.
Strafford (N. H.), Bible Society, work done by, 124.
Stringfield, Rev. Thomas, Agent of Society, 178.
Strong, Caleb, Vice-President, 29.
Strong, Rev. W. S., Sub-Agent in China, 500.
Stuart, George Hay, quoted on work of Christian Commission during Civil War, 275–276; President of Christian Commission, 291; Vice-President of Society, 352.
Stuntz, Rev. Homer C., of the Philippines, quoted, 508–509.
Sturges, Rev. A. A., translator of Ponape version, 362.
Sturges, Frederick, death of, 445.
Sturges, Jonathan, death of, 354.
Stuyvesant, Peter G., death of, 196.
Suckley, George, on first Board of Managers, 29.
Surinam, Bibles sent to, 97.
Sussex County (N. J.) Auxiliary, mentioned, 457.
Sutton, Rev. A., Baptist Missionary in India, 239.
Suydam, James, Vice-President of Society, 353.
Swan, Benjamin L., death of, 288.
Swedish Scriptures, 126, 382.
Swift, Gen. J. G., death of, 287.

T

Taft, J. H., death of, 443.
Talbot, Charles N., member of Finance Committee, 353.
Tamil Version, in Ceylon, 103, 104, 106, 238, 239.
Tank, Rev. Otto, translator of Book of Acts into Arawack, 223.
Tappan, John, Vice-President of Society, 349.
Taylor, A. L., Assistant Treasurer of Society, 289, 356.
Taylor, Rev. Dr. Lachlin, representative to Jubilee, 320.
Taylor, Rev. Dr. Nathaniel W., delegate to first Convention American Bible Society, 22.
Taylor, Rev. Dr. W. J. R., 285; service as Corresponding Secretary of Bible Society, 290.
Taylor, Zachary, quoted on value of Bible, 204, 205.
Telmonde, Father, destruction of Bibles by, 203.
Telugu Bible, revision of, 363.
Tenney, E. P., death of, 445.
Tenth Anniversary, sympathy with Latin Americans expressed at, 75.

Texas Auxiliaries, Bibles sent to, for soldiers (1845–47), 183.
Texas Auxiliary Bible Society, 112.
Thibet, distribution in, 404.
Thompson, Rev. B. P., Agent of Society in Mexico, 220.
Thompson, Rev. Henry C., member of Committee on Revision of Spanish Version, 480, 481.
Thompson, James, Agent of British and Foreign Bible Society, 57, 76.
Thompson, Smith, Vice-President, 29.
Thompson, Mr. W. L., Panama, 397.
Thomson, Archdeacon, mentioned, 498.
Thorne, Mr., colporteur in China, 405.
Tilghman, William, Vice-President, 29; death of, 98.
Tonga Version, 362.
Torrance, Rev. Thomas, Sub-Agent in China, 501.
Tower, Rev. W. H., Eastern Agency Secretary, 463.
Tracy, Charles, Vice-President of Society, 353.
Translations, regulations respecting appropriations for, 559.
Translators and revisors, list of missionary, 565–569.
Travelling Agents, appointed to animate Auxiliaries, 125.
Treasurers of Society, list of, 554–555.
Troup, Robert, death of, 99.
Trowbridge, C. C., Vice-President of Society, 351.
Trumbull, Rev. D., work of, in Chile, 222, 390; in Valparaiso, 303; mentioned, 392.
Tsuda, Mr., Japanese official, conversion of, 417.
Tucker, Rev. H. C., Agent in Brazil, 397, 474.
Tucker, Rev. W. J., quoted, 357.
Turkey, American missions in, 227; origin of Protestant Evangelical Community in, 230; progress of work of Bible Society in, 231–235; donations from, to be used in giving the Bible to freedmen, 284; opposition to distribution in, 421, 512; Agency in, 422; distribution in, 422, 424; German Emperor's visit to, 514; disturbances in 1898–1914, 514–515; unexpected encouragement in, 517.
Turkish version of Bible, 65, 149, 360, 425.
Turner, Madam Clorinda Matto de, translation of Gospels for Quechua Indians undertaken by, 476.
Turner, Rev. Dr. Samuel H., member of Committee on Versions, 249.
Tuttle, E. B., death of, 444.
Tuttle, Rev. Samuel L., services and death of, 289.
Tyng, Rev. Dr. S. H., mentioned, 194, 210.
Tyrol, Bible given to chapel in the, 383.

U

Underwood, Rev. H. G., work of, on Korean Version, 418, 486.
Union Revision in China, 497.
United States Navy, grant of Bibles to (1820), 54.
Urdu, Scriptures printed in, at Lucknow, 239, 308.
Uriya, Scriptures printed in, 135, 308; grants for translations, 239.
Uruguay, mentioned, 222, 223; Mr. Milne in, 390.
Utah, Bible distribution in, 177.
Utica, Bibles supplied to immigrants passing through, 126.

V

Valera Version, adopted, 130; revised (1860), 199, 478, 480, 481.
Valez, Don Justo, Life Directorship of Society offered to, 77.
Valparaiso, American Consul distributes Bibles in, 57; Scriptures distributed from, 77; Mr. Wheelwright arrives in, 147.
Valparaiso Bible Society, mentioned, 303, 390, 476.
Van Diessel, Rev. S., translator of Bible into Creolese, 329.
Van Dyck, Rev. Dr. C. V. A., translator of Bible into Arabic, 234; gift to Society by, 284; Arabic translation revised and completed by, 331.
Van Norden, Mr., mentioned, 396.
Van Rensselaer, Alexander, death of, 354.
Van Rensselaer, Stephen, on first Board of Managers, 29; mentioned, 32.
Van Wagenen, Hubert, elected Treasurer, 100; resignation of, 120; death of, 196.

Varick, Richard, on first Board of Managers, 29; elected Treasurer of Society, 30; relations of, with Washington, 32; resignation of, as Treasurer, 66; elected Vice-President, 66; elected President, 72; mentioned, 74; death of, 97.
Venezuela, work of Agent of Society in, 221–222; Society established in, 470, 477.
Vera Cruz, distribution in, 220.
Verbeck, Rev. Dr., one of first missionaries to Japan, 313; translator of Scriptures, 361, 414.
Vermilye, Rev. Dr., Jubilee sermon by, 319.
Vermilye, Washington R., member of Finance Committee, 353.
Vermont Bible Society, tries to aid French Canadian, 63; donation from, to American Society, 88; distribution by, 175; Bibles given to soldiers in Civil War by, 272.
Vernon, Rev. L. M., missionary in Rome, 387.
Version Moderna, issued, 130, 479.
Versions. *See* Foreign Languages.
Vice-Presidents of Society, mentioned, 349–352, 353; list of, 542–546.
Vienna, Scriptures printed in, 366.
Vieques, missionary work on island of, 388.
Villegagnon, betrayer of French Huguenots in Brazil, 223.
Vinita, conference at, 366.
Vinton, Rev. Dr. Alexander, Jubilee sermon by, 320.
Virginia, Bibles sent to mountain districts of, 64.
Virginia Bible Society, mentioned, 114, 340; distribution by, 175; course followed by, during Civil War, 263–264; resumes Auxiliary relationship, 280; co-operation of, in organisation of South Atlantic Agency, 461.
Vroom, Peter D., Vice-President, 350.
Vulgate Version of Bible, 129–130.

W

Waite, Rev. H. C., distribution by, in Italy, 387.
Waite, W. B., of the New York Institution for the Blind, 524; gift of printing press to Society by, 524.
Waldensian Committee in Florence, money granted to, 305.
Walker, Samuel J., urges preparation of Spanish Testament for use in California, 189.
Walker expedition to Nicaragua, Bible distribution stopped by, 220–221.
Wallace, Joshua M., Chairman of first Convention of American Bible Society, 22, 24.
Walsh, A. Robertson, Vice-President, 353.
Ward, Rev. Mr., connection with Bible printing in India, 59.
Ward, Rev. Dr., retirement of, as District Superintendent, 370.
Warder, John, on first Board of Managers, 29.
Ware, James, colporteur, manager of Shanghai office and translator, 406; Agent ad interim in China, 409.
Warner, George, on first Board of Managers, 29.
Warner, Henry W., delegate to Convention of 1816, 347–348.
Washington, Bushrod, Vice-President, 29; death of, 99.
Washington, D. C., general Bible Convention at (1844), 204.
Washington City Bible Society, donations of, 154; adopts Walker resolution, 189; distribution to soldiers by, 272–273.
Washington County (N. Y.) Bible Society, distribution by, 85; mentioned, 86, 109, 340.
Watts, Dr. John, on first Board of Managers, 29; death of, 99.
Wayland, Rev. Dr. Francis, mentioned, 140; quoted, 143.
Weakley, Rev. R. H., on Committee for revision of Turkish Scriptures, 426.
Welsh Auxiliaries, donations from, 340.
Welsh Scriptures, 126; printed at Bible House, 199.
Wenli Version, decision to make, 497.
Westchester County Auxiliary Bible Society, extract from report of, 62; mentioned, 340, 457.
Western Agency, organised, 461; circulation in, 465.
West Indies, Scriptures sent to, for distribution, 77; work in desultory (1866), 304; problem of, for Society's labours, 470–471.

Westrup, Thomas, Agent in Mexico, 301, 302, 393.
Wharton, Rev. Dr., member of Committee on Resolutions to unite Bible Societies, 16.
Wheeler, Rev. D. H., Agent of American Bible Society, killed in Nicaragua, 220–221.
Wheeler, Rev. L. L., Agent in China, 409; death of, 493.
Wheeling, Bibles supplied to immigrants passing through, 126.
Wheelwright, Rev. Isaac W., Agent in Chile, 146, 222.
Whipple, Rev. W. L., Agent for Persia, 424, 526.
White, Bishop, President of Philadelphia Bible Society, 34; quoted, 37.
White, Norman, Vice-President of Society, 353.
Whitlock, William, Treasurer of Society, 356.
Whitten, Rev. S. P., retirement of, as District Superintendent, 370.
Wilder, S. V. S., mentioned, 58.
Williams, Bishop D. C., translator of Scriptures, 361.
Williams, John L., death of, 444.
Williams, Rev. Dr. M. H., delegate to seventy-fifth anniversary, 431.
Williams, Dr. S. Wells, mentioned, 23; supplying of Bibles to overland stage stations due to, 201; missionary to China, 244; Japanese translation attempted by, 313; elected Presidest of Society, 348; death of, 349.
Williams, William, delegate to first Convention American Bible Society, 23.
Williams, Rev. Dr. W. R., Jubilee sermon by, 320.
Williamson, Rev. Dr. T. S., money granted to, for translations into Dakota language, 200; mentioned, 329; story of method, 359.
Wilmer, Rev. Simon, member of Committee on Constitution, 25; mentioned, 30.
Wilson, Mr., sells Spanish Bibles in Mexico City, 77.
Wilson, Peter, on first Board of Managers, 29.
Winslow, R. F., elected Recording Secretary, 99; resignation of, 121.
Winslow, Rev. Mr., missionary in India, urges world supply, 117; quoted, 122, 131; receives grant for printing Tamil Scriptures, 159.
Winston, Frederick S., Vice-President, 352.
Winthrop, Robert C., address by, at Jubilee, 323; death of, 444.
Wix, Archdeacon, missionary to Labrador fishermen, 112; money sent to, for fishermen, 144.
Wolcott, F. H., Vice-President, 352.
Wood, James, elected President of Society, 443; visit of, to Panama, 480.
Woodbridge, Dr., President of Virginia Bible Society, 281.
Woodhull, Rev. Dr. S. S., elected Secretary for Domestic Correspondence, 66; resignation and re-election of, 99.
Woolsey, Edward J., death of, 354.
Woolsey, W. W., elected Treasurer, 66; elected Vice-President, 99.
Worcester's Dictionary, copyright and income from sales donated to American Bible Society and American Peace Society, 284.
Worthington, Thomas, Vice-President, 30; death of, 98.
Wragg, Rev. Dr., distribution by, among coloured people, 466.
Wright, Charles, member of Committee on Constitution, 25; on first Board of Managers, 29.
Wright, G. G., death of, 444.
Wright, J. A., death of, 288.
Wright, Rev. Dr. J. N., work of, as translator, 363.

Y

Yokohama, Scriptures printed in, 366; depository in, opened, 412; Bible House in, burned, 483; headquarters of Society in, 484.
Young Men's Bible Society of Cincinnati, co-operation of, in organisation of Central Agency, 462.
Young Men's Christian Association, organisation of Christian Commission by, during Civil War, 275; quartered in Bible House, 333.
Young Men's New York Bible Society, becomes Auxiliary, 93, 94; offers money for Chinese Scriptures, 124; takes name of New York Bible Society, 94.

Z

Zaccheus, J. W., teacher and missionary in island of Vieques, 388.

Zapotec, Gospel of St. John published in, 473.

Zulu Version, translating and printing of 242, 316, 362; large shipment of, to South Africa, 366.

Printed in the United States of America.